FEIFFER   Feiffer, Jules.

The ghost script.

$26.95   32026010109319

DATE			

The
Ghost Script

The Ghost Script

A Graphic Novel

Jules Feiffer

Liveright Publishing Corporation

A Division of W. W. Norton & Company

Independent Publishers Since 1923

New York   London

For information about permission to reproduce selections from this book,
write to Permissions, Liveright Publishing Corporation, a division of
W. W. Norton & Company, Inc., 500 Fifth Avenue, New York, NY 10110

For information about special discounts for bulk purchases, please contact
W. W. Norton Special Sales at specialsales@wwnorton.com or 800-233-4830

Manufacturing by Toppan Leefung
Production manager: Anna Oler

ISBN 978-1-63149-313-3

Liveright Publishing Corporation
500 Fifth Avenue, New York, N.Y. 10110
www.wwnorton.com

W. W. Norton & Company Ltd.
15 Carlisle Street, London W1D 3BS

1 2 3 4 5 6 7 8 9 0

To: I. F. Stone
Murray Kempton
and
Leonard Boudin

Foreword

The *Kill My Mother* trilogy (this is the final volume) was never meant to be political. It was dreamed up as an old man's homage to the noir fiction and films of my boyhood, drawn in a style based on the works of the two cartoonists who were my adventure strip deities: Milton Caniff and Will Eisner.

Nonetheless, by the middle of book two, *Cousin Joseph*, it became clear that I had tricked myself into writing about that time, nearly seventy years ago, when my Bronx-boy, left-wing leanings fixed on the Hollywood blacklist, and I found myself shaped as a political being, from that time to this.

A week or so after I was discharged from the army in 1953, I went down to Foley Square in downtown Manhattan to hear Jerome Robbins testify before the House Un-American Activities Committee. From his *Fancy Free* ballet to his Broadway musicals *On The Town* and *West Side Story*, Robbins had revitalized theater and dance. The Committee chair swore him in and asked what he did for a living. Robbins answered that he was a director and choreographer. That last term had not yet entered common parlance, and Robbins was asked to explain what in the world it meant. But first, every Committee member took his turn mispronouncing it for the folks listening on TV or radio back home in Real America—"You're a choreogawhagawhut?" "You're a cory-corywhatzis?" "You're a corwaggawufer?"—thus indicating to the voters who counted that they were uncontaminated by this fairy–Jew York City word.

Not long after, I attended a memorial service in Brooklyn for the blacklisted actor J. Edward Bromberg, one of the founders of the Group Theatre. Midway through, another founding member, playwright Clifford Odets, made an unscheduled appearance. Odets gave a speech that had the audience on its feet, cheering. It was as if, lost in Hollywood hackdom for years, he was reclaiming his title as our most important left-wing voice. With the poetic-oratorical sway of his *Waiting for Lefty*, he denounced the Committee for killing his old friend Joe. But Joe's death would not go unavenged. Joe would be redeemed, the Committee would be vanquished, American idealism would be restored.

"Odets is back! Odets is back!" we in the audience cried, as we wept.

A week later, Odets appeared before the Committee. As a friendly witness! He named names. And when Odets was asked who had recruited him into the Communist Party, he came up with his first name: "J. Edward Bromberg."

"Where am I? Am I going crazy? What kind of country am I living in?"

All these thoughts stuttered through my mind at that moment—and for seventy years after.

With the conclusion of this trilogy, I offer my last words on the subject.

Part One: Murchison

Chapter One: Archie Goldman

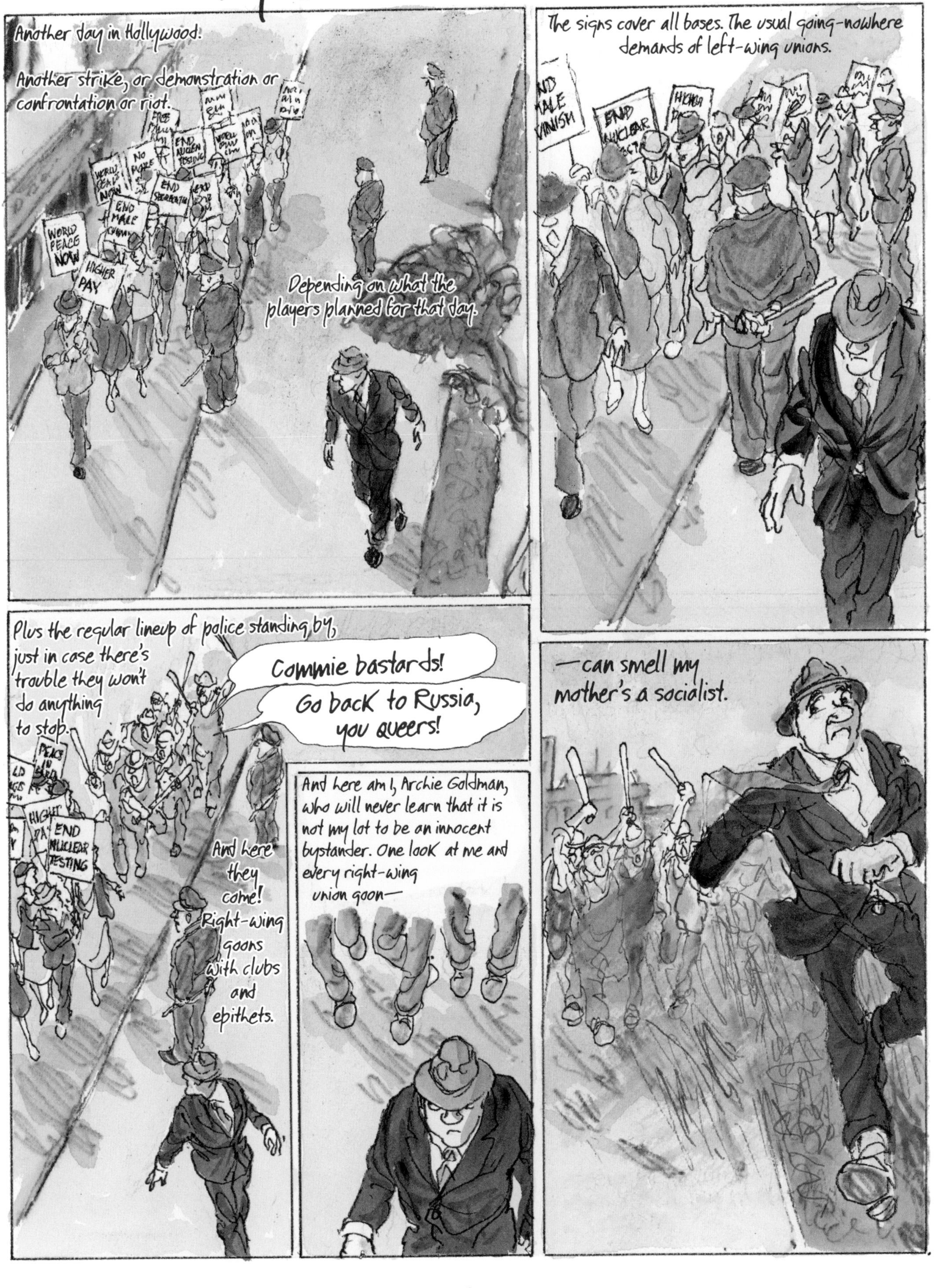

Another day in Hollywood.
Another strike, or demonstration or confrontation or riot.
WORLD PEACE NOW
HIGHER PAY
Depending on what the players planned for that day.
The signs cover all bases. The usual going-nowhere demands of left-wing unions.
Plus the regular lineup of police standing by, just in case there's trouble they won't do anything to stop.
Commie bastards!
Go back to Russia, you queers!
END NUCLEAR TESTING
And here they come! Right-wing goons with clubs and epithets.
And here am I, Archie Goldman, who will never learn that it is not my lot to be an innocent bystander. One look at me and every right-wing union goon—
—can smell my mother's a socialist.

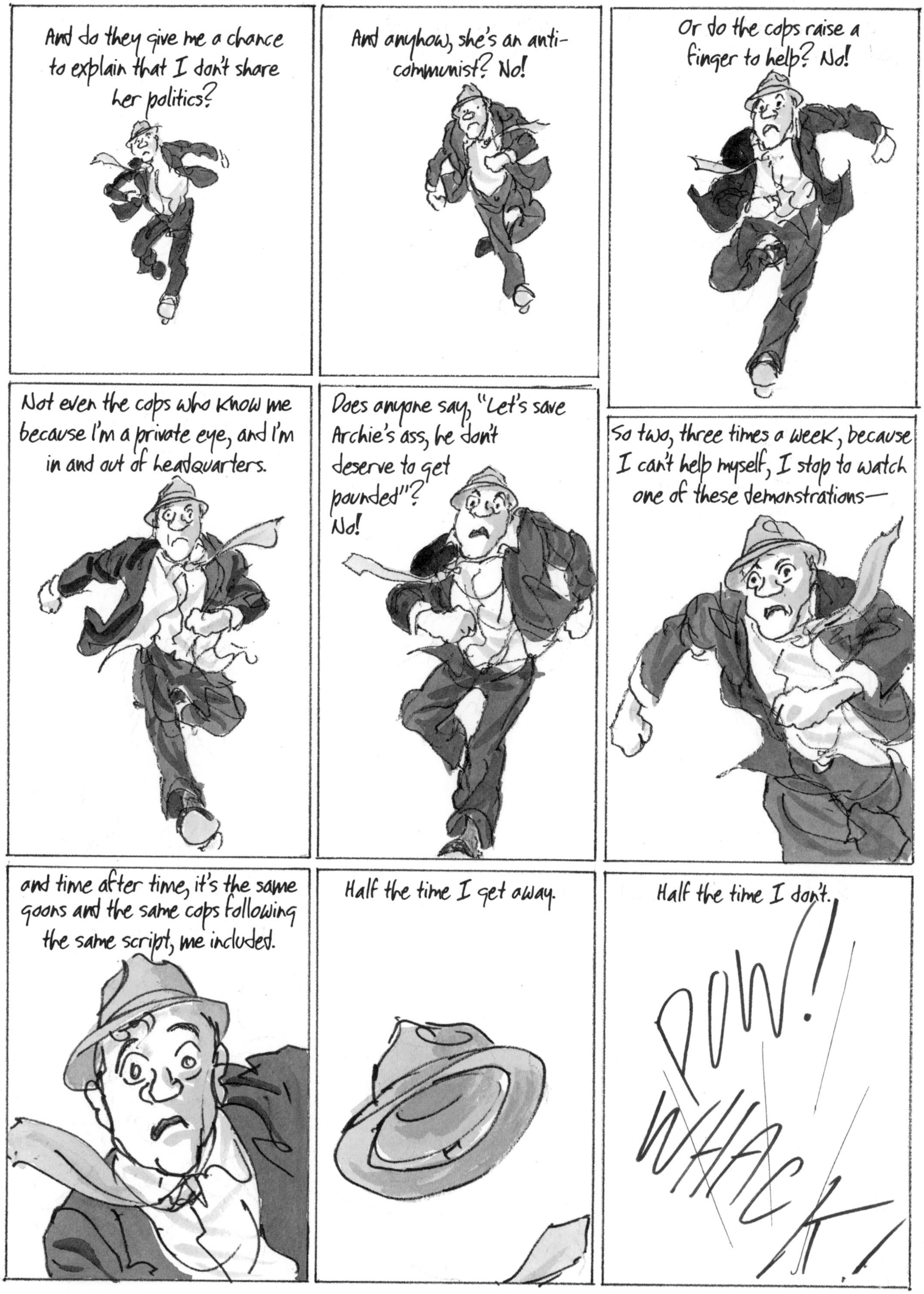
And do they give me a chance to explain that I don't share her politics?
And anyhow, she's an anti-communist? No!
Or do the cops raise a finger to help? No!
Not even the cops who know me because I'm a private eye, and I'm in and out of headquarters.
Does anyone say, "Let's save Archie's ass, he don't deserve to get pounded"? No!
So two, three times a week, because I can't help myself, I stop to watch one of these demonstrations—
and time after time, it's the same goons and the same cops following the same script, me included.
Half the time I get away.
Half the time I don't.
POW!
WHACK!

Chapter Two: A Night at Addie's

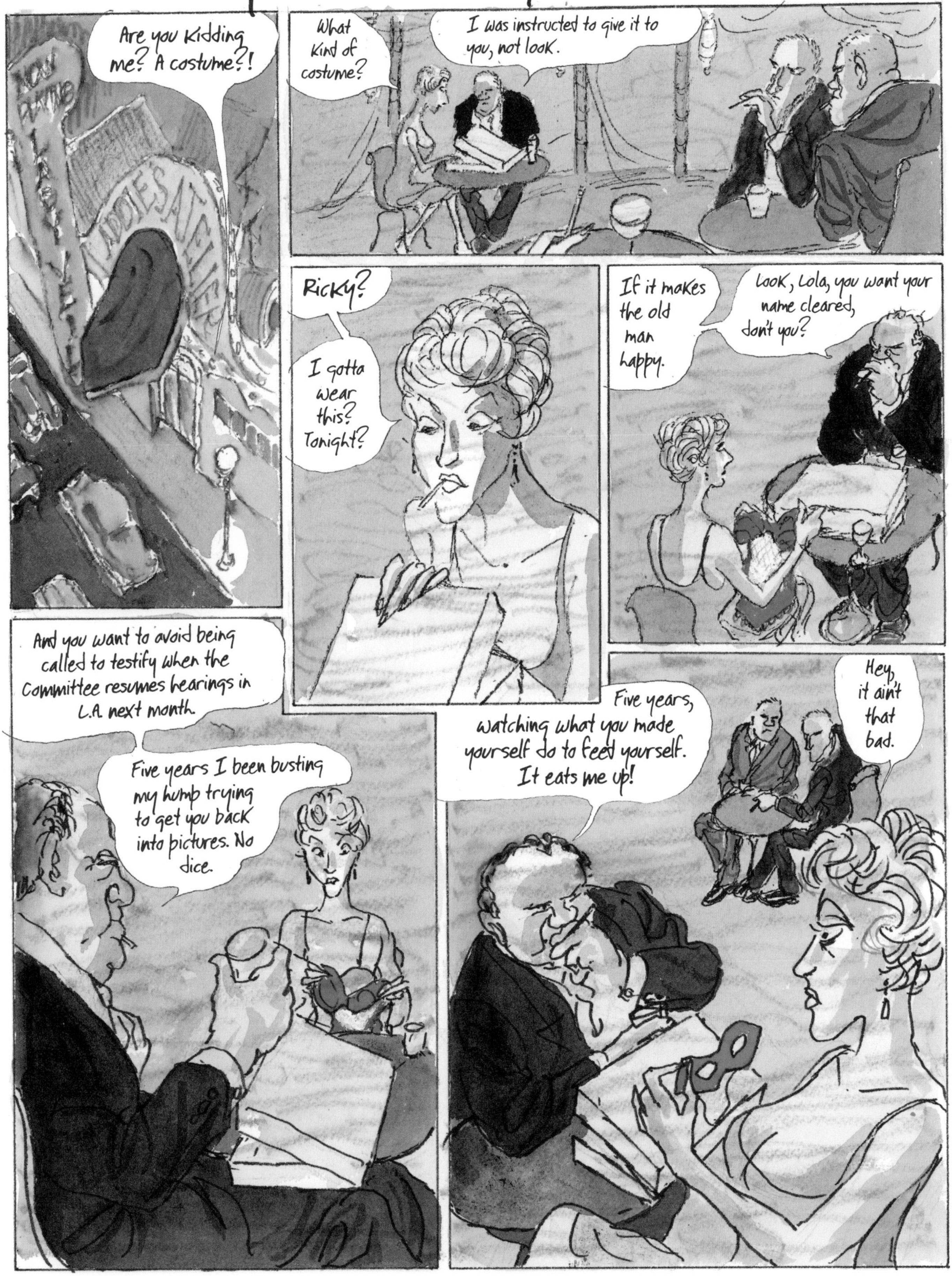

Are you kidding me? A costume?!
What kind of costume?
I was instructed to give it to you, not look.
Ricky?
I gotta wear this? Tonight?
If it makes the old man happy.
Look, Lola, you want your name cleared, don't you?
And you want to avoid being called to testify when the Committee resumes hearings in L.A. next month.
Five years I been busting my hump trying to get you back into pictures. No dice.
Five years, watching what you made yourself do to feed yourself. It eats me up!
Hey, it ain't that bad.

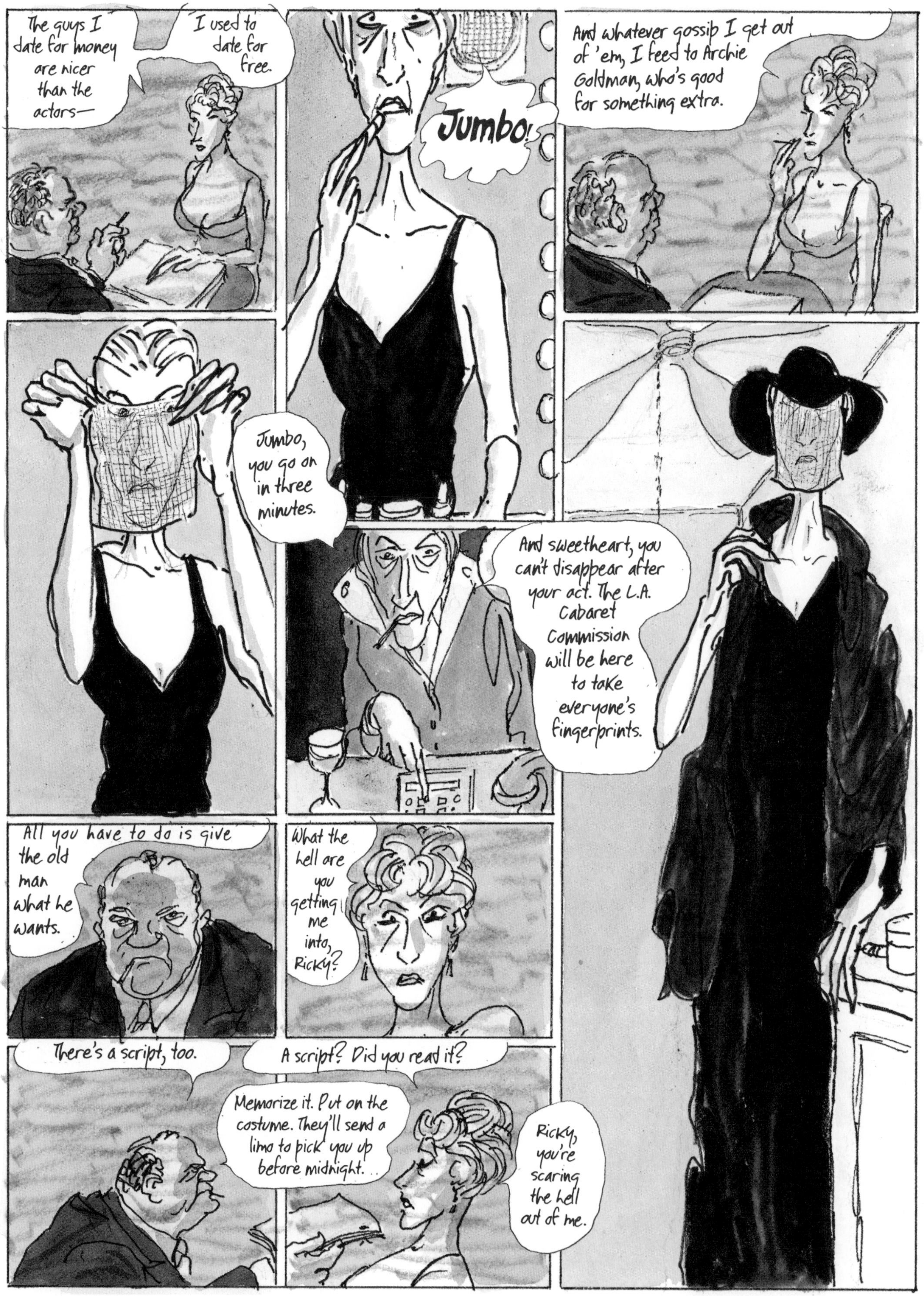
The guys I date for money are nicer than the actors—
I used to date for free.
Jumbo!
And whatever gossip I get out of 'em, I feed to Archie Goldman, who's good for something extra.
Jumbo, you go on in three minutes.
And sweetheart, you can't disappear after your act. The L.A. Cabaret Commission will be here to take everyone's fingerprints.
All you have to do is give the old man what he wants.
What the hell are you getting me into, Ricky?
There's a script, too.
A script? Did you read it?
Memorize it. Put on the costume. They'll send a limo to pick you up before midnight...
Ricky, you're scaring the hell out of me.

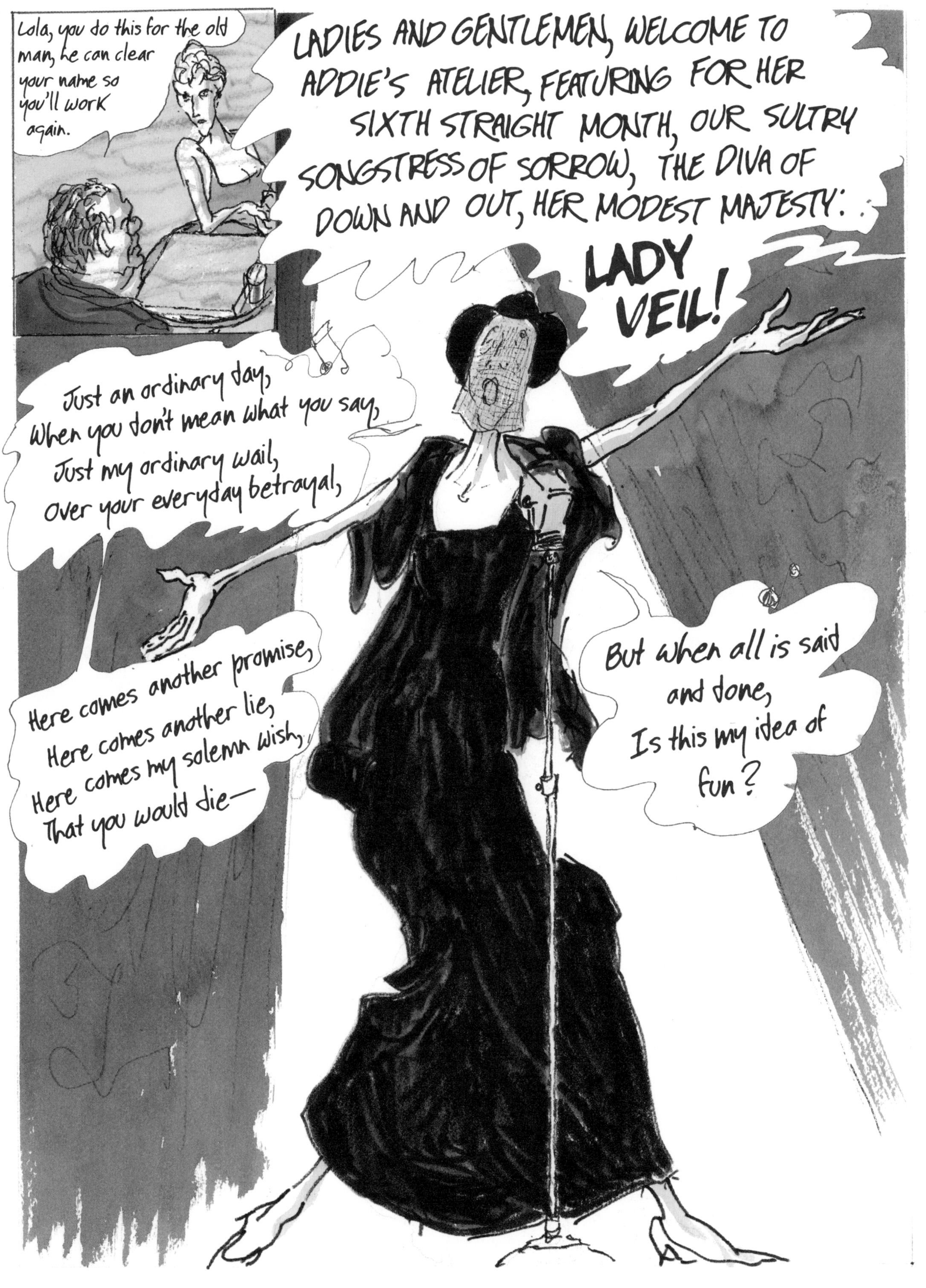
Lola, you do this for the old man, he can clear your name so you'll work again.
LADIES AND GENTLEMEN, WELCOME TO ADDIE'S ATELIER, FEATURING FOR HER SIXTH STRAIGHT MONTH, OUR SULTRY SONGSTRESS OF SORROW, THE DIVA OF DOWN AND OUT, HER MODEST MAJESTY:
LADY VEIL!
Just an ordinary day, When you don't mean what you say, Just my ordinary wail, Over your everyday betrayal,
Here comes another promise, Here comes another lie, Here comes my solemn wish, That you would die—
But when all is said and done, Is this my idea of fun?

Chapter Three: Flashback—Bay City, 1931

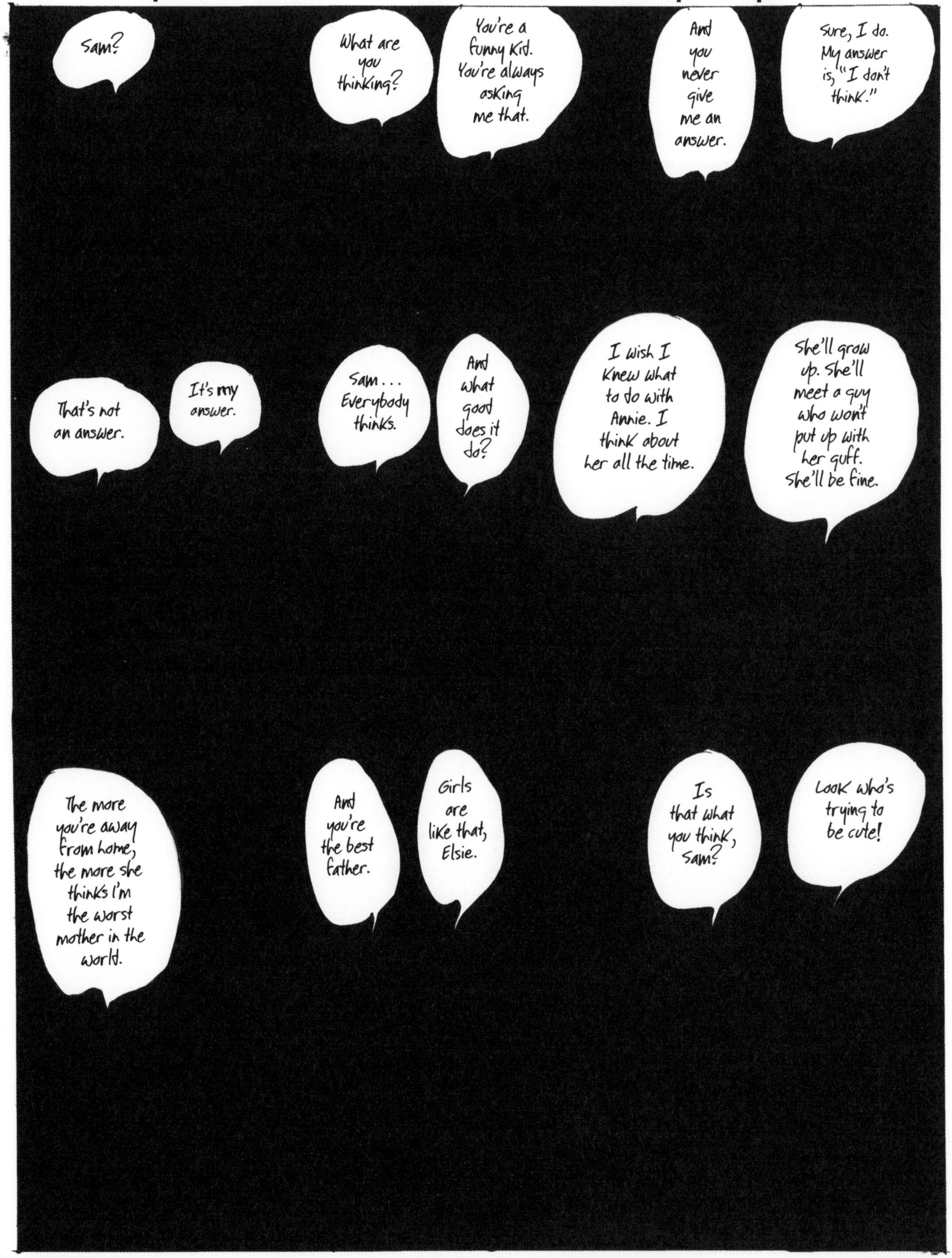
Sam?
What are you thinking?
You're a funny kid. You're always asking me that.
And you never give me an answer.
Sure, I do. My answer is, "I don't think."
That's not an answer.
It's my answer.
Sam . . . Everybody thinks.
And what good does it do?
I wish I knew what to do with Annie. I think about her all the time.
She'll grow up. She'll meet a guy who won't put up with her guff. She'll be fine.
The more you're away from home, the more she thinks I'm the worst mother in the world.
And you're the best father.
Girls are like that, Elsie.
Is that what you think, Sam?
Look who's trying to be cute!

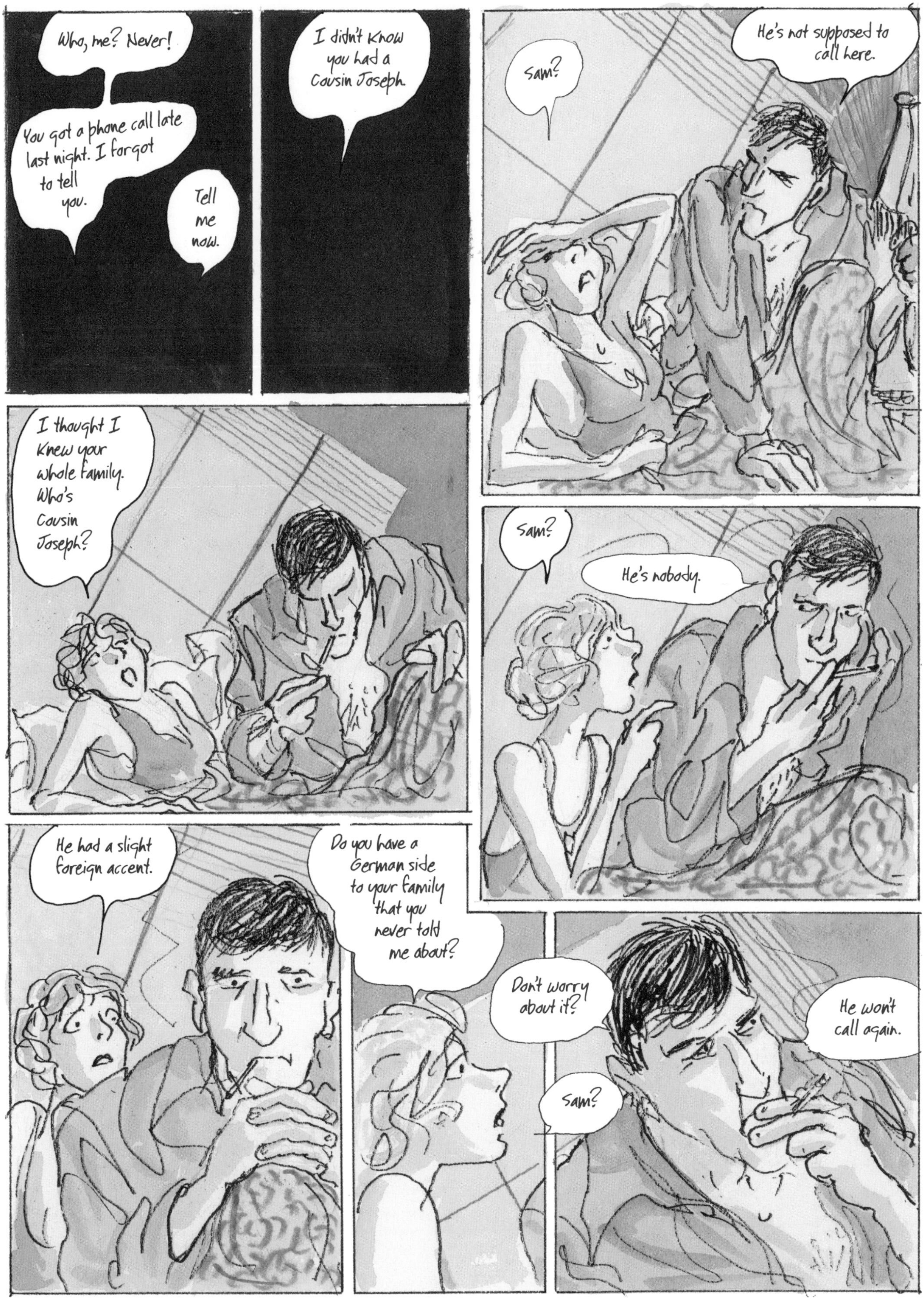

Who, me? Never!
You got a phone call late last night. I forgot to tell you.
Tell me now.
I didn't know you had a Cousin Joseph.
Sam?
He's not supposed to call here.
I thought I knew your whole family. Who's Cousin Joseph?
Sam?
He's nobody.
He had a slight foreign accent.
Do you have a German side to your family that you never told me about?
Don't worry about it?
Sam?
He won't call again.

Chapter Four: Shamus

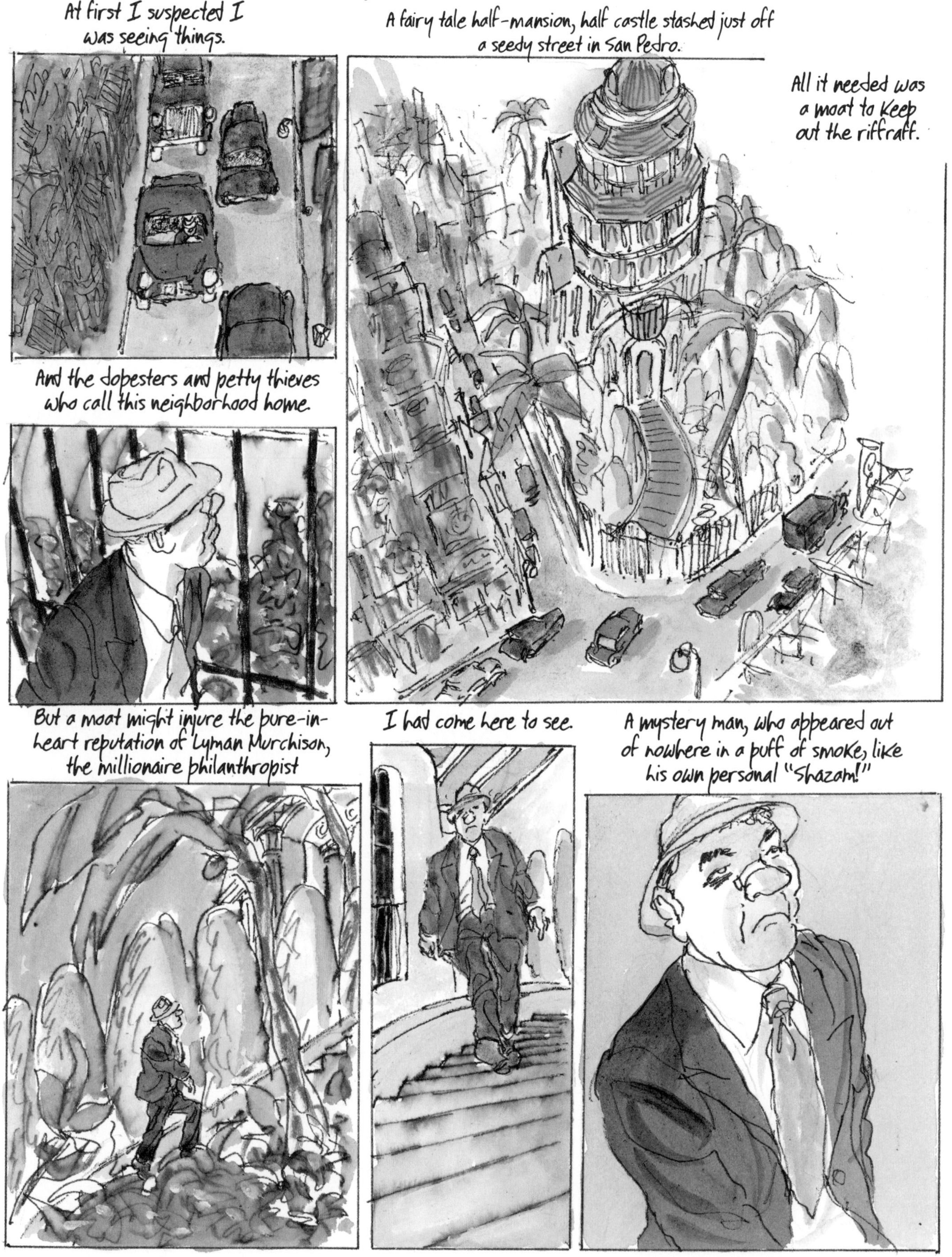

At first I suspected I was seeing things.
A fairy tale half-mansion, half castle stashed just off a seedy street in San Pedro.
All it needed was a moat to keep out the riffraff.
And the dopesters and petty thieves who call this neighborhood home.
But a moat might injure the pure-in-heart reputation of Lyman Murchison, the millionaire philanthropist
I had come here to see.
A mystery man, who appeared out of nowhere in a puff of smoke, like his own personal "Shazam!"

But he's less Captain Marvel than Captain America.

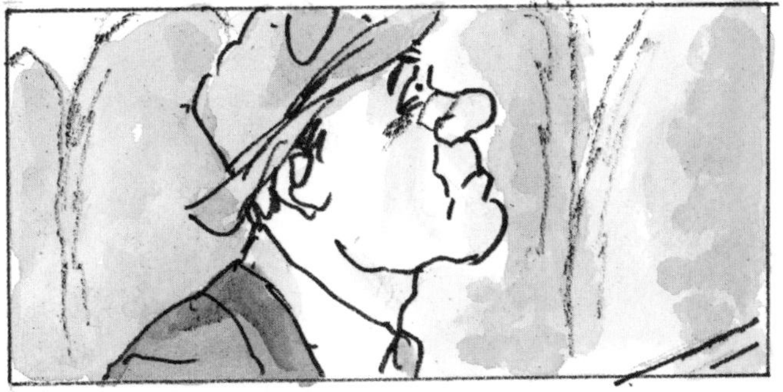

He doesn't fight crime, he fights Reds. And all the Red sympathizers, who, once upon a time, were in fashion out here.

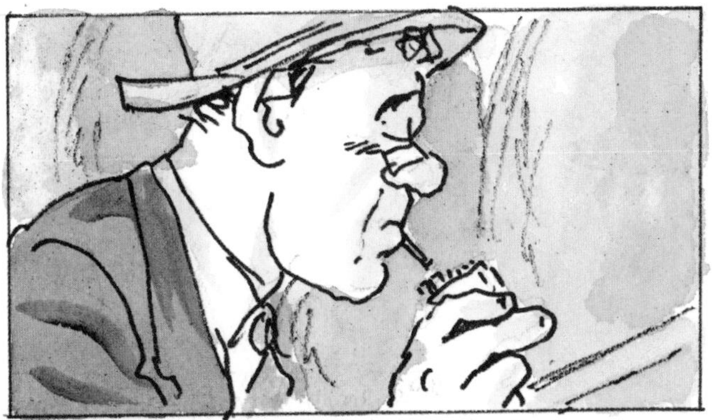

Until the war ended. And faster than a speeding bullet, Red went out of style.

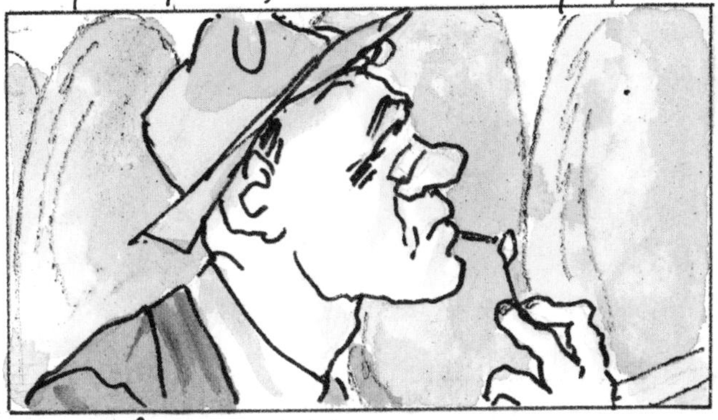

That is, if you wanted to keep your movie job.

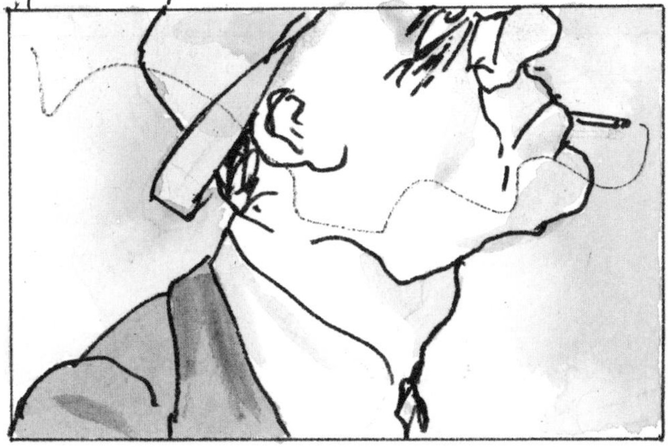

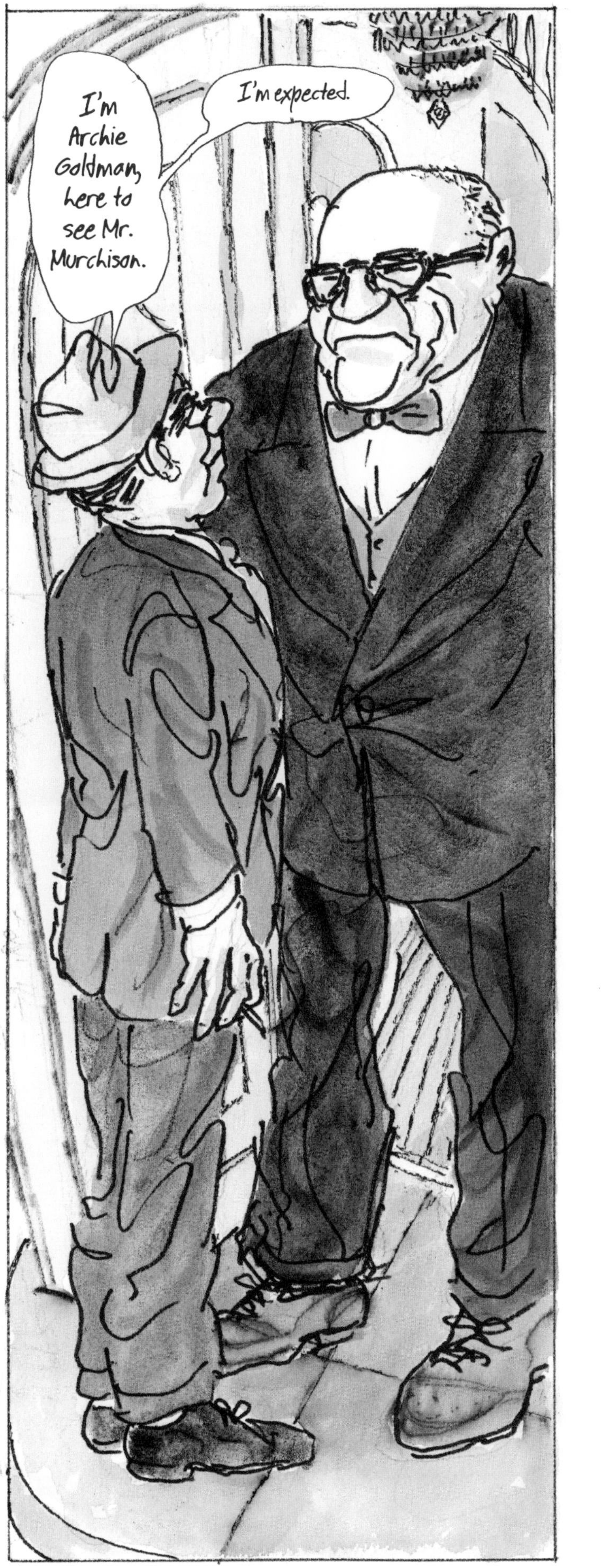
I'm Archie Goldman, here to see Mr. Murchison.
I'm expected.

Chapter Five: Miss Know-It-All

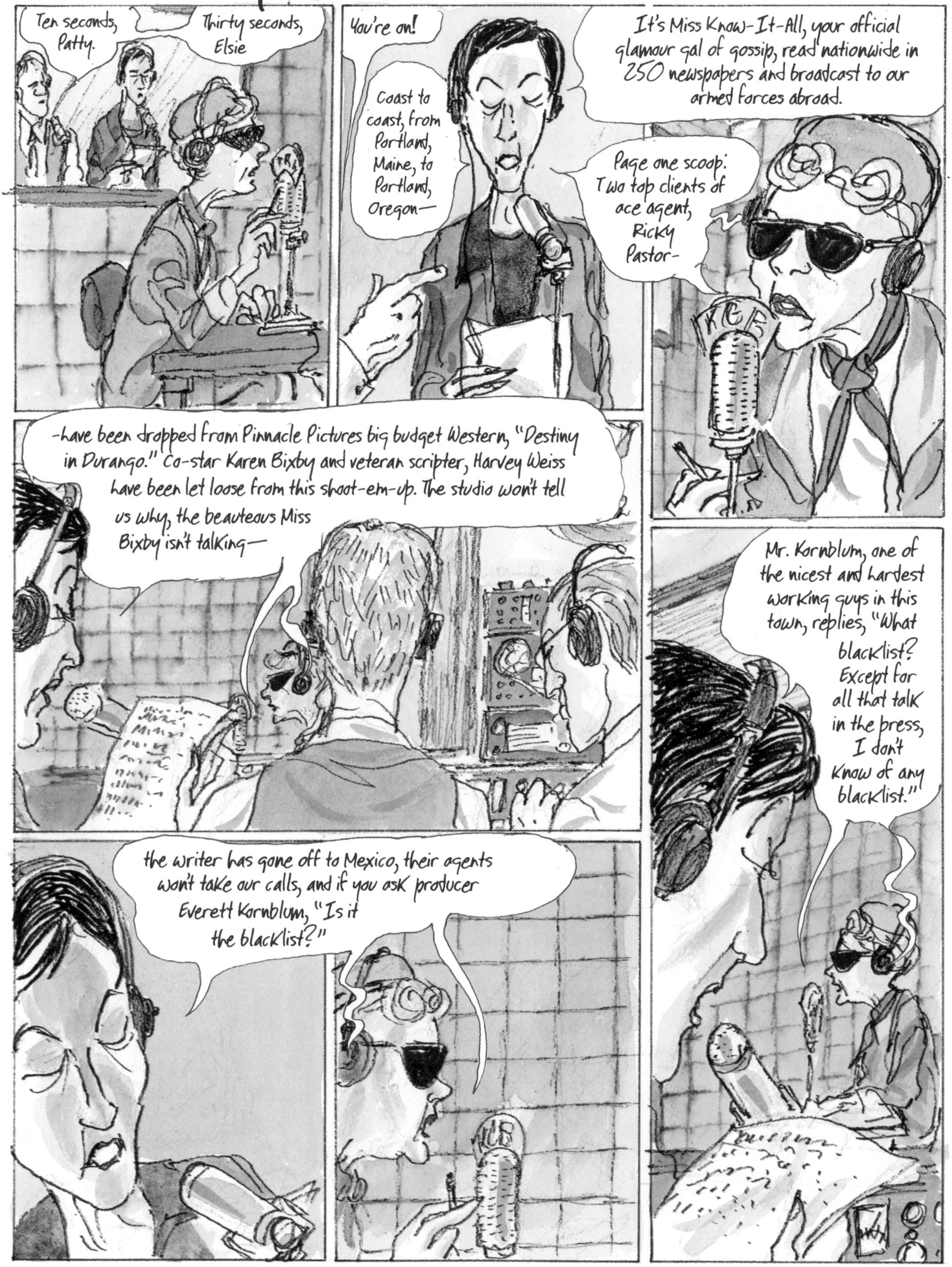

Ten seconds, Patty.
Thirty seconds, Elsie
You're on!
Coast to coast, from Portland, Maine, to Portland, Oregon—
It's Miss Know-It-All, your official glamour gal of gossip, read nationwide in 250 newspapers and broadcast to our armed forces abroad.
Page one scoop: Two top clients of ace agent, Ricky Pastor-
KCF
-have been dropped from Pinnacle Pictures big budget Western, "Destiny in Durango." Co-star Karen Bixby and veteran scripter, Harvey Weiss have been let loose from this shoot-em-up. The studio won't tell us why, the beauteous Miss Bixby isn't talking—
Mr. Kornblum, one of the nicest and hardest working guys in this town, replies, "What blacklist? Except for all that talk in the press, I don't know of any blacklist."
the writer has gone off to Mexico, their agents won't take our calls, and if you ask producer Everett Kornblum, "Is it the blacklist?"

Chapter Six: The Greenhouse

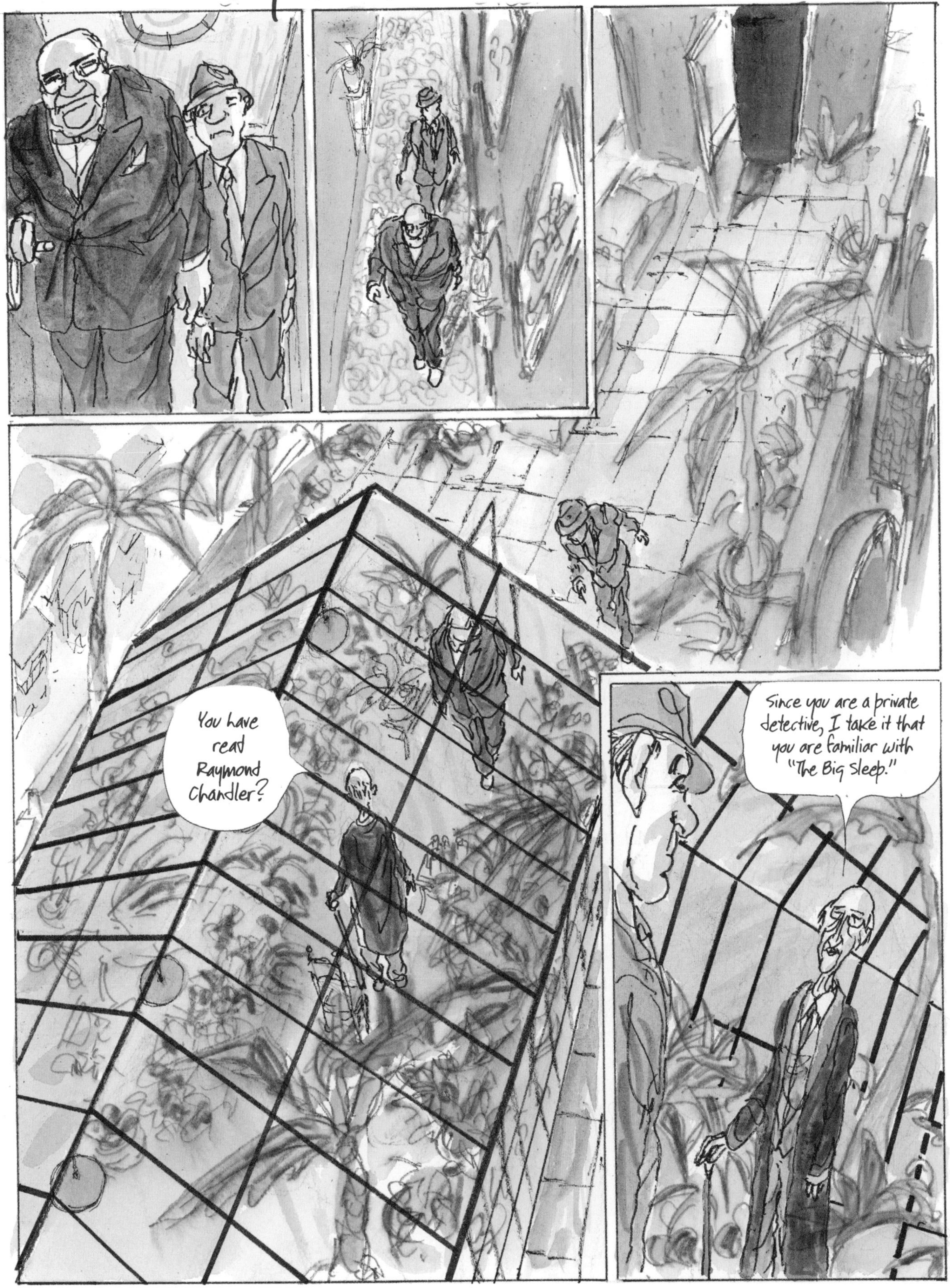
You have read Raymond Chandler?
Since you are a private detective, I take it that you are familiar with "The Big Sleep."

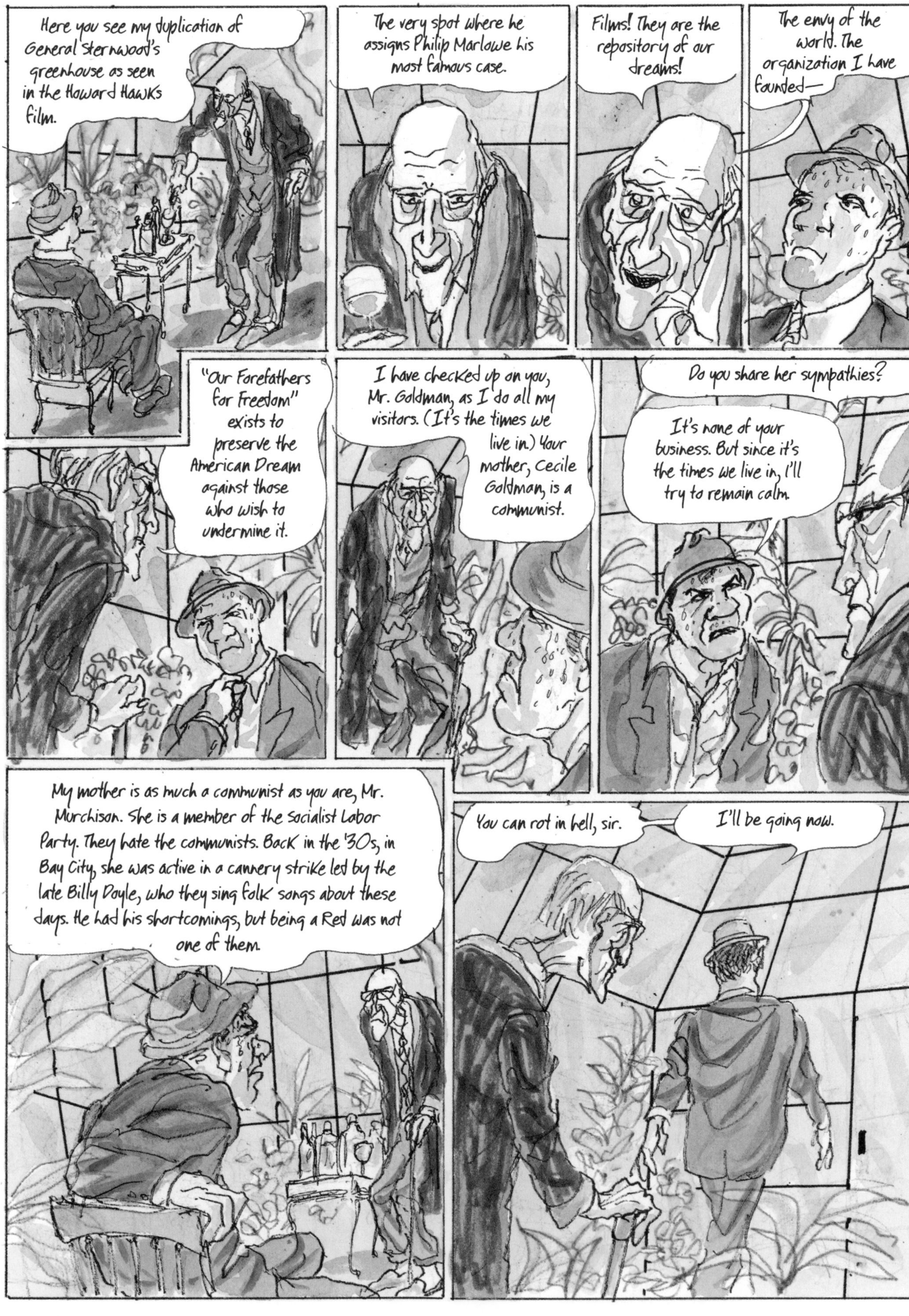
Here you see my duplication of General Sternwood's greenhouse as seen in the Howard Hawks film.
The very spot where he assigns Philip Marlowe his most famous case.
Films! They are the repository of our dreams!
The envy of the world. The organization I have founded—
"Our Forefathers for Freedom" exists to preserve the American Dream against those who wish to undermine it.
I have checked up on you, Mr. Goldman, as I do all my visitors. (It's the times we live in.) Your mother, Cecile Goldman, is a communist.
Do you share her sympathies?
It's none of your business. But since it's the times we live in, I'll try to remain calm.
My mother is as much a communist as you are, Mr. Murchison. She is a member of the Socialist Labor Party. They hate the communists. Back in the '30s, in Bay City, she was active in a cannery strike led by the late Billy Doyle, who they sing folk songs about these days. He had his shortcomings, but being a Red was not one of them.
You can rot in hell, sir.
I'll be going now.

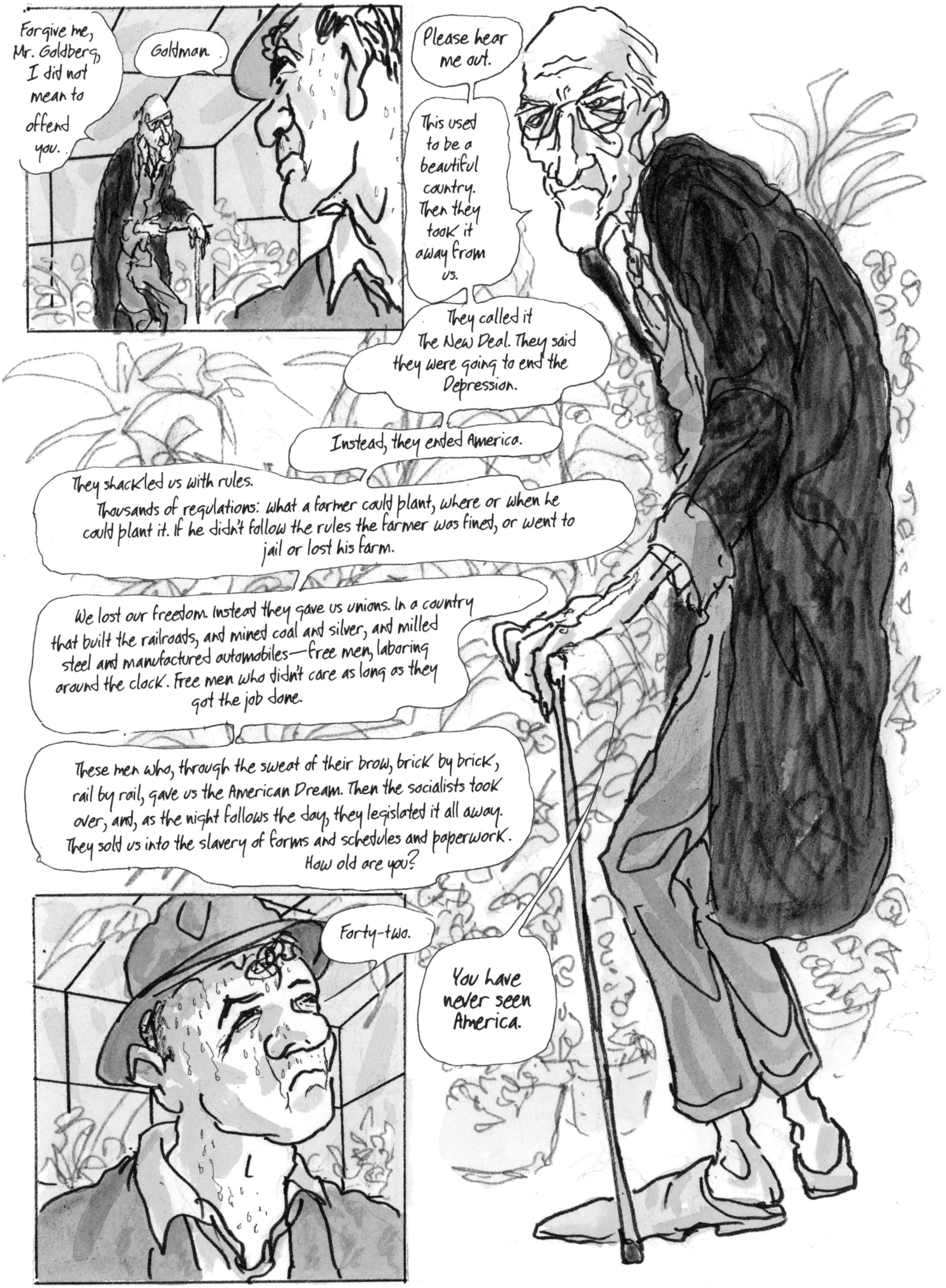

Forgive me, Mr. Goldberg, I did not mean to offend you.
Goldman.
Please hear me out.
This used to be a beautiful country. Then they took it away from us.
They called it The New Deal. They said they were going to end the Depression.
Instead, they ended America.
They shackled us with rules. Thousands of regulations: what a farmer could plant, where or when he could plant it. If he didn't follow the rules the farmer was fined, or went to jail or lost his farm.
We lost our freedom. Instead they gave us unions. In a country that built the railroads, and mined coal and silver, and milled steel and manufactured automobiles—free men, laboring around the clock. Free men who didn't care as long as they got the job done.
These men who, through the sweat of their brow, brick by brick, rail by rail, gave us the American Dream. Then the socialists took over, and, as the night follows the day, they legislated it all away. They sold us into the slavery of forms and schedules and paperwork. How old are you?
Forty-two.
You have never seen America.

Chapter Seven: The Kornblum Metaphor

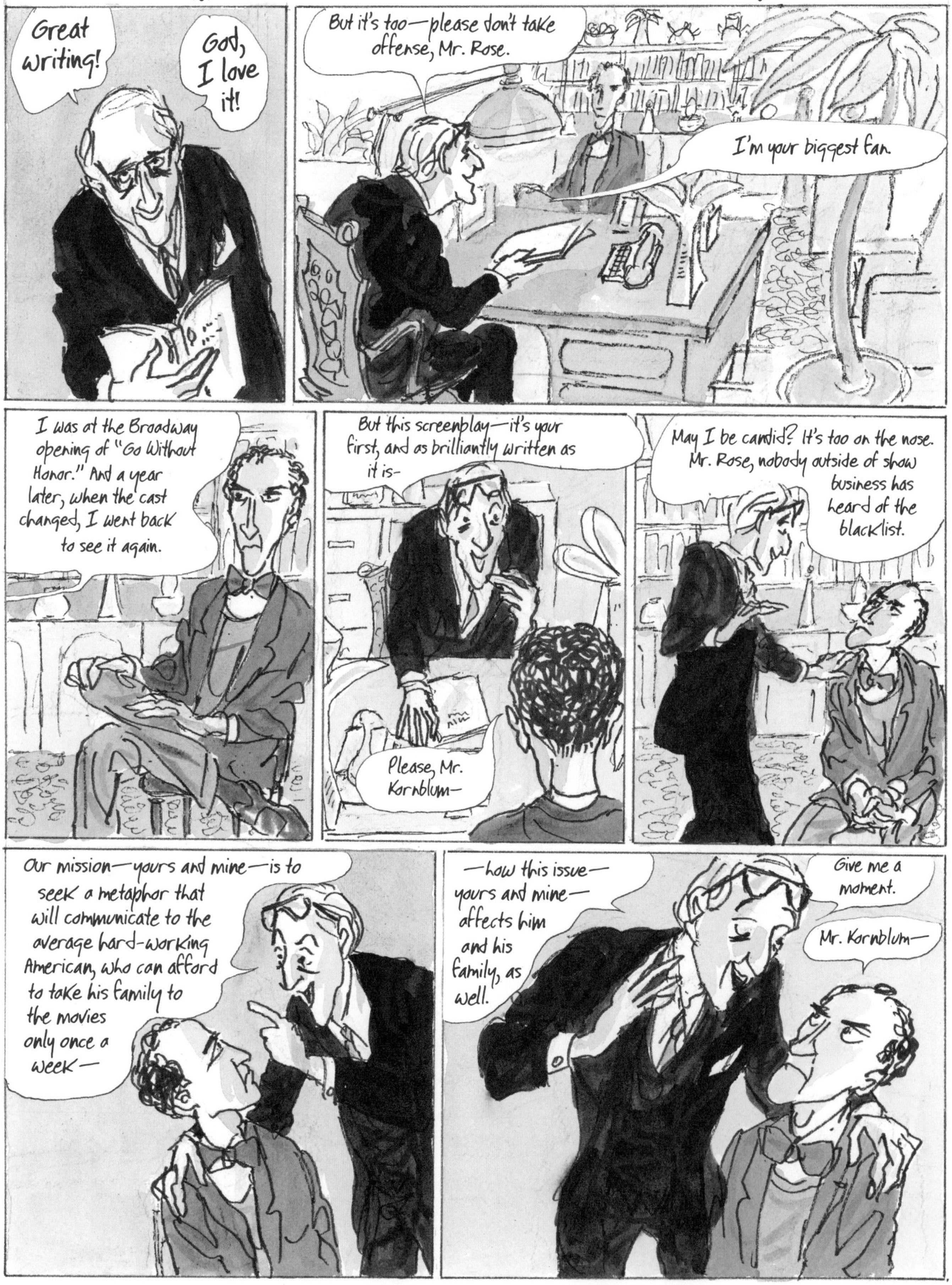

Great writing!
God, I love it!
But it's too—please don't take offense, Mr. Rose.
I'm your biggest fan.
I was at the Broadway opening of "Go Without Honor." And a year later, when the cast changed, I went back to see it again.
But this screenplay—it's your first, and as brilliantly written as it is-
Please, Mr. Kornblum—
May I be candid? It's too on the nose. Mr. Rose, nobody outside of show business has heard of the blacklist.
Our mission—yours and mine—is to seek a metaphor that will communicate to the average hard-working American, who can afford to take his family to the movies only once a week—
—how this issue—yours and mine—affects him and his family, as well.
Give me a moment.
Mr. Kornblum—

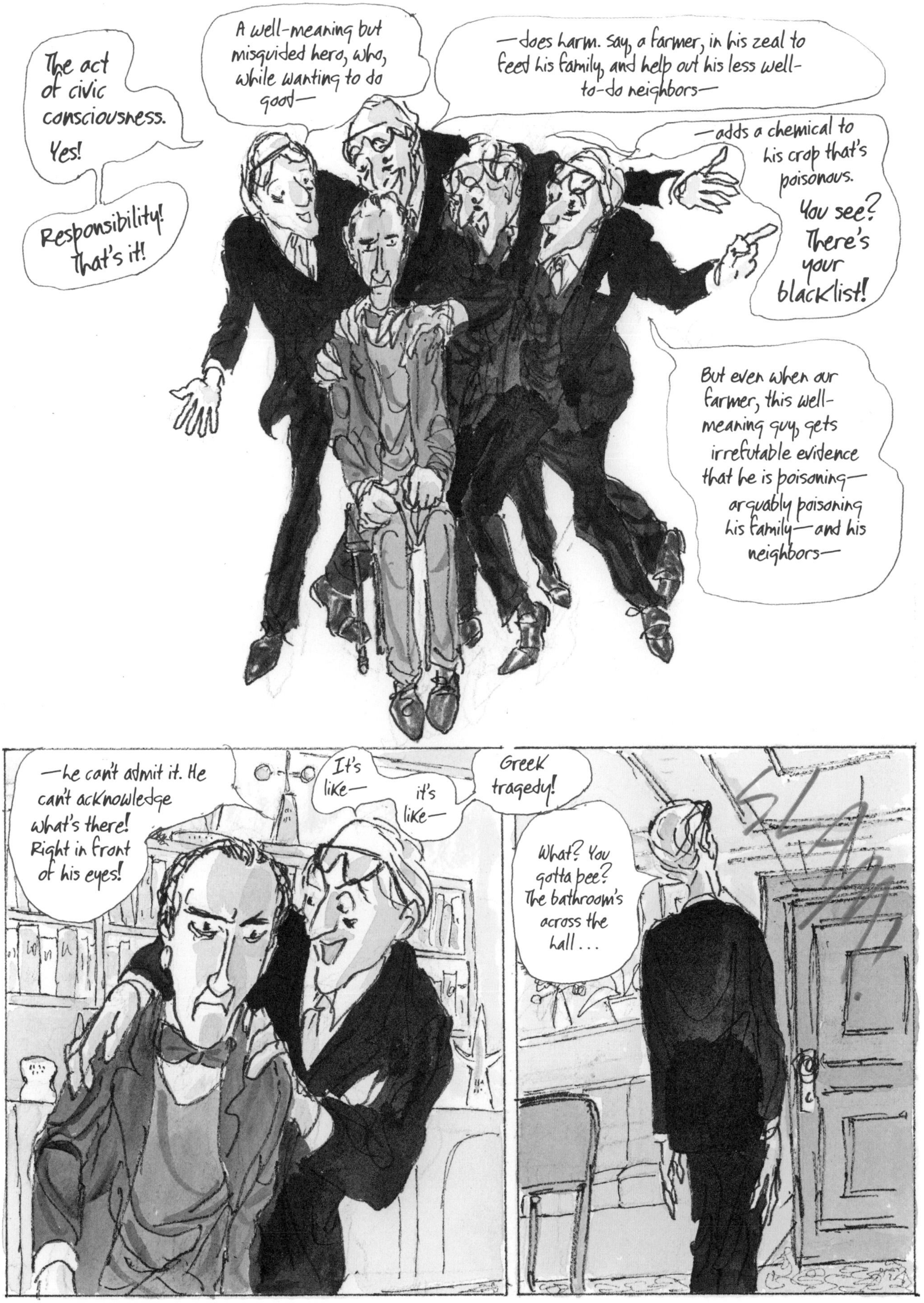
The act of civic consciousness.
Yes!
Responsibility! That's it!
A well-meaning but misguided hero, who, while wanting to do good—
—does harm. Say, a farmer, in his zeal to feed his family, and help out his less well-to-do neighbors—
—adds a chemical to his crop that's poisonous.
You see? There's your blacklist!
But even when our farmer, this well-meaning guy, gets irrefutable evidence that he is poisoning—arguably poisoning his family—and his neighbors—
—he can't admit it. He can't acknowledge what's there! Right in front of his eyes!
It's like—
it's like—
Greek tragedy!
What? You gotta pee? The bathroom's across the hall . . .
SLAM

Chapter Eight: The Ghost Script

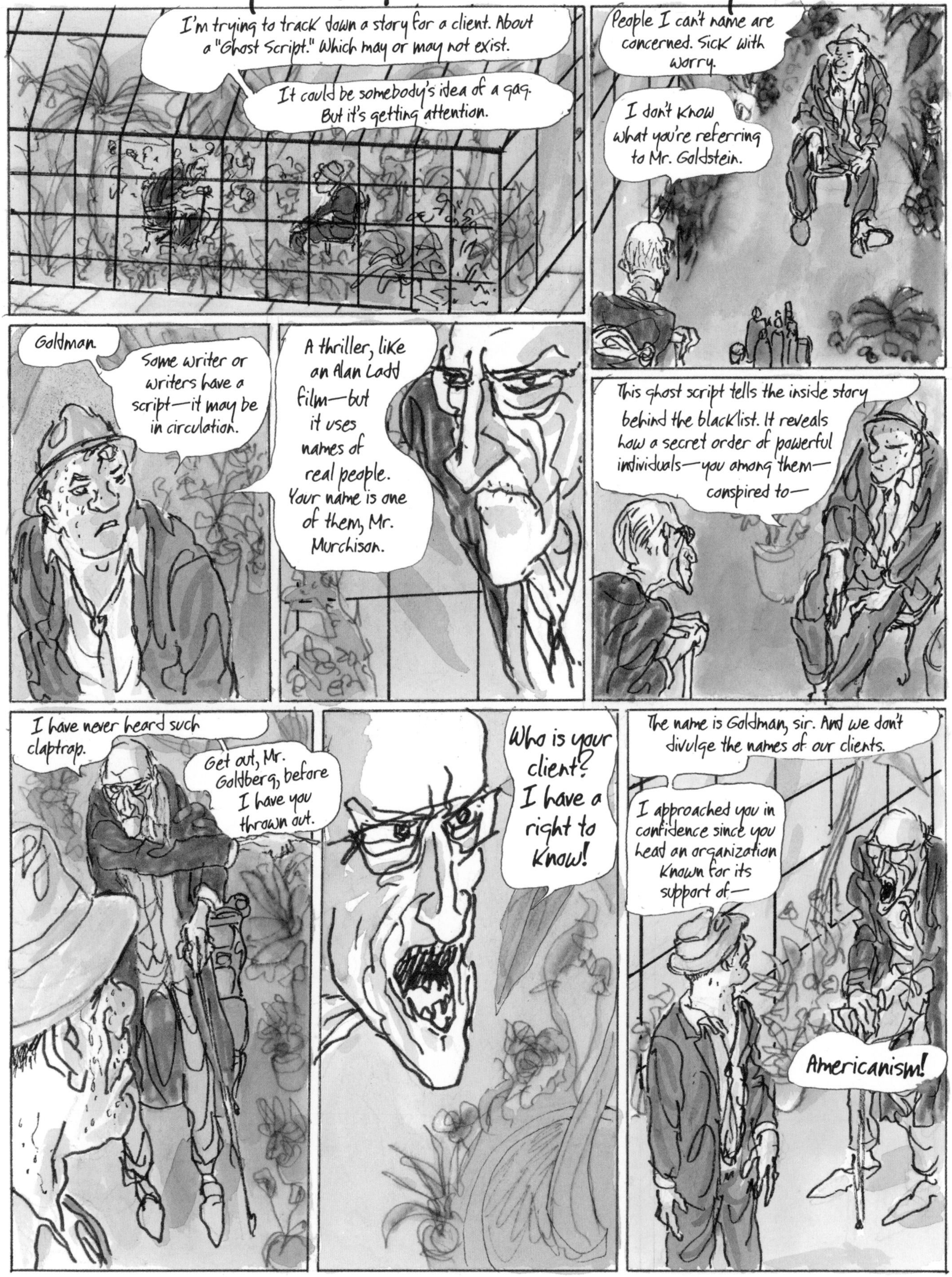

I'm trying to track down a story for a client. About a "Ghost Script." Which may or may not exist.
It could be somebody's idea of a gag. But it's getting attention.
People I can't name are concerned. Sick with worry.
I don't know what you're referring to Mr. Goldstein.
Goldman.
Some writer or writers have a script—it may be in circulation.
A thriller, like an Alan Ladd film—but it uses names of real people. Your name is one of them, Mr. Murchison.
This ghost script tells the inside story behind the blacklist. It reveals how a secret order of powerful individuals—you among them—conspired to—
I have never heard such claptrap.
Get out, Mr. Goldberg, before I have you thrown out.
Who is your client? I have a right to know!
The name is Goldman, sir. And we don't divulge the names of our clients.
I approached you in confidence since you head an organization known for its support of—
Americanism!

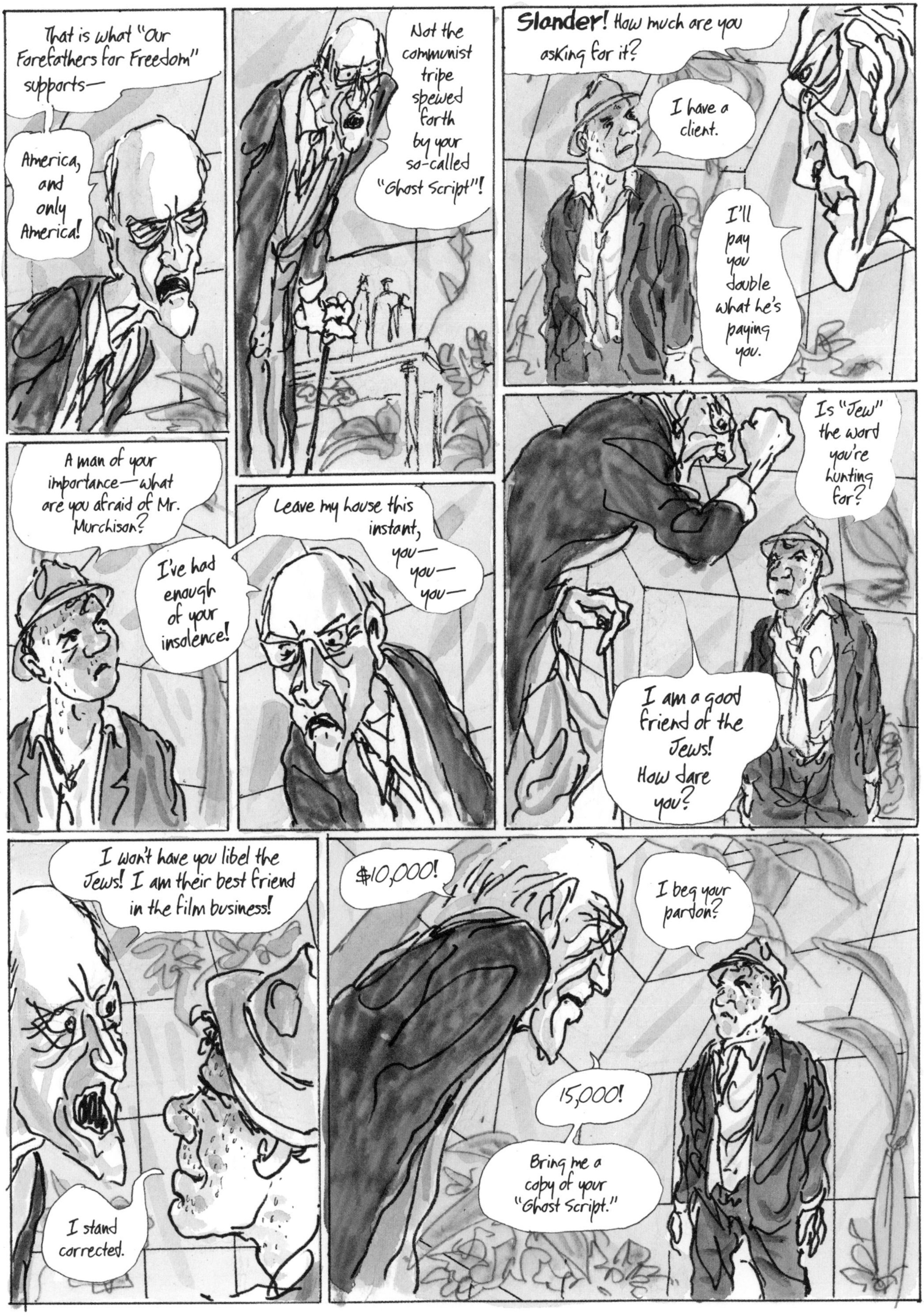
That is what "Our Forefathers for Freedom" supports—
America, and only America!
Not the communist tripe spewed forth by your so-called "Ghost Script"!
Slander! How much are you asking for it?
I have a client.
I'll pay you double what he's paying you.
A man of your importance—what are you afraid of Mr. Murchison?
I've had enough of your insolence!
Leave my house this instant, you— you— you—
Is "Jew" the word you're hunting for?
I am a good friend of the Jews! How dare you?
I won't have you libel the Jews! I am their best friend in the film business!
I stand corrected.
$10,000!
I beg your pardon?
15,000!
Bring me a copy of your "Ghost Script."

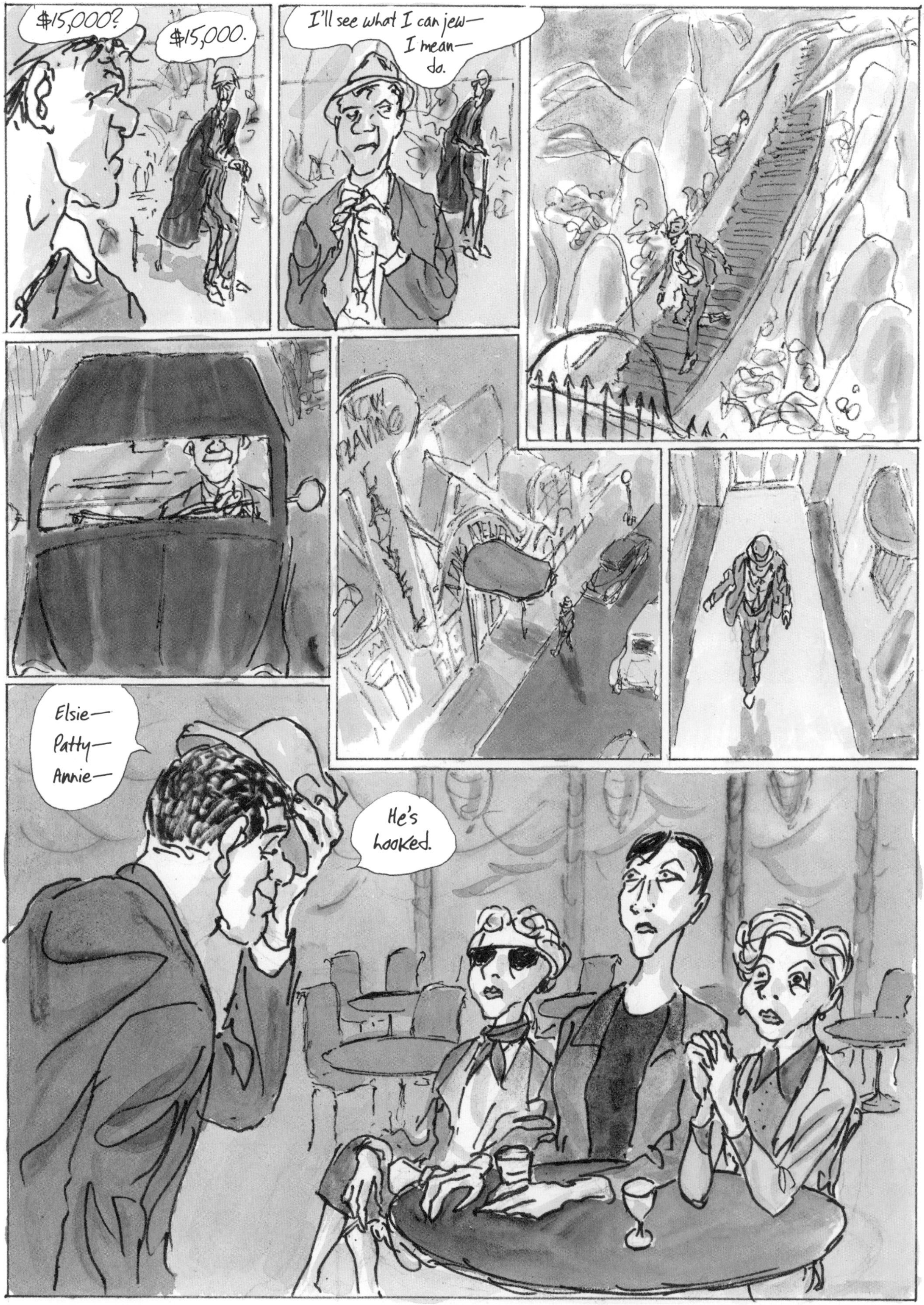
$15,000?
$15,000.
I'll see what I can jew—
I mean—
do.
NOW PLAYING
Elsie—
Patty—
Annie—
He's hooked.

Chapter Nine: Sam's Ghost

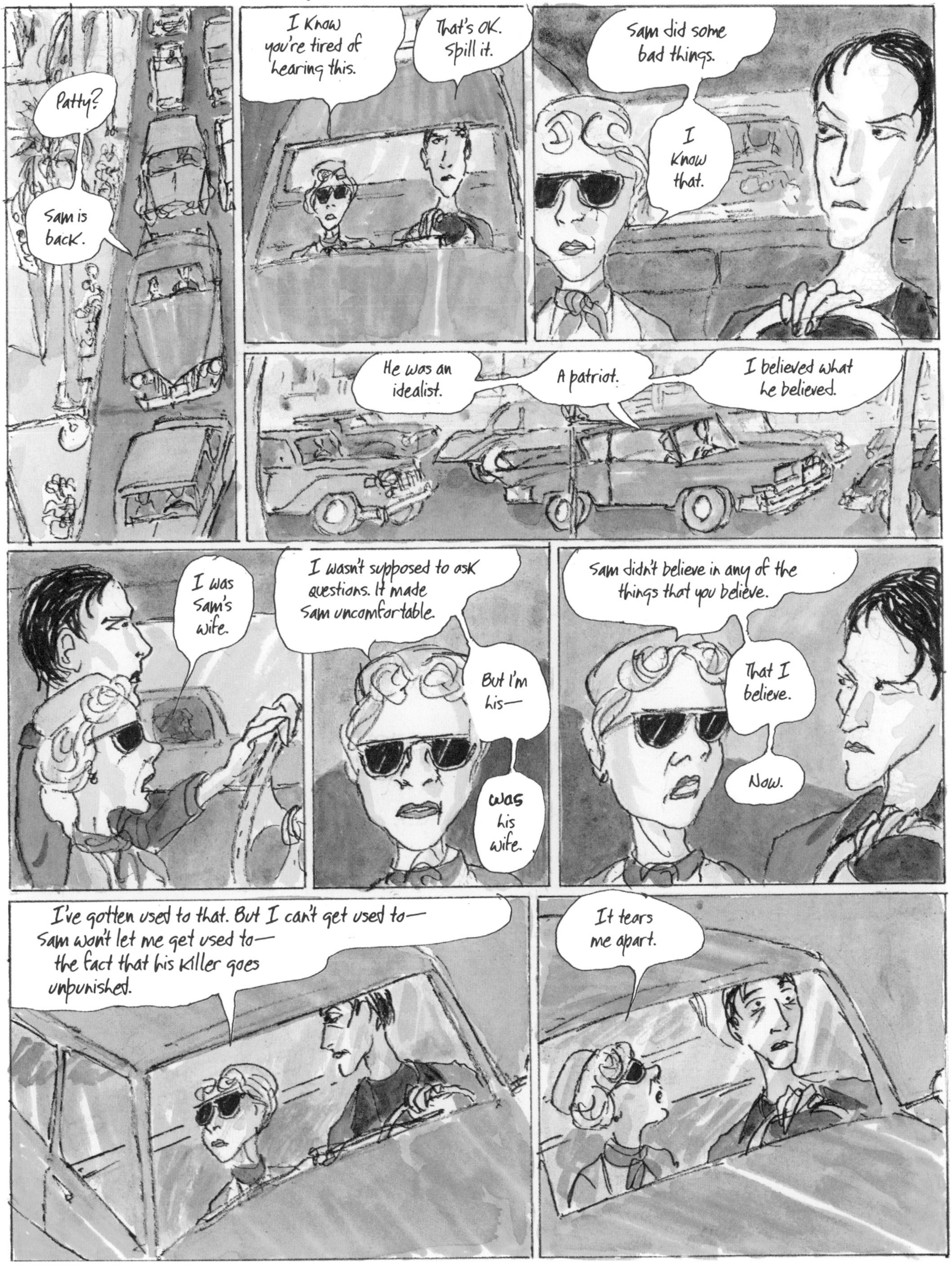

Patty?
Sam is back.
I Know you're tired of hearing this.
That's OK. Spill it.
Sam did some bad things.
I Know that.
He was an idealist.
A patriot.
I believed what he believed.
I was Sam's wife.
I wasn't supposed to ask questions. It made Sam uncomfortable.
But I'm his—
was his wife.
Sam didn't believe in any of the things that you believe.
That I believe.
Now.
I've gotten used to that. But I can't get used to— Sam won't let me get used to— the fact that his Killer goes unpunished.
It tears me apart.

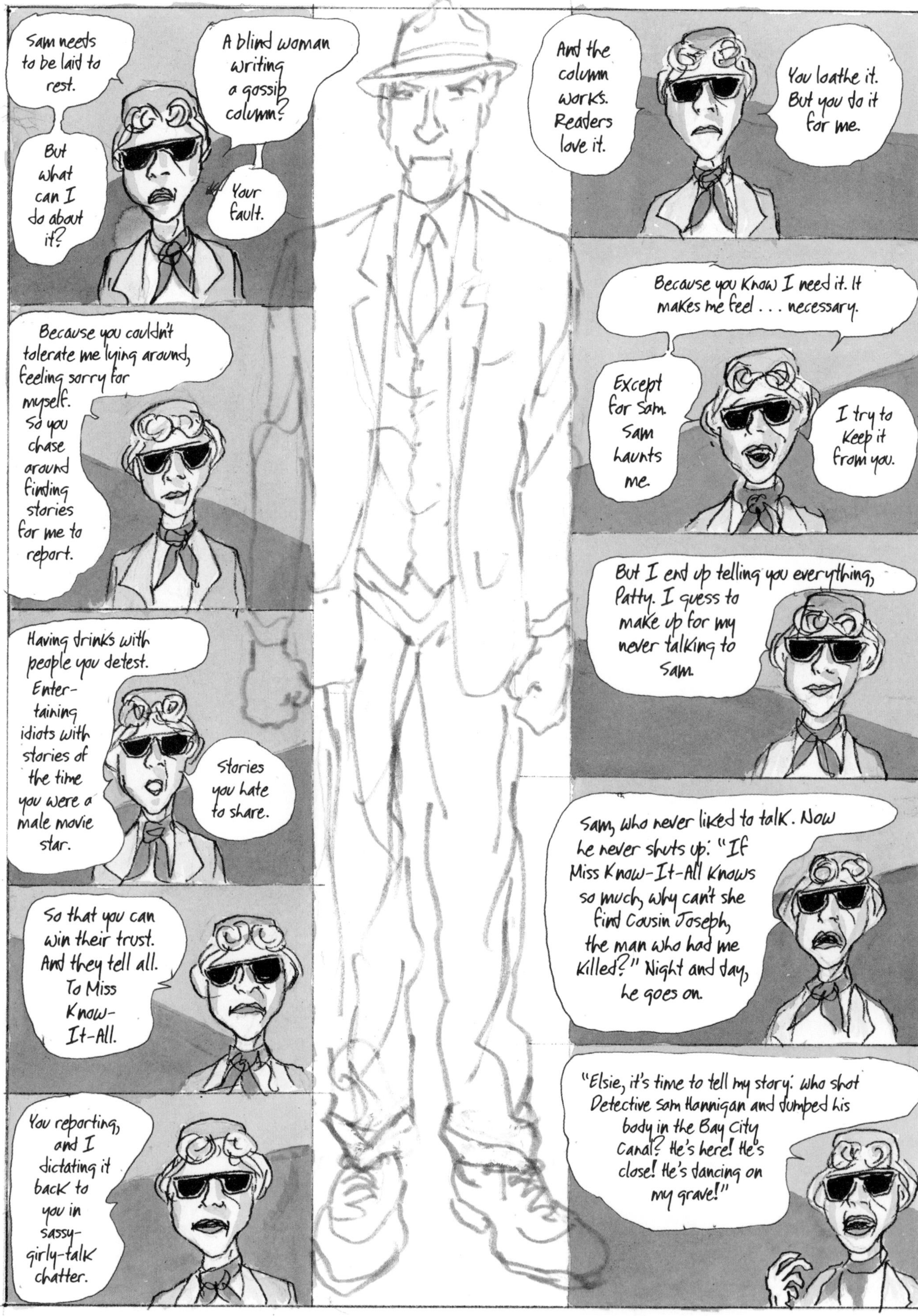

Sam needs to be laid to rest.
A blind woman writing a gossip column?
But what can I do about it?
Your fault.
And the column works. Readers love it.
You loathe it. But you do it for me.
Because you couldn't tolerate me lying around, feeling sorry for myself. So you chase around finding stories for me to report.
Because you know I need it. It makes me feel . . . necessary.
Except for Sam. Sam haunts me.
I try to keep it from you.
Having drinks with people you detest. Enter-taining idiots with stories of the time you were a male movie star.
Stories you hate to share.
But I end up telling you everything, Patty. I guess to make up for my never talking to Sam.
So that you can win their trust. And they tell all. To Miss Know-It-All.
Sam, who never liked to talk. Now he never shuts up: "If Miss Know-It-All knows so much, why can't she find Cousin Joseph, the man who had me killed?" Night and day, he goes on.
You reporting, and I dictating it back to you in sassy-girly-talk chatter.
"Elsie, it's time to tell my story: who shot Detective Sam Hannigan and dumped his body in the Bay City Canal? He's here! He's close! He's dancing on my grave!"

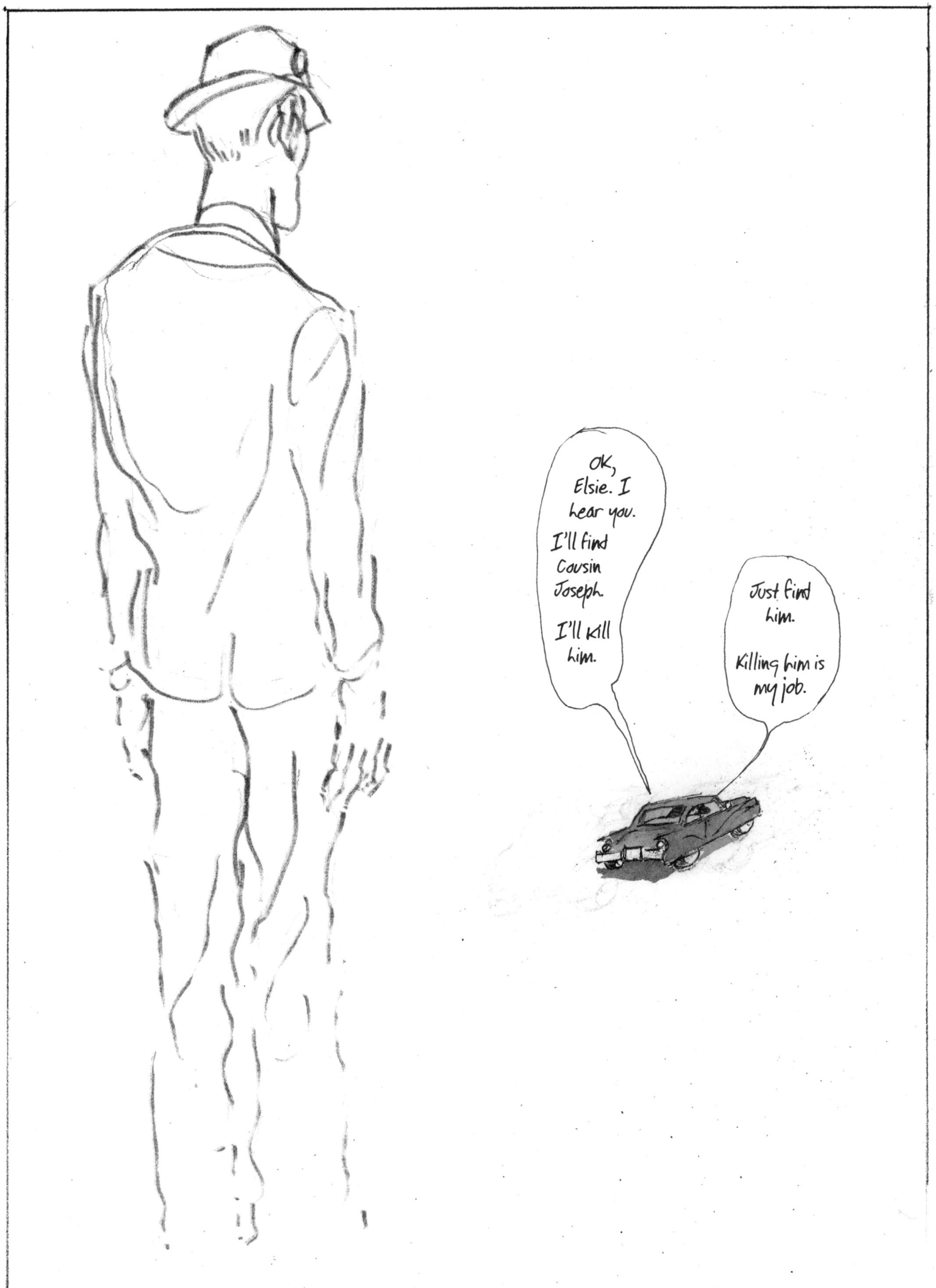
OK, Elsie. I hear you. I'll find Cousin Joseph. I'll kill him.
Just find him. Killing him is my job.

Chapter Ten: Flashback—Bay City, 1931

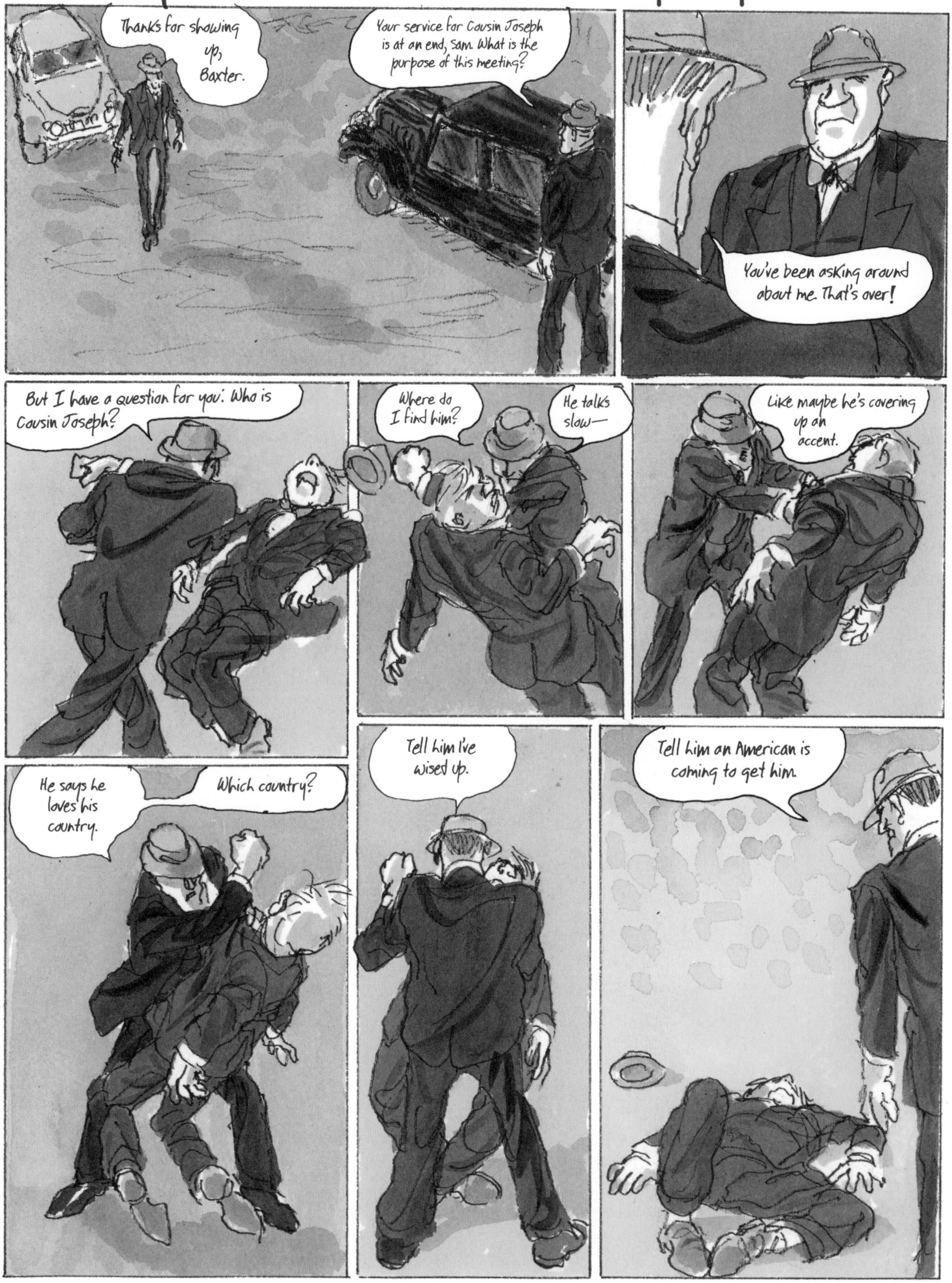

Thanks for showing up, Baxter.
Your service for Cousin Joseph is at an end, Sam. What is the purpose of this meeting?
You've been asking around about me. That's over!
But I have a question for you: Who is Cousin Joseph?
Where do I find him?
He talks slow—
Like maybe he's covering up an accent.
He says he loves his country.
Which country?
Tell him I've wised up.
Tell him an American is coming to get him.

Chapter Eleven: Cissy Goldman's Late-Night Visitor

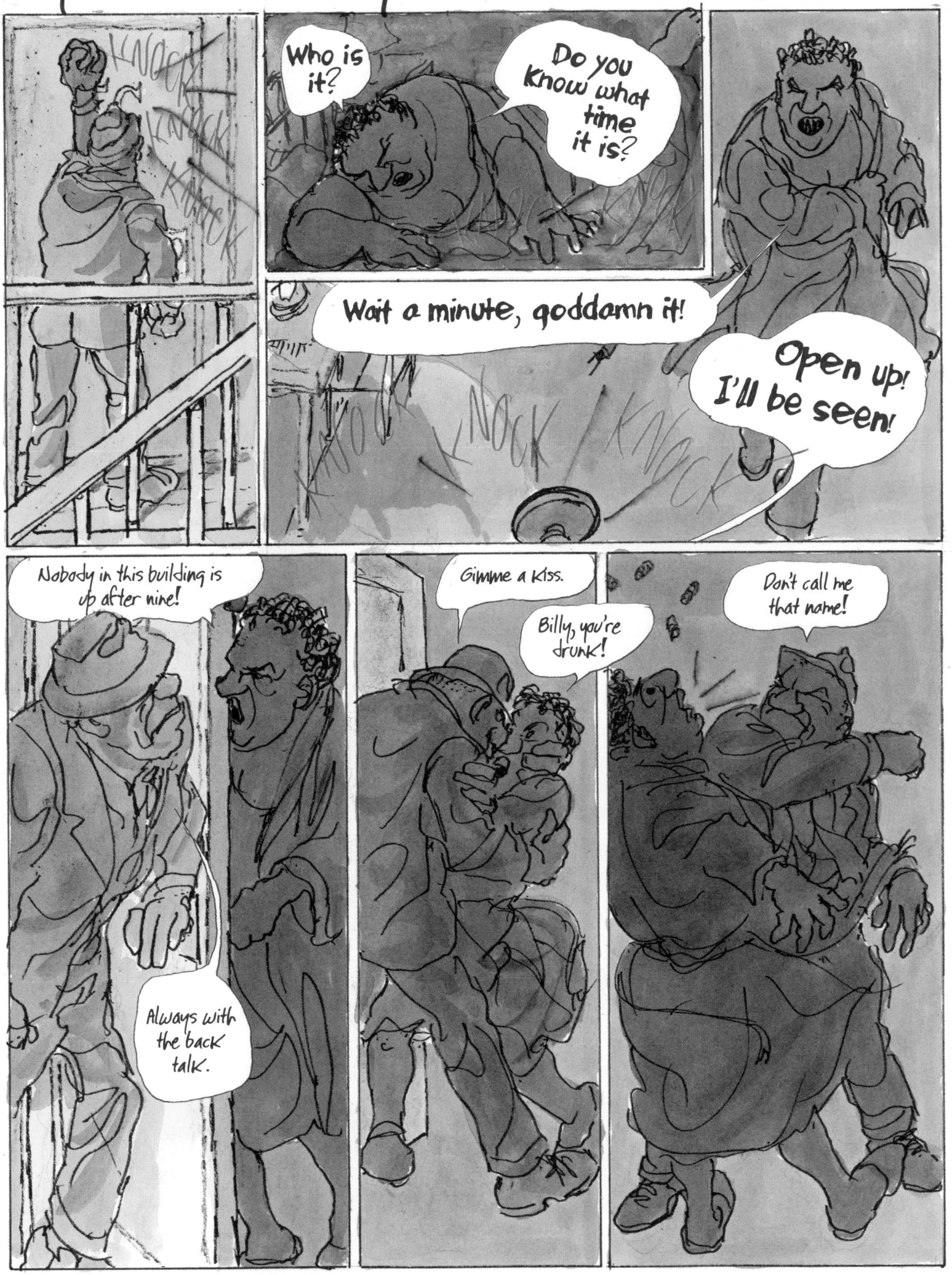
KNOCK KNOCK KNOCK
Who is it?
Do you know what time it is?
Wait a minute, goddamn it!
KNOCK KNOCK KNOCK
Open up! I'll be seen!
Nobody in this building is up after nine!
Always with the back talk.
Gimme a kiss.
Billy, you're drunk!
Don't call me that name!

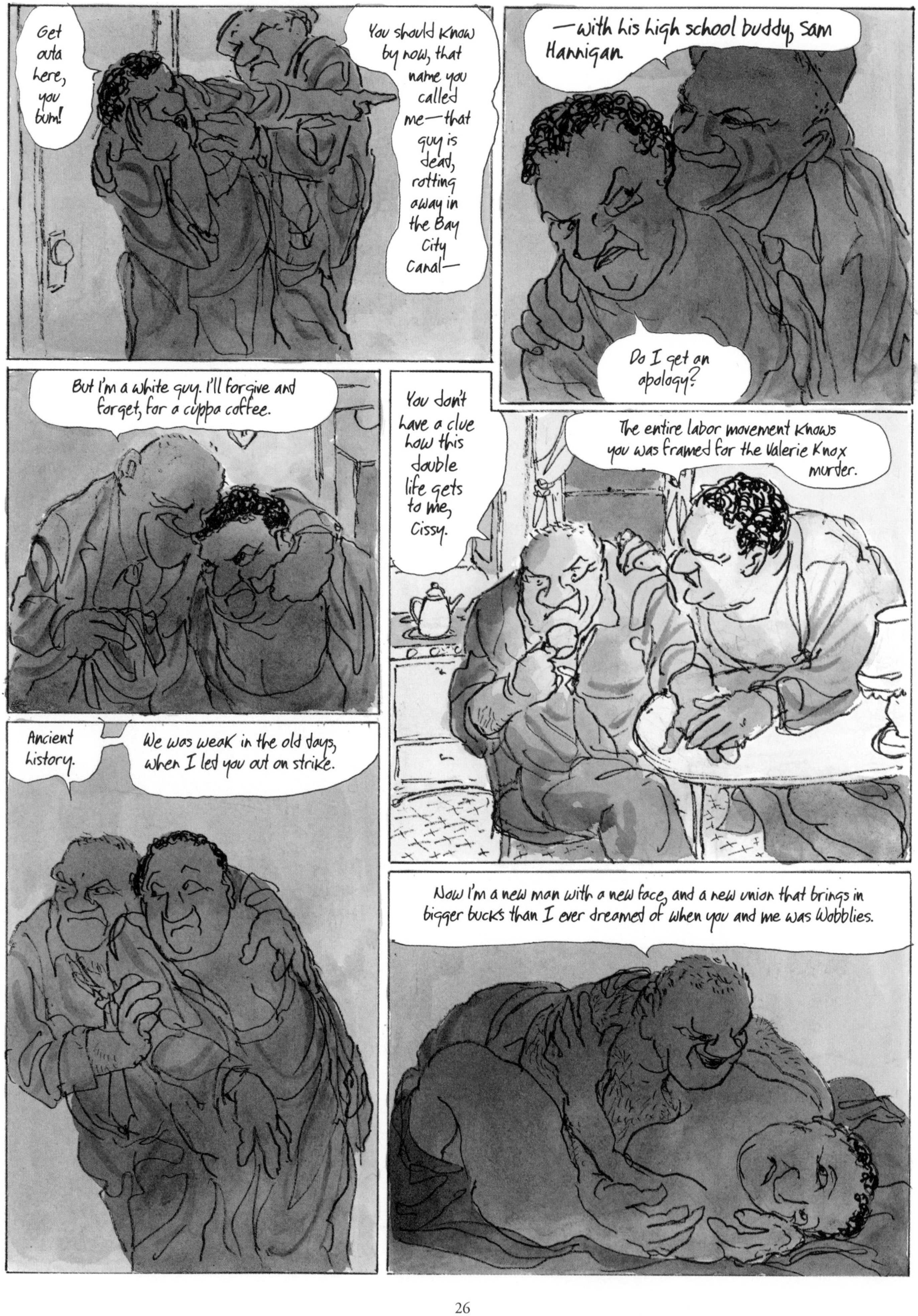
Get outa here, you bum!
You should know by now, that name you called me—that guy is dead, rotting away in the Bay City Canal—
—with his high school buddy, Sam Hannigan.
Do I get an apology?
But I'm a white guy. I'll forgive and forget, for a cuppa coffee.
You don't have a clue how this double life gets to me, Cissy.
The entire labor movement knows you was framed for the Valerie Knox murder.
Ancient history.
We was weak in the old days, when I led you out on strike.
Now I'm a new man with a new face, and a new union that brings in bigger bucks than I ever dreamed of when you and me was Wobblies.

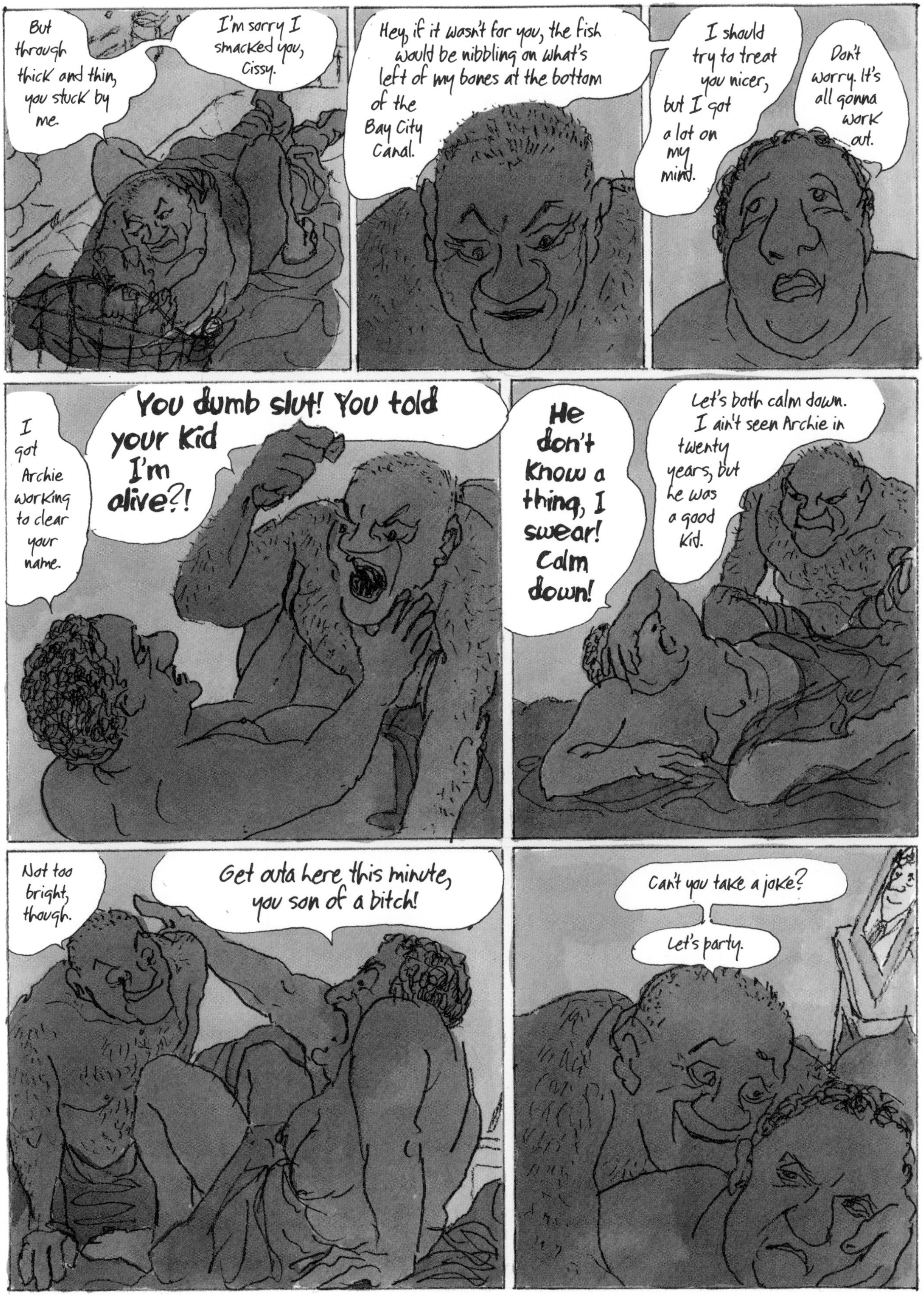
But through thick and thin, you stuck by me.
I'm sorry I smacked you, Cissy.
Hey, if it wasn't for you, the fish would be nibbling on what's left of my bones at the bottom of the Bay City Canal.
I should try to treat you nicer, but I got a lot on my mind.
Don't worry. It's all gonna work out.
I got Archie working to clear your name.
You dumb slut! You told your kid I'm alive?!
He don't know a thing, I swear! Calm down!
Let's both calm down. I ain't seen Archie in twenty years, but he was a good kid.
Not too bright, though.
Get outa here this minute, you son of a bitch!
Can't you take a joke?
Let's party.

Chapter Twelve: Sammy Hannigan

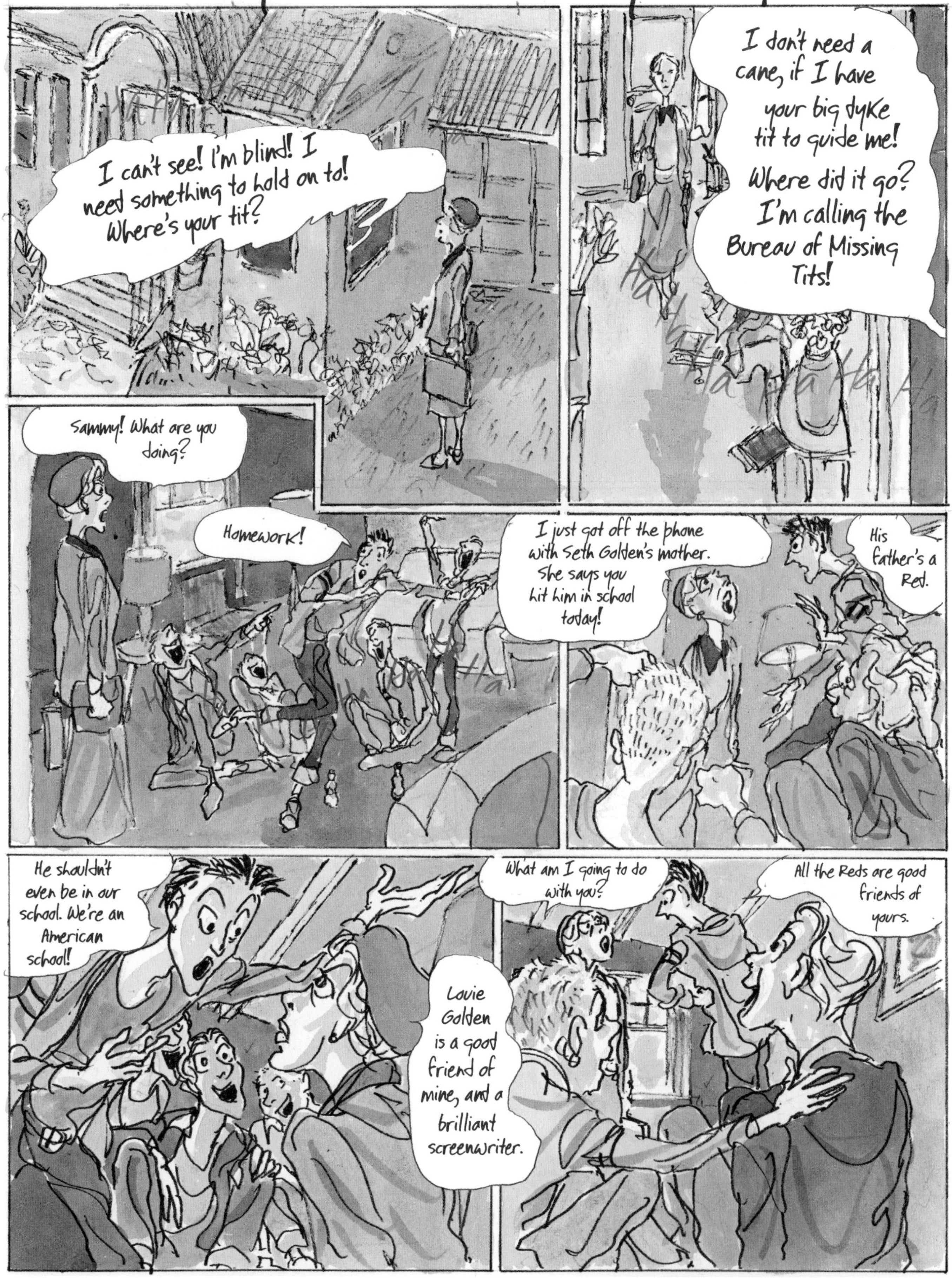

I can't see! I'm blind! I need something to hold on to! Where's your tit?
I don't need a cane, if I have your big dyke tit to guide me!
Where did it go? I'm calling the Bureau of Missing Tits!
Sammy! What are you doing?
Homework!
I just got off the phone with Seth Golden's mother. She says you hit him in school today!
His father's a Red.
He shouldn't even be in our school. We're an American school!
Louie Golden is a good friend of mine, and a brilliant screenwriter.
What am I going to do with you?
All the Reds are good friends of yours.

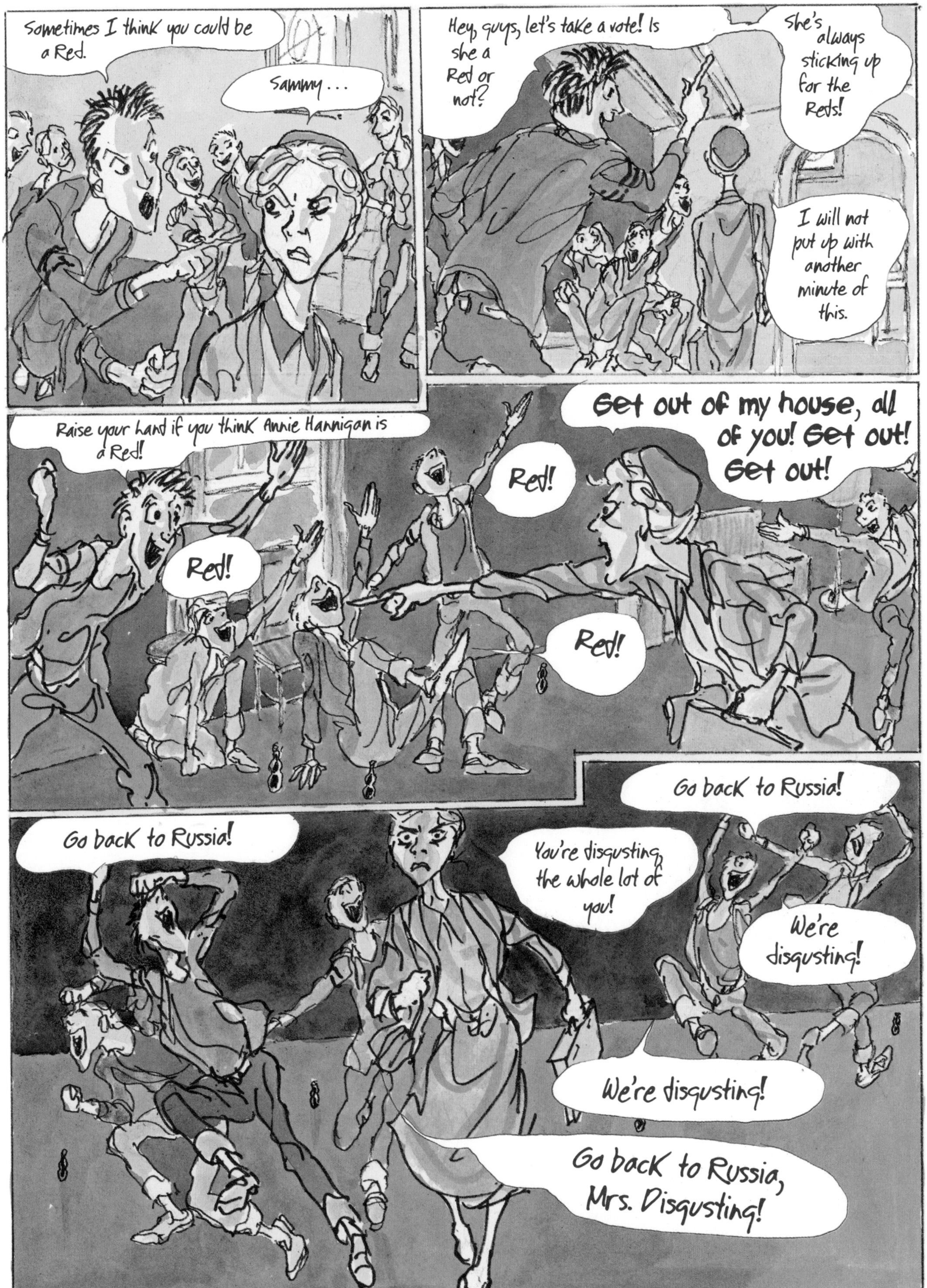
Sometimes I think you could be a Red.
Sammy . . .
Hey, guys, let's take a vote! Is she a Red or not?
She's always sticking up for the Reds!
I will not put up with another minute of this.
Raise your hand if you think Annie Hannigan is a Red!
Red!
Red!
Get out of my house, all of you! Get out! Get out!
Red!
Go back to Russia!
Go back to Russia!
You're disgusting, the whole lot of you!
We're disgusting!
We're disgusting!
Go back to Russia, Mrs. Disgusting!

Chapter Thirteen: The Blacklisted Dominatrix

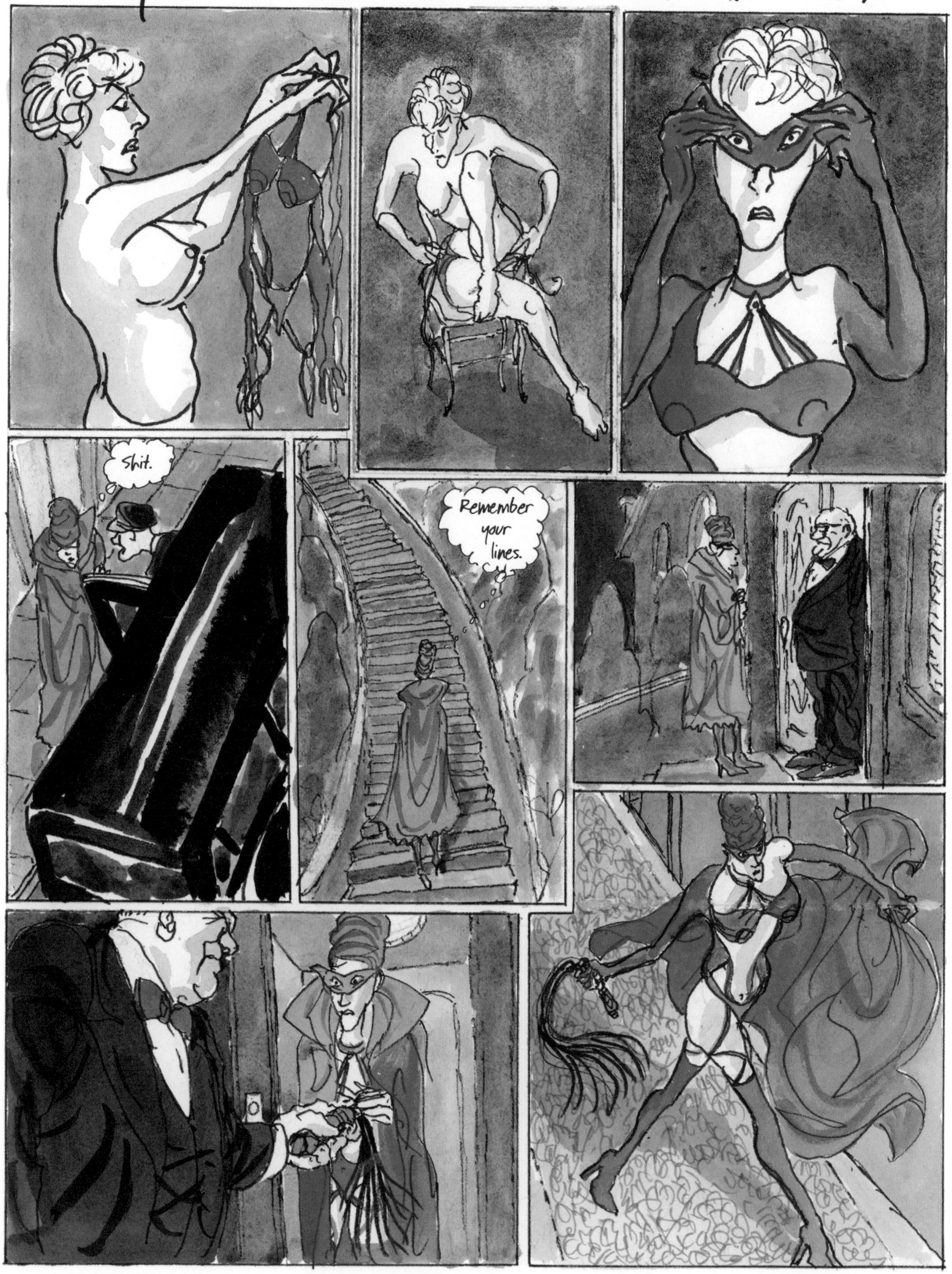

Shit.
Remember your lines.

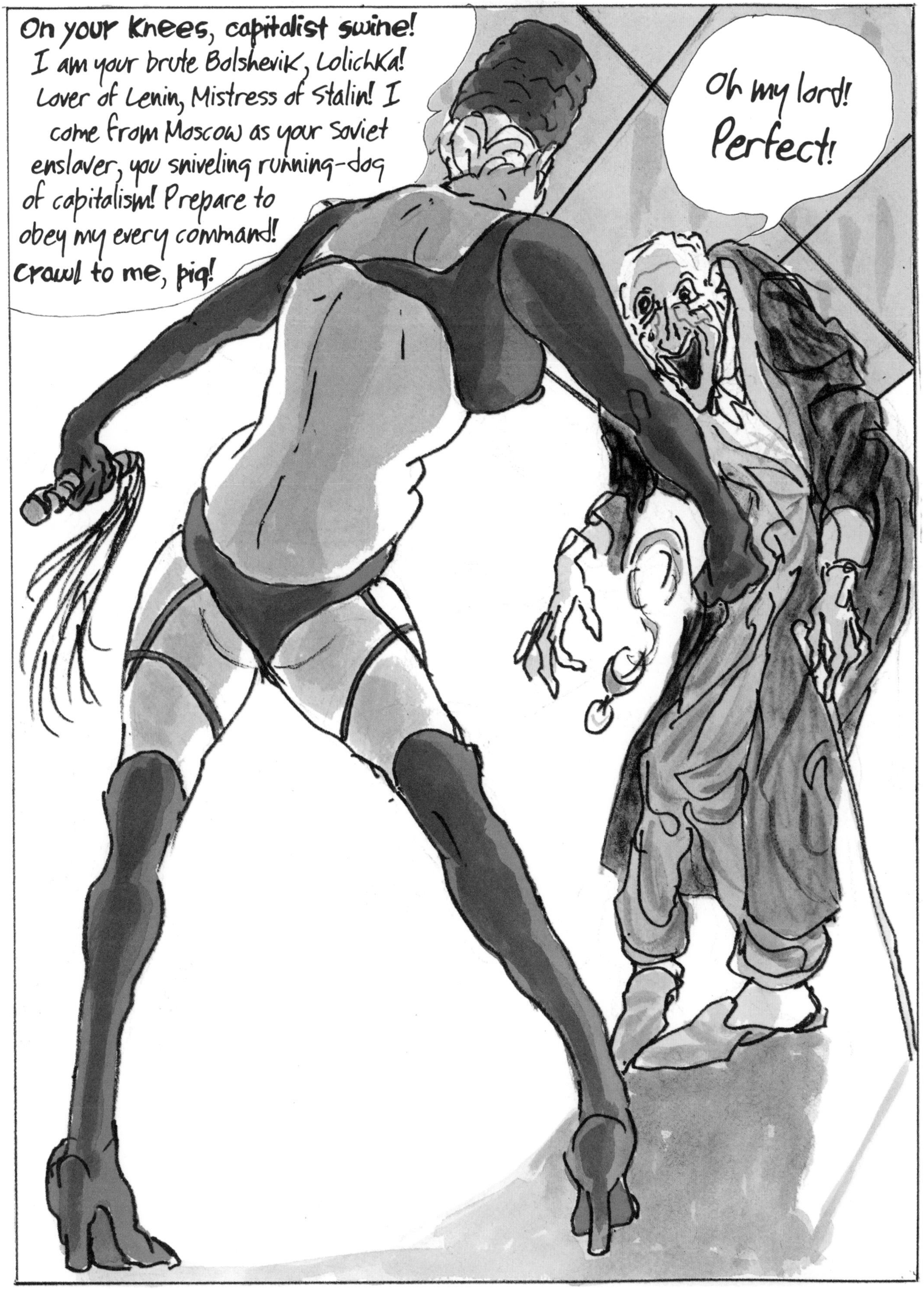
On your knees, capitalist swine! I am your brute Bolshevik, Lolichka! Lover of Lenin, Mistress of Stalin! I come from Moscow as your Soviet enslaver, you sniveling running-dog of capitalism! Prepare to obey my every command! Crawl to me, pig!
Oh my lord! Perfect!

Chapter Fourteen: On the Run

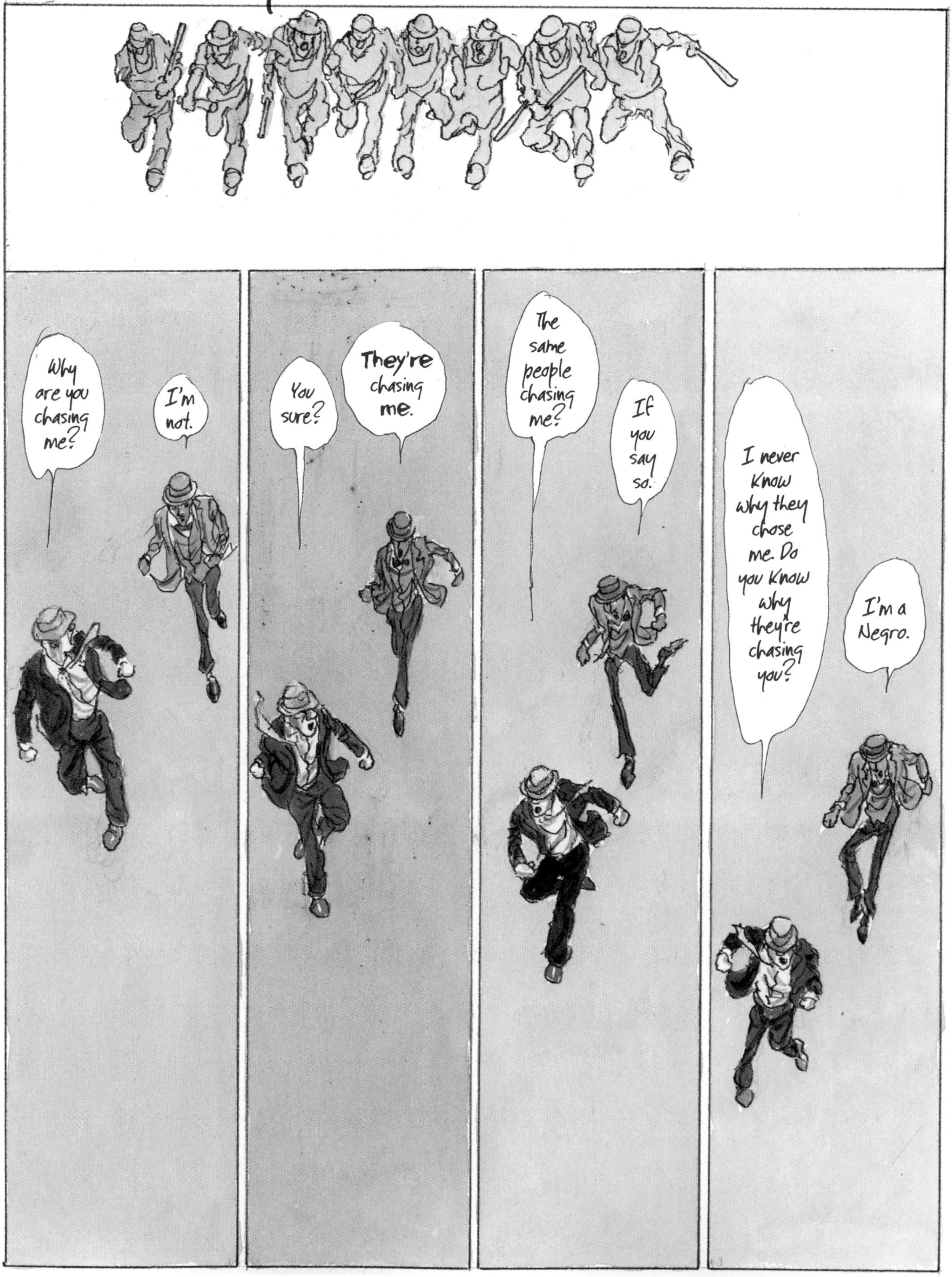

Why are you chasing me?
I'm not.
You sure?
They're chasing me.
The same people chasing me?
If you say so.
I never know why they chose me. Do you know why they're chasing you?
I'm a Negro.

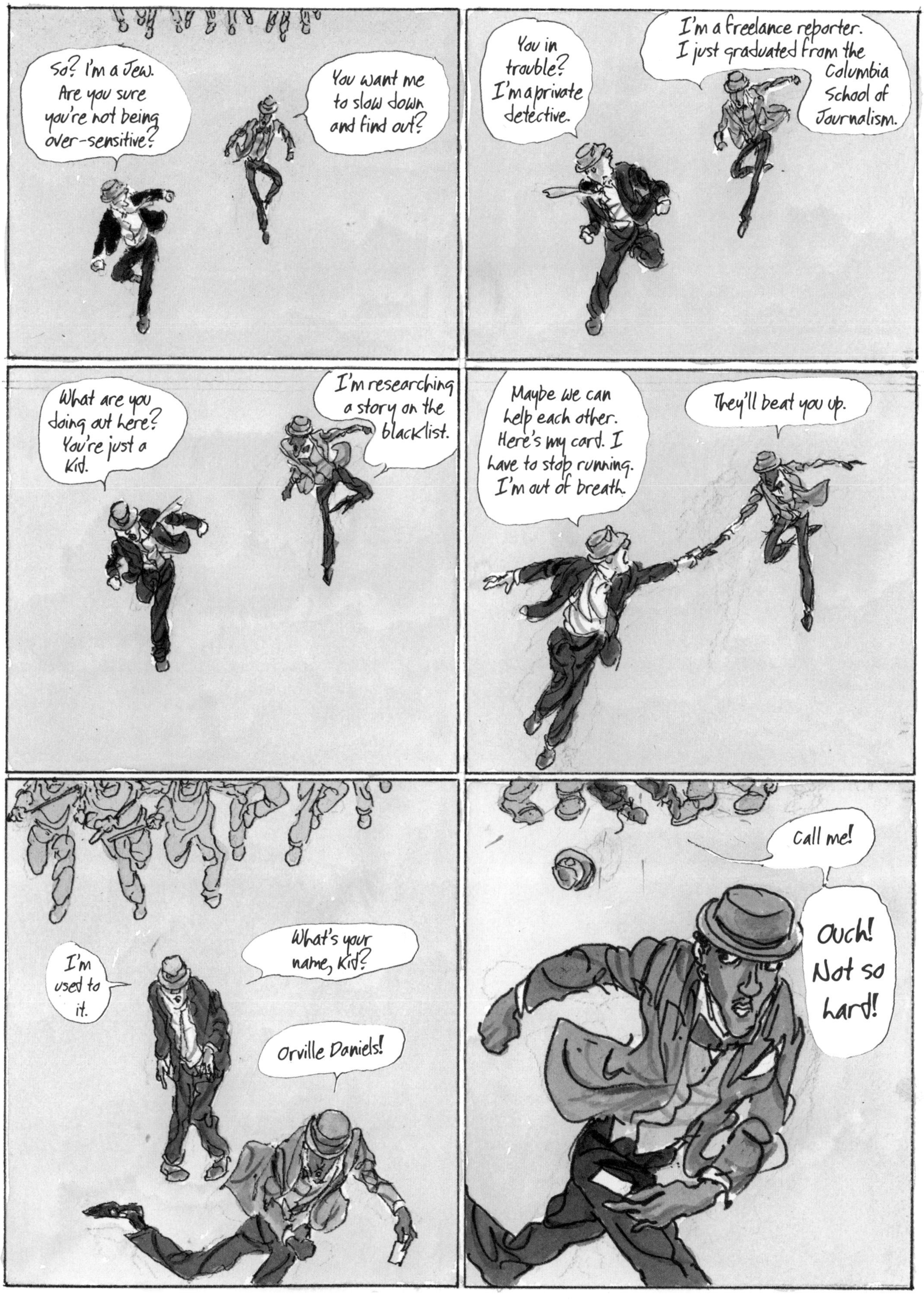
So? I'm a Jew. Are you sure you're not being over-sensitive?
You want me to slow down and find out?
You in trouble? I'm a private detective.
I'm a freelance reporter. I just graduated from the Columbia School of Journalism.
What are you doing out here? You're just a kid.
I'm researching a story on the blacklist.
Maybe we can help each other. Here's my card. I have to stop running. I'm out of breath.
They'll beat you up.
I'm used to it.
What's your name, kid?
Orville Daniels!
Call me!
Ouch! Not so hard!

Chapter Fifteen: A Man Called Sox

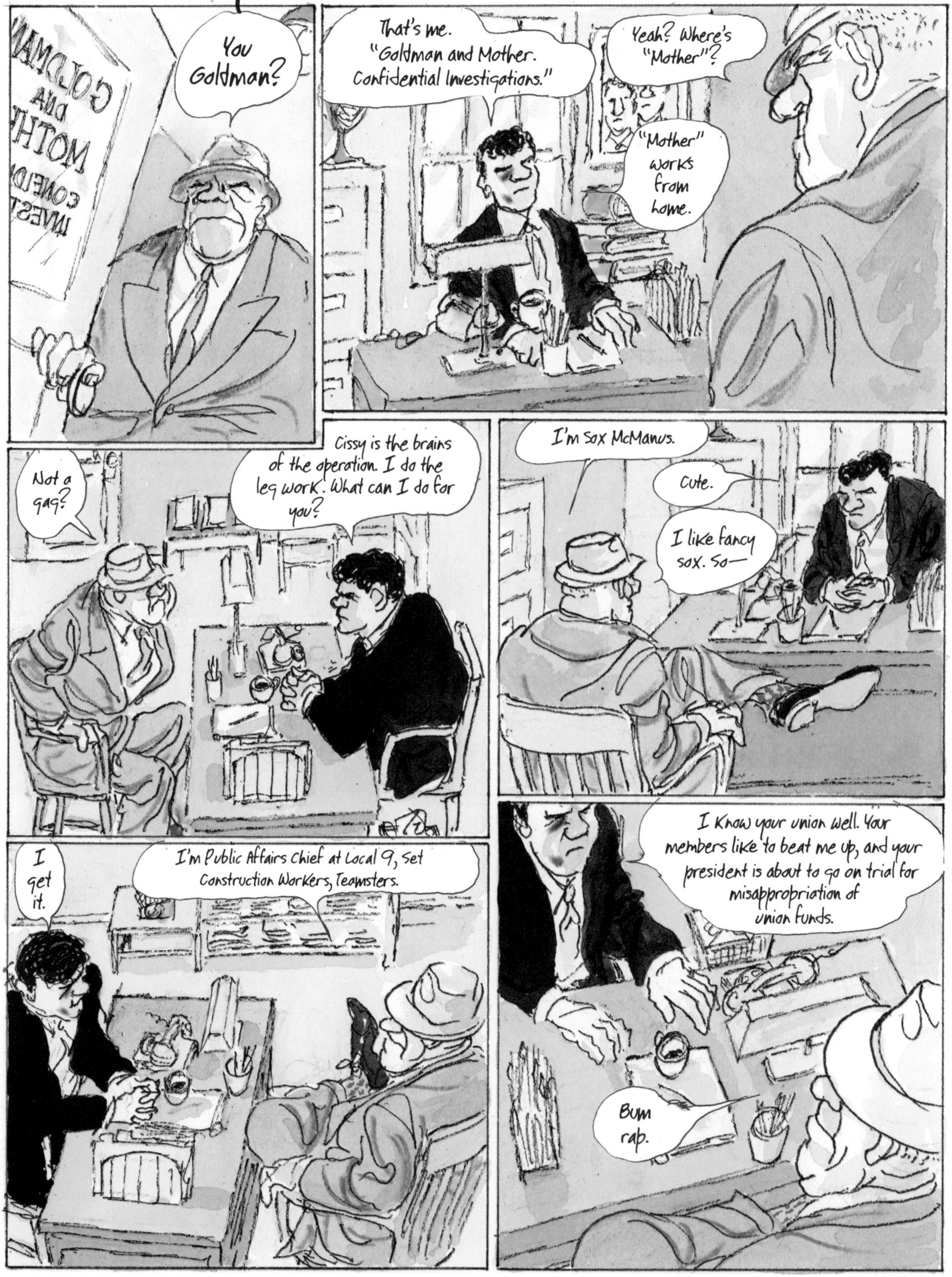
GOLDMAN AND MOTHER CONFIDENTIAL INVESTIGATIONS
You Goldman?
That's me. "Goldman and Mother. Confidential Investigations."
Yeah? Where's "Mother"?
"Mother" works from home.
Not a gag?
Cissy is the brains of the operation. I do the leg work. What can I do for you?
I'm Sox McManus.
Cute.
I like fancy sox. So—
I get it.
I'm Public Affairs Chief at Local 9, Set Construction Workers, Teamsters.
I know your union well. Your members like to beat me up, and your president is about to go on trial for misappropriation of union funds.
Bum rap.

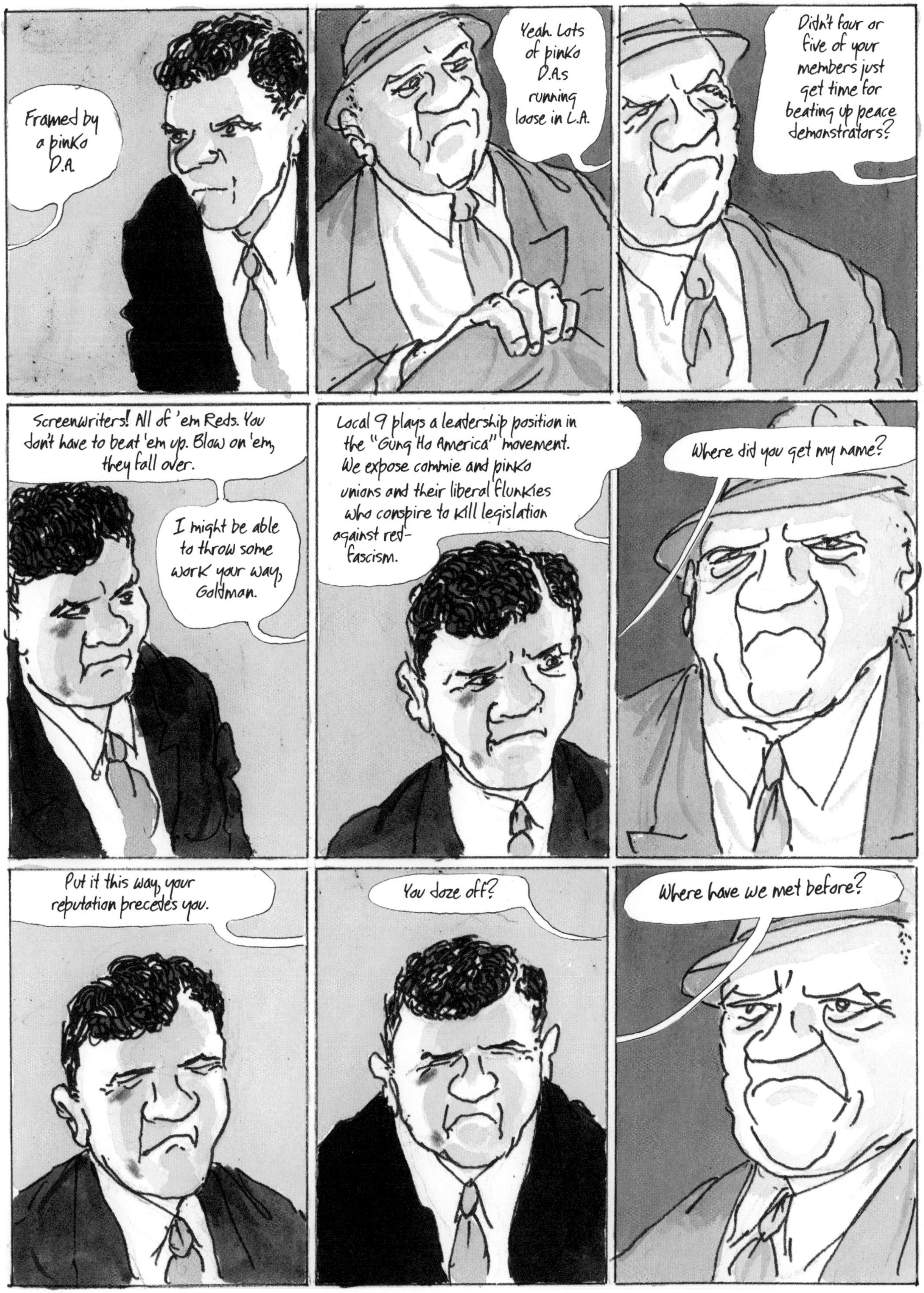
Framed by a pinko D.A.
Yeah. Lots of pinko D.A.s running loose in L.A.
Didn't four or five of your members just get time for beating up peace demonstrators?
Screenwriters! All of 'em Reds. You don't have to beat 'em up. Blow on 'em, they fall over.
I might be able to throw some work your way, Goldman.
Local 9 plays a leadership position in the "Gung Ho America" movement. We expose commie and pinko unions and their liberal flunkies who conspire to kill legislation against red-fascism.
Where did you get my name?
Put it this way, your reputation precedes you.
You doze off?
Where have we met before?

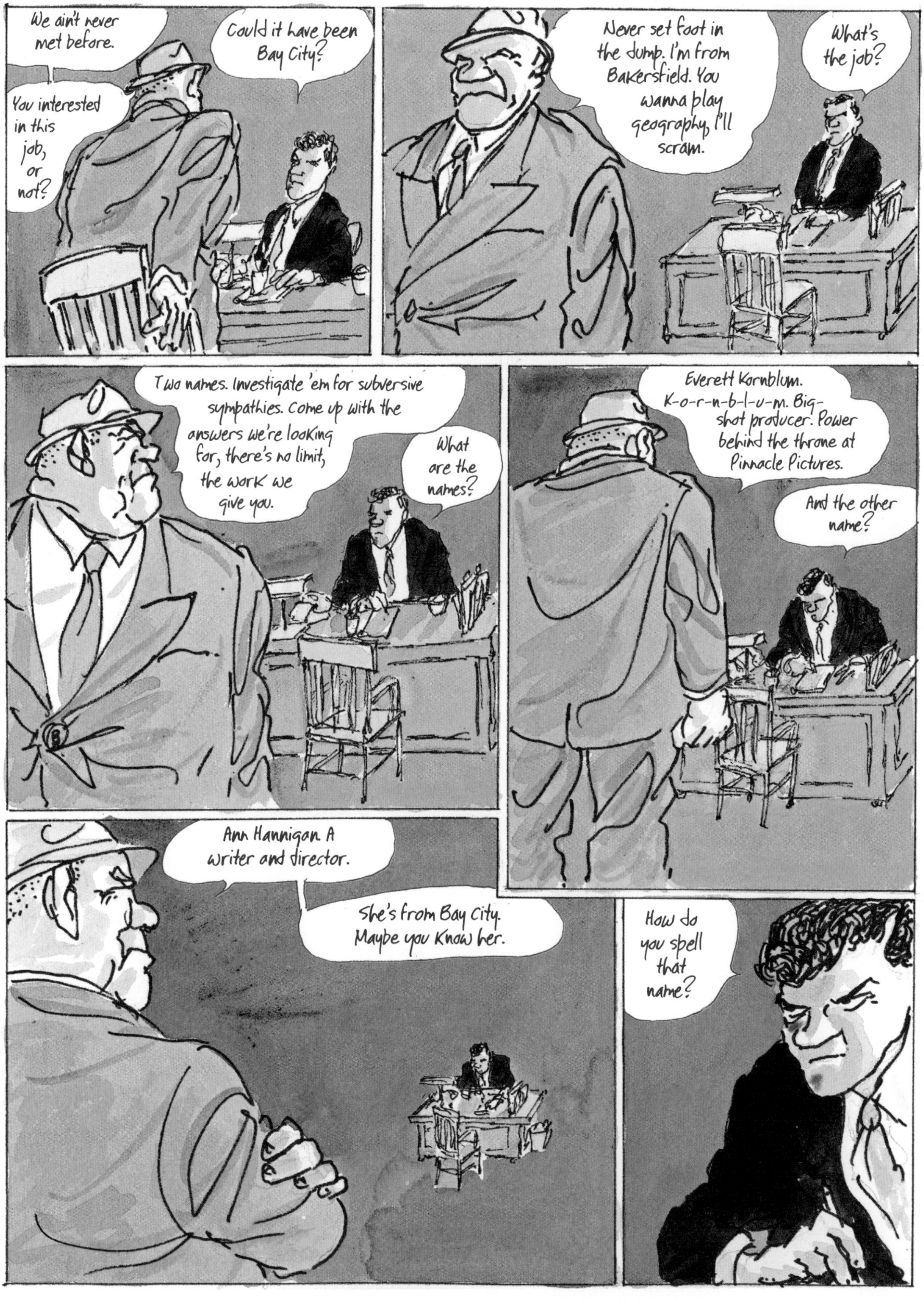
We ain't never met before.
You interested in this job, or not?
Could it have been Bay City?
Never set foot in the dump. I'm from Bakersfield. You wanna play geography, I'll scram.
What's the job?
Two names. Investigate 'em for subversive sympathies. Come up with the answers we're looking for, there's no limit, the work we give you.
What are the names?
Everett Kornblum. K-o-r-n-b-l-u-m. Big-shot producer. Power behind the throne at Pinnacle Pictures.
And the other name?
Ann Hannigan. A writer and director.
She's from Bay City. Maybe you know her.
How do you spell that name?

Chapter Sixteen: Bedroom Scene

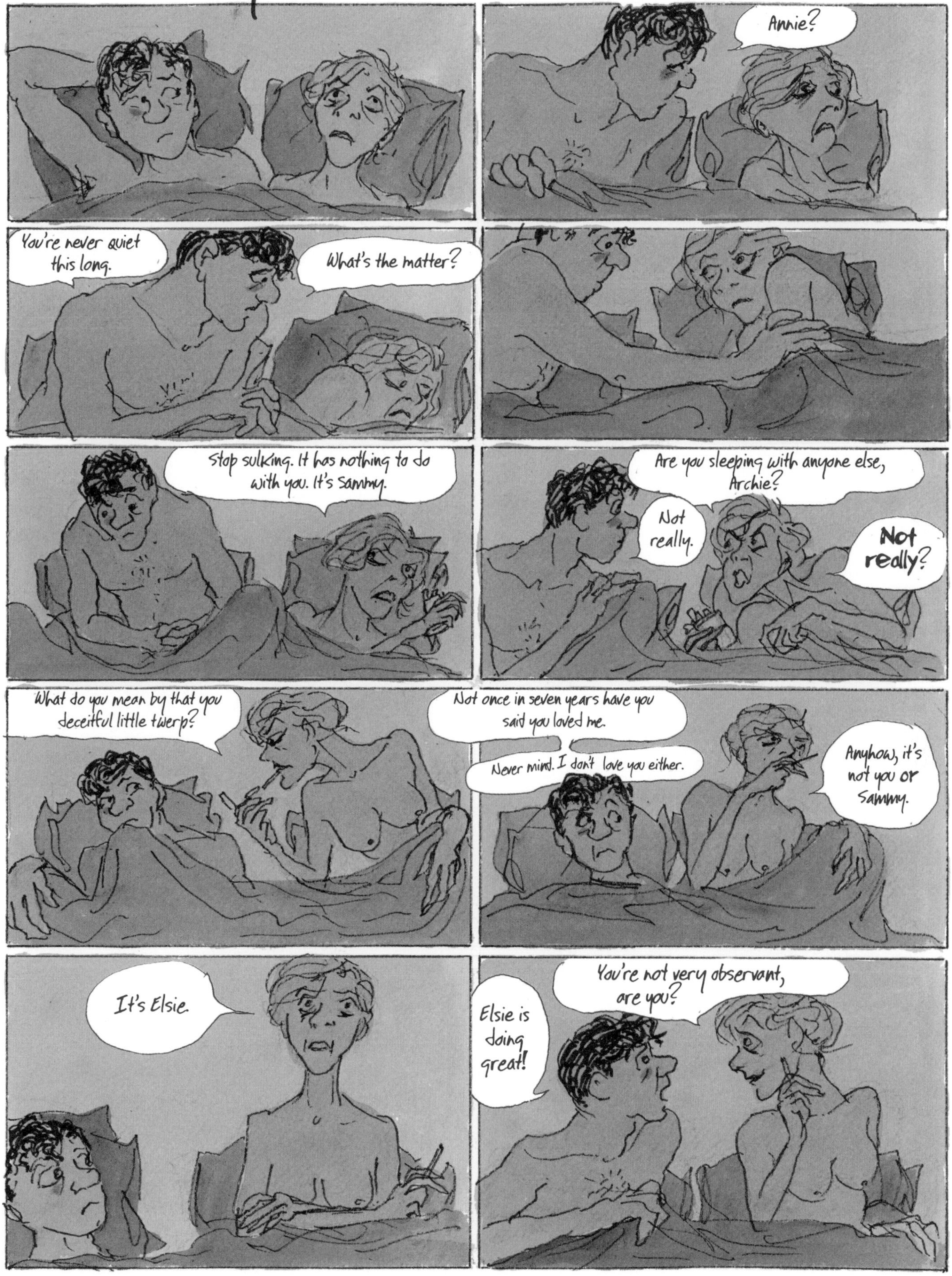

Annie?
You're never quiet this long.
What's the matter?
Stop sulking. It has nothing to do with you. It's Sammy.
Are you sleeping with anyone else, Archie?
Not really.
Not really?
What do you mean by that you deceitful little twerp?
Not once in seven years have you said you loved me.
Never mind. I don't love you either.
Anyhow, it's not you or Sammy.
It's Elsie.
Elsie is doing great!
You're not very observant, are you?

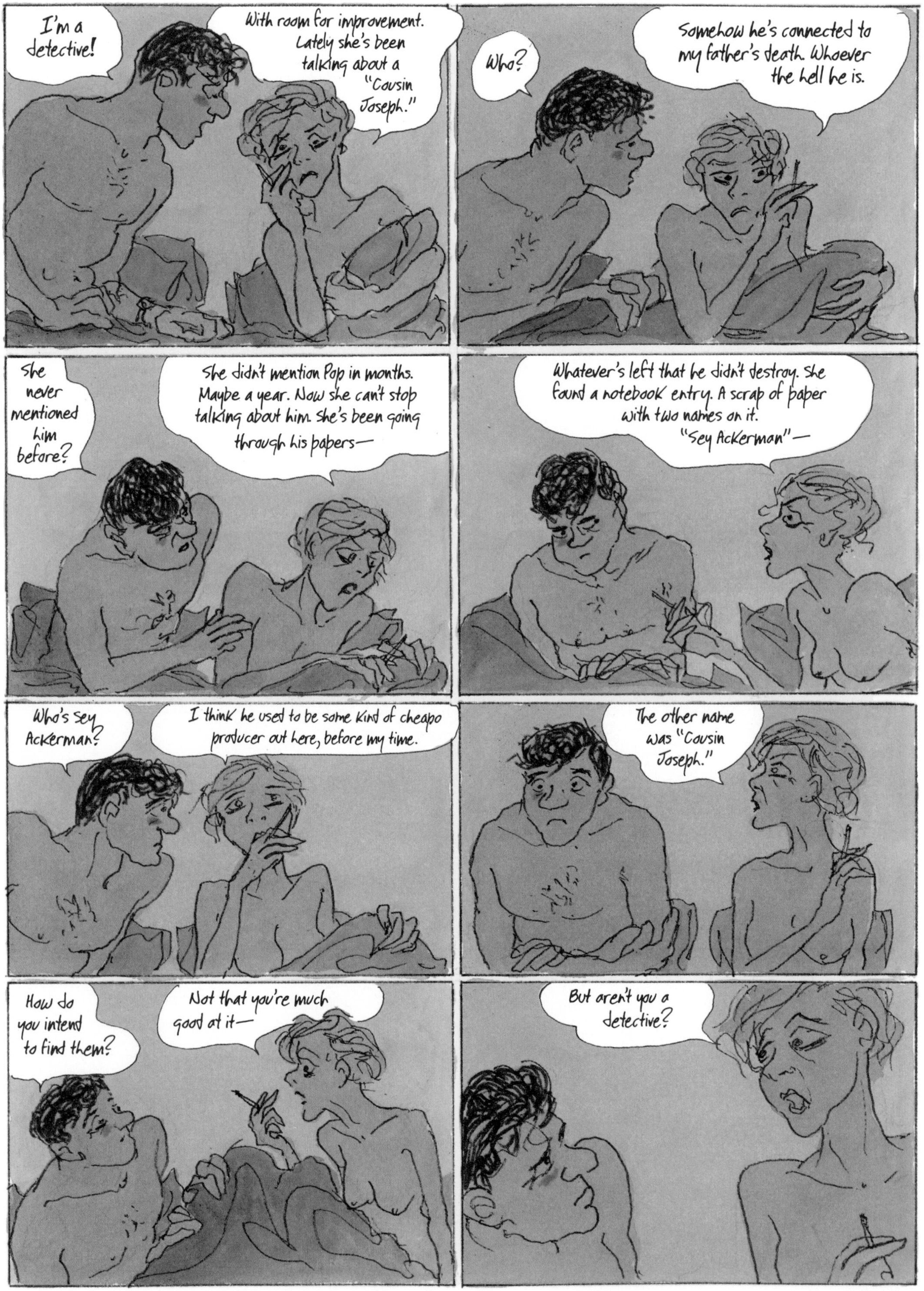

I'm a detective!
With room for improvement. Lately she's been talking about a "Cousin Joseph."
Who?
Somehow he's connected to my father's death. Whoever the hell he is.
She never mentioned him before?
She didn't mention Pop in months. Maybe a year. Now she can't stop talking about him. She's been going through his papers—
Whatever's left that he didn't destroy. She found a notebook entry. A scrap of paper with two names on it. "Sey Ackerman"—
Who's Sey Ackerman?
I think he used to be some kind of cheapo producer out here, before my time.
The other name was "Cousin Joseph."
How do you intend to find them?
Not that you're much good at it—
But aren't you a detective?

Chapter Seventeen: Reds

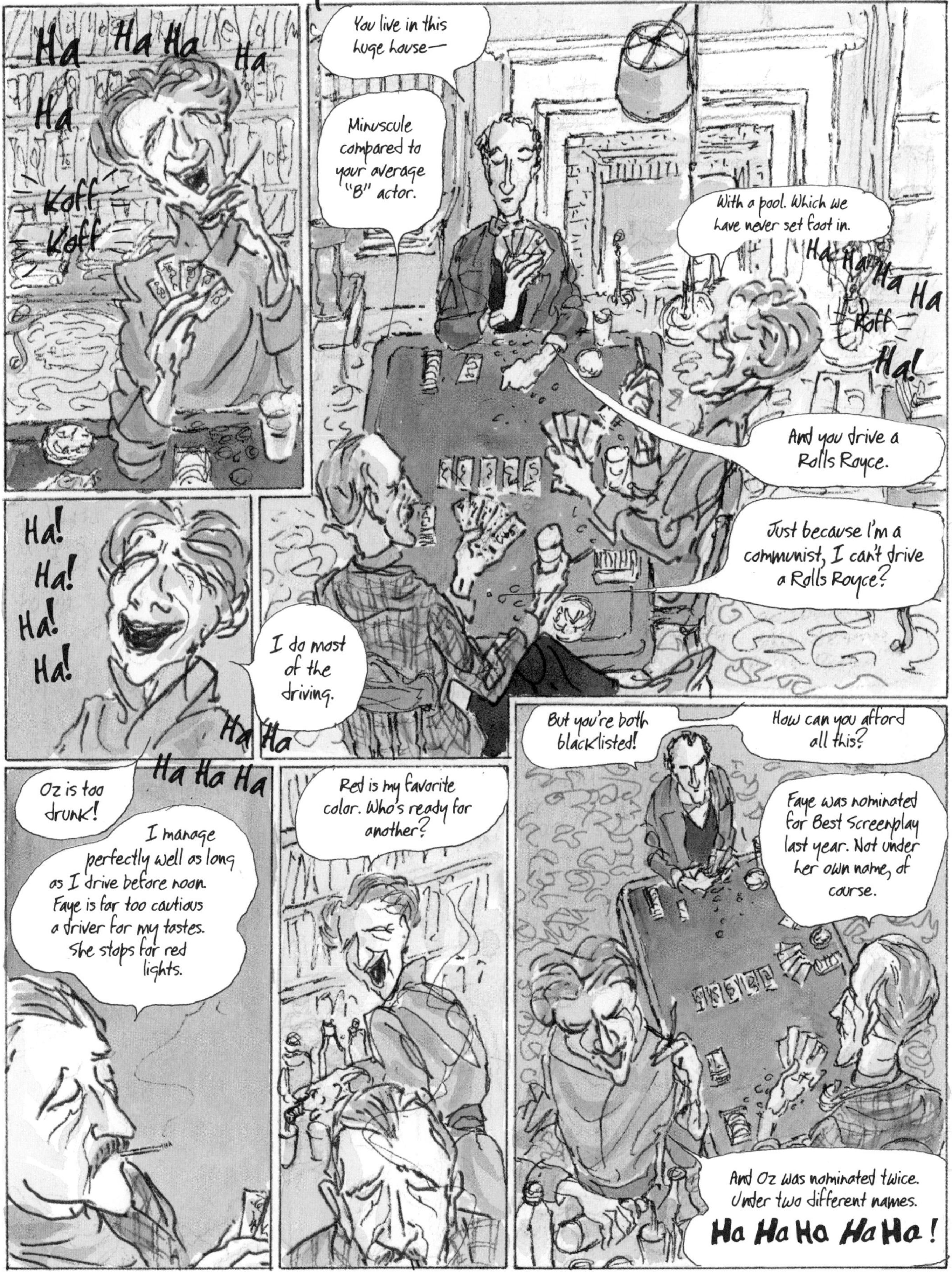

Ha Ha Ha Ha Ha
Koff Koff
You live in this huge house—
Minuscule compared to your average "B" actor.
With a pool. Which we have never set foot in.
Ha Ha Ha Ha Koff Ha!
And you drive a Rolls Royce.
Just because I'm a communist, I can't drive a Rolls Royce?
Ha! Ha! Ha! Ha!
I do most of the driving.
Ha Ha
Ha Ha Ha
Oz is too drunk!
I manage perfectly well as long as I drive before noon. Faye is far too cautious a driver for my tastes. She stops for red lights.
Red is my favorite color. Who's ready for another?
But you're both blacklisted!
How can you afford all this?
Faye was nominated for Best Screenplay last year. Not under her own name, of course.
And Oz was nominated twice. Under two different names.
Ha Ha Ha Ha Ha!

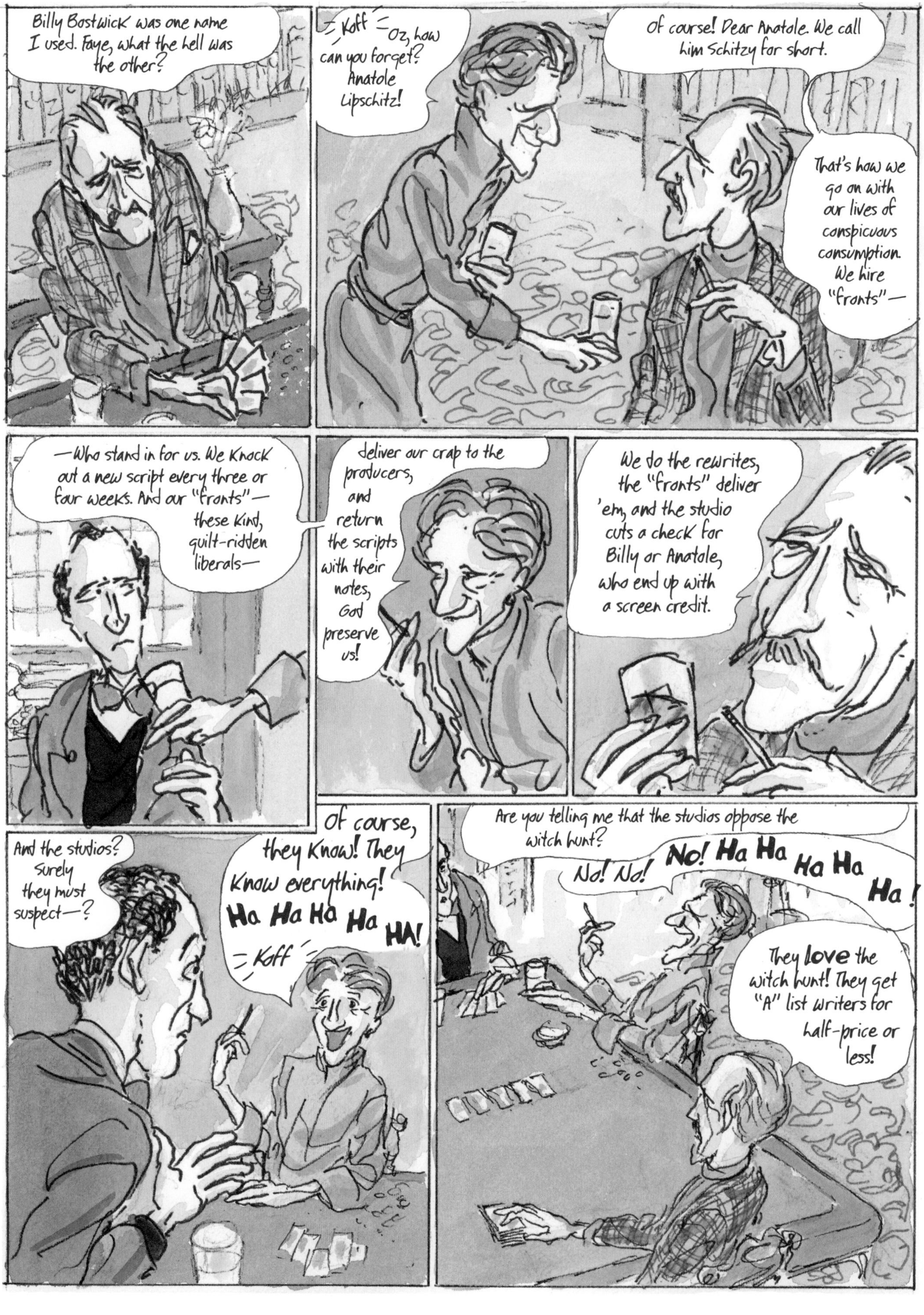
Billy Bostwick was one name I used. Faye, what the hell was the other?
Koff
Oz, how can you forget? Anatole Lipschitz!
Of course! Dear Anatole. We call him Schitzy for short.
That's how we go on with our lives of conspicuous consumption. We hire "fronts"—
—Who stand in for us. We knock out a new script every three or four weeks. And our "fronts"—
these kind, guilt-ridden liberals—
deliver our crap to the producers,
and return the scripts with their notes, God preserve us!
We do the rewrites, the "fronts" deliver 'em, and the studio cuts a check for Billy or Anatole, who end up with a screen credit.
And the studios? Surely they must suspect—?
Of course, they know! They know everything!
Ha Ha Ha Ha HA!
Koff
Are you telling me that the studios oppose the witch hunt?
No! No!
No! Ha Ha Ha Ha Ha!
They love the witch hunt! They get "A" list writers for half-price or less!

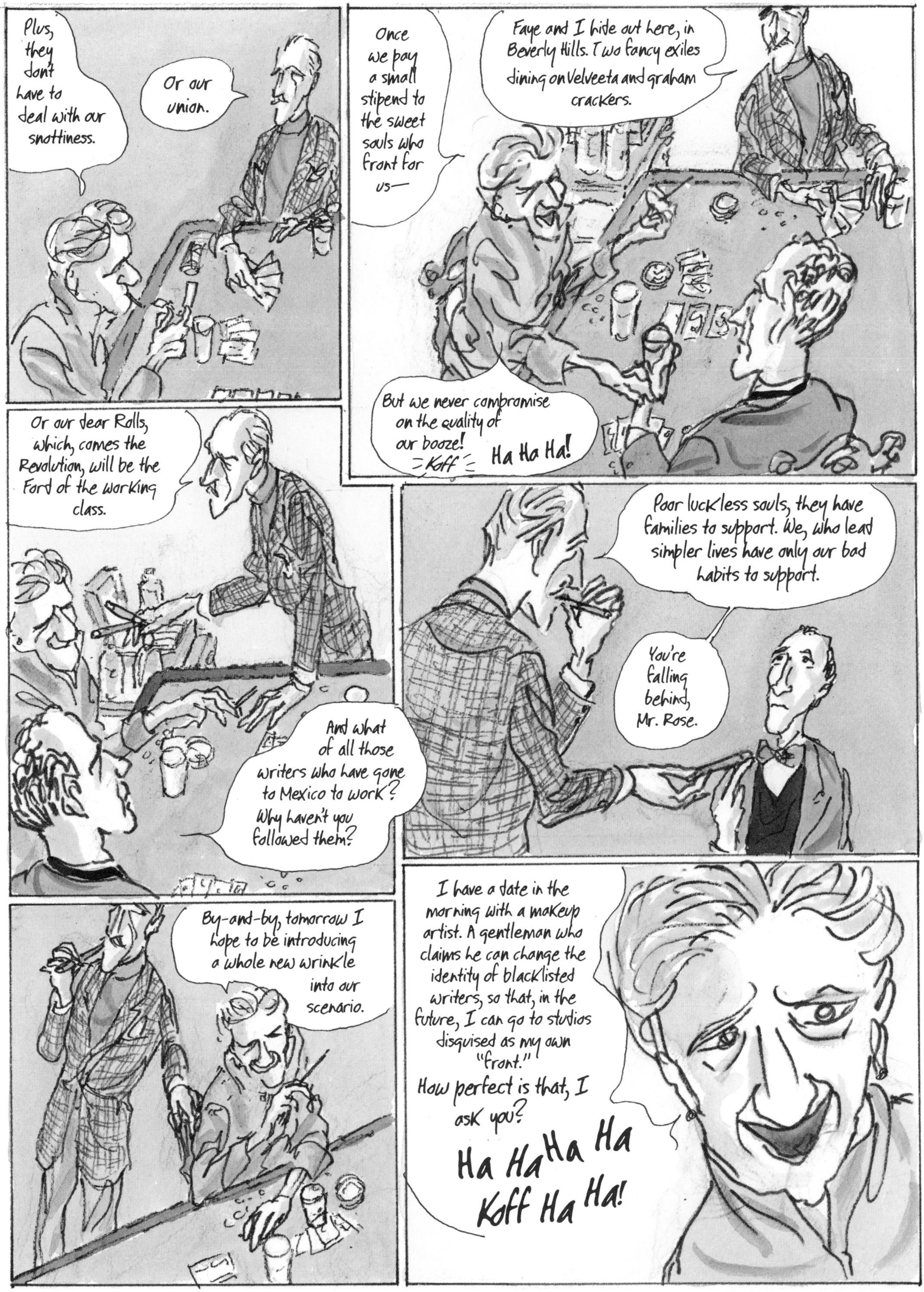

Plus, they don't have to deal with our snottiness.
Or our union.
Once we pay a small stipend to the sweet souls who front for us—
Faye and I hide out here, in Beverly Hills. Two fancy exiles dining on Velveeta and graham crackers.
But we never compromise on the quality of our booze!
Koff
Ha Ha Ha!
Or our dear Rolls, which, comes the Revolution, will be the Ford of the working class.
And what of all those writers who have gone to Mexico to work? Why haven't you followed them?
Poor luckless souls, they have families to support. We, who lead simpler lives have only our bad habits to support.
You're falling behind, Mr. Rose.
By-and-by, tomorrow I hope to be introducing a whole new wrinkle into our scenario.
I have a date in the morning with a makeup artist. A gentleman who claims he can change the identity of blacklisted writers, so that, in the future, I can go to studios disguised as my own "front."
How perfect is that, I ask you?
Ha Ha Ha Ha
Koff Ha Ha!

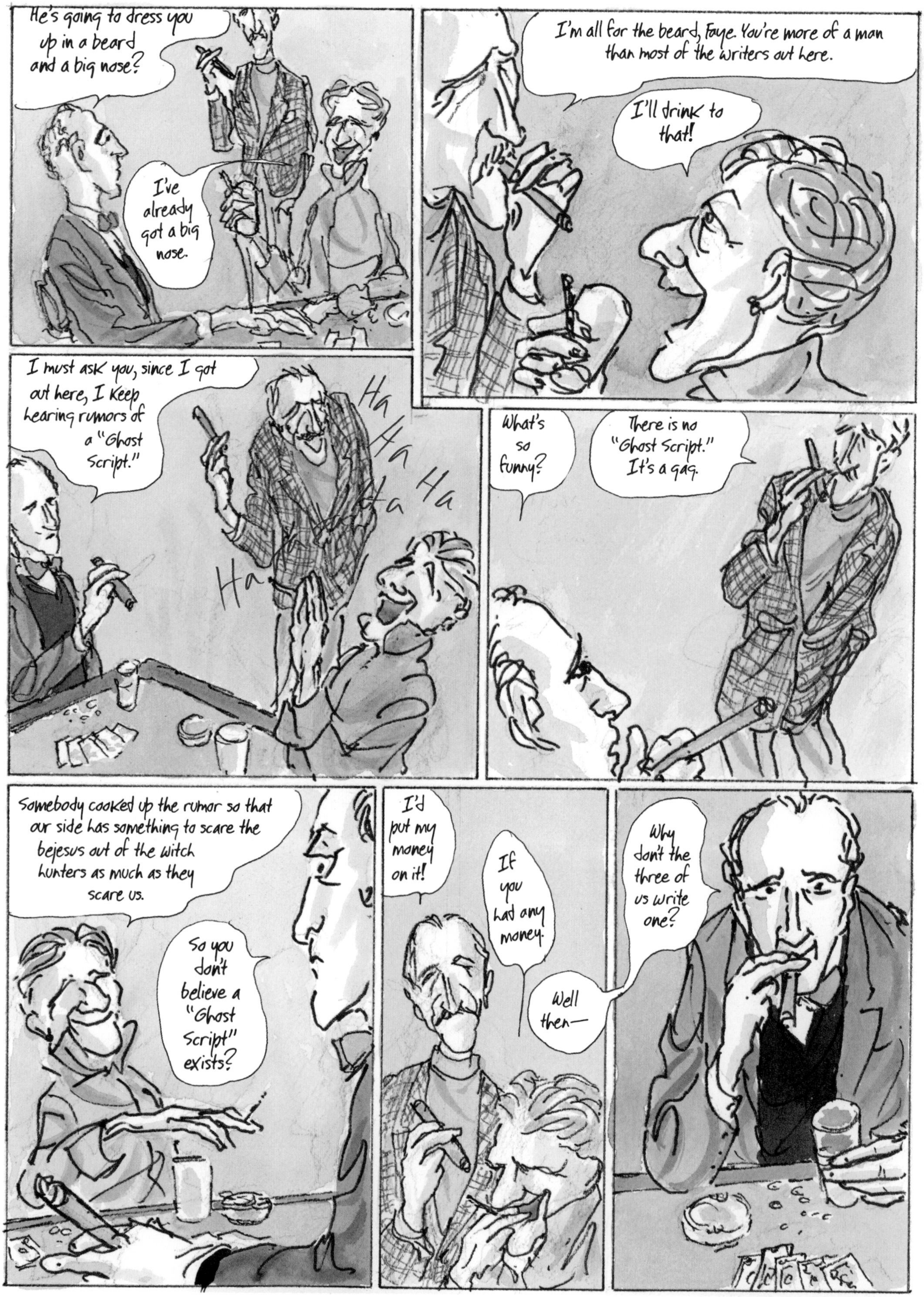
He's going to dress you up in a beard and a big nose?
I've already got a big nose.
I'm all for the beard, Faye. You're more of a man than most of the writers out here.
I'll drink to that!
I must ask you, since I got out here, I keep hearing rumors of a "Ghost Script."
Ha Ha Ha Ha Ha
What's so funny?
There is no "Ghost Script." It's a gag.
Somebody cooked up the rumor so that our side has something to scare the bejesus out of the witch hunters as much as they scare us.
So you don't believe a "Ghost Script" exists?
I'd put my money on it!
If you had any money.
Well then—
Why don't the three of us write one?

Chapter Eighteen: Makeover

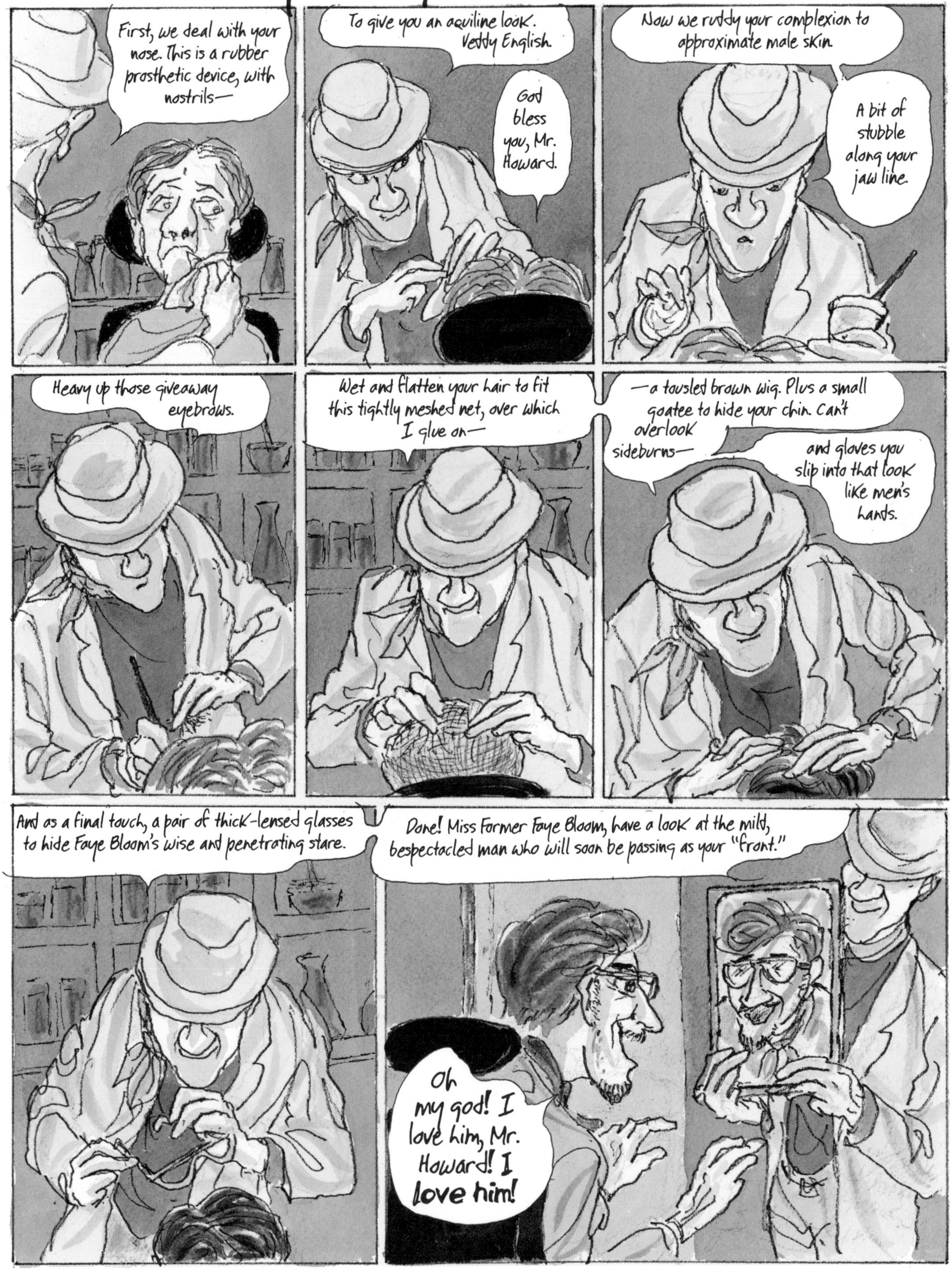

First, we deal with your nose. This is a rubber prosthetic device, with nostrils—
To give you an aquiline look. Veddy English.
God bless you, Mr. Howard.
Now we ruddy your complexion to approximate male skin.
A bit of stubble along your jaw line.
Heavy up those giveaway eyebrows.
Wet and flatten your hair to fit this tightly meshed net, over which I glue on—
—a tousled brown wig. Plus a small goatee to hide your chin. Can't overlook sideburns—
and gloves you slip into that look like men's hands.
And as a final touch, a pair of thick-lensed glasses to hide Faye Bloom's wise and penetrating stare.
Done! Miss Former Faye Bloom, have a look at the mild, bespectacled man who will soon be passing as your "front."
Oh my god! I love him, Mr. Howard! I love him!

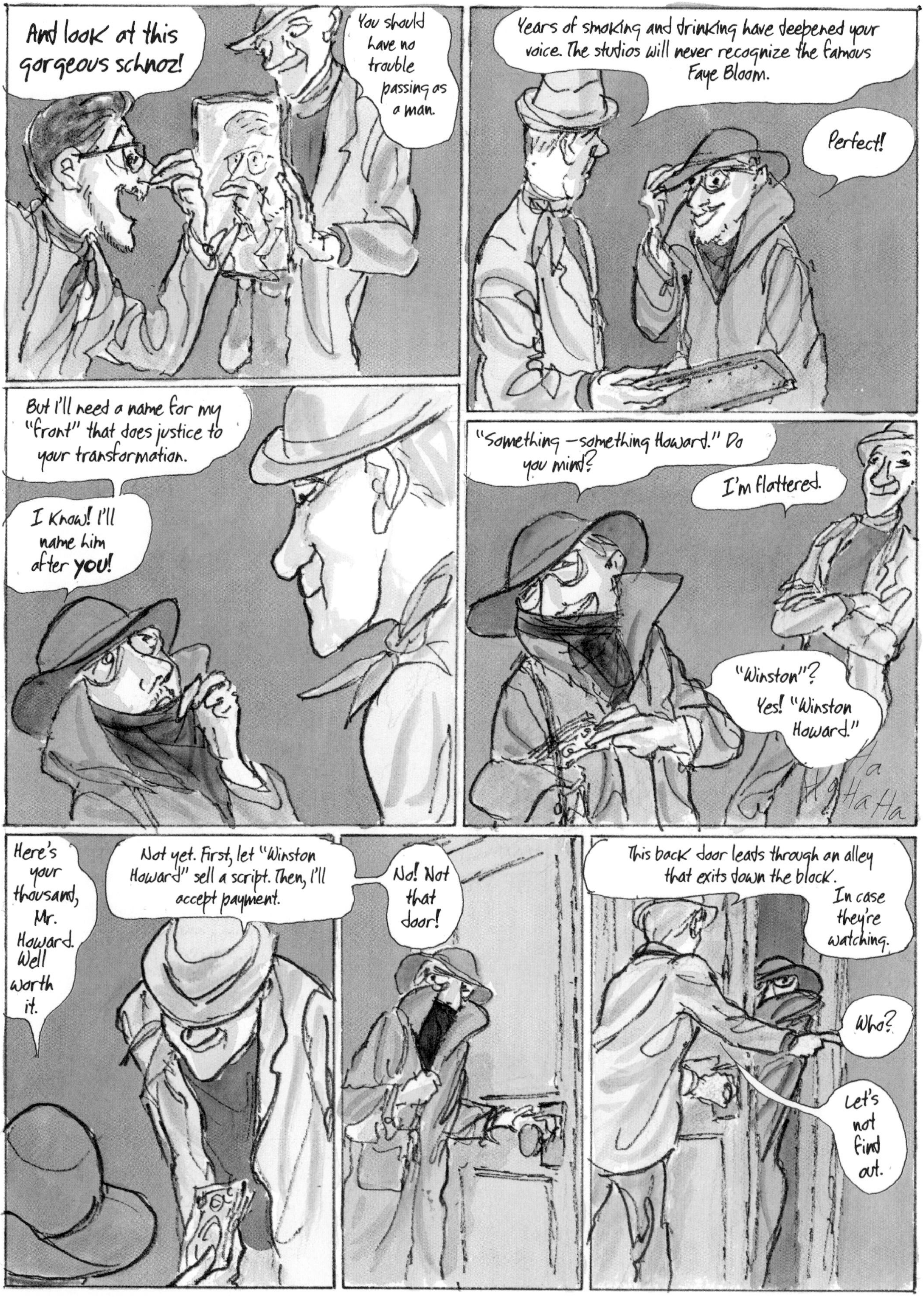

And look at this gorgeous schnoz!
You should have no trouble passing as a man.
Years of smoking and drinking have deepened your voice. The studios will never recognize the famous Faye Bloom.
Perfect!
But I'll need a name for my "front" that does justice to your transformation.
I Know! I'll name him after YOU!
"Something —something Howard." Do you mind?
I'm flattered.
"Winston"? Yes! "Winston Howard."
Ha Ha Ha Ha
Here's your thousand, Mr. Howard. Well worth it.
Not yet. First, let "Winston Howard" sell a script. Then, I'll accept payment.
No! Not that door!
This back door leads through an alley that exits down the block.
In case they're watching.
Who?
Let's not find out.

Chapter Nineteen: The Spooks

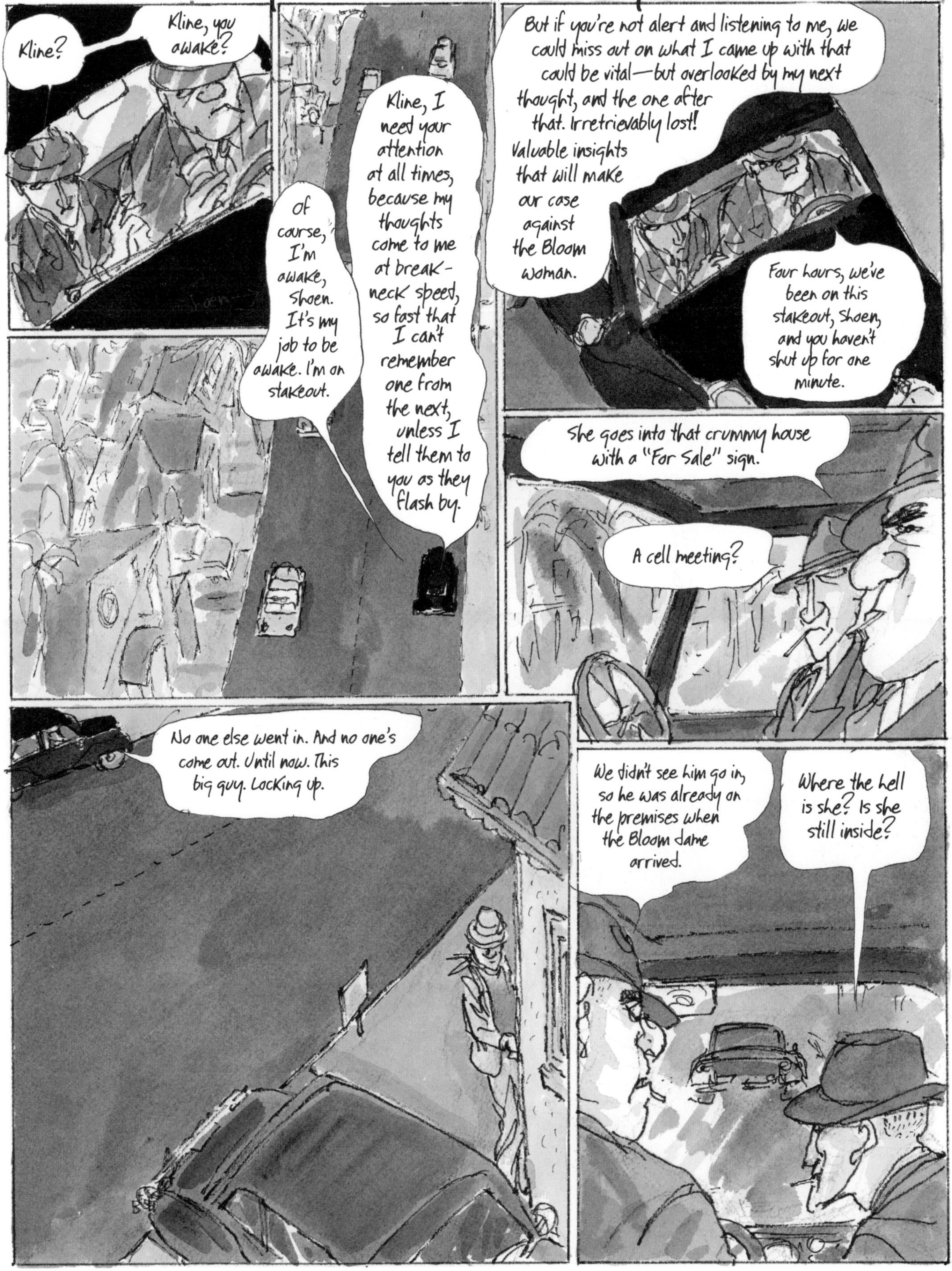

Kline?
Kline, you awake?
Of course, I'm awake, Shoen. It's my job to be awake. I'm on stakeout.
Kline, I need your attention at all times, because my thoughts come to me at break-neck speed, so fast that I can't remember one from the next, unless I tell them to you as they flash by.
But if you're not alert and listening to me, we could miss out on what I came up with that could be vital—but overlooked by my next thought, and the one after that. Irretrievably lost! Valuable insights that will make our case against the Bloom woman.
Four hours, we've been on this stakeout, Shoen, and you haven't shut up for one minute.
She goes into that crummy house with a "For Sale" sign.
A cell meeting?
No one else went in. And no one's come out. Until now. This big guy. Locking up.
We didn't see him go in, so he was already on the premises when the Bloom dame arrived.
Where the hell is she? Is she still inside?

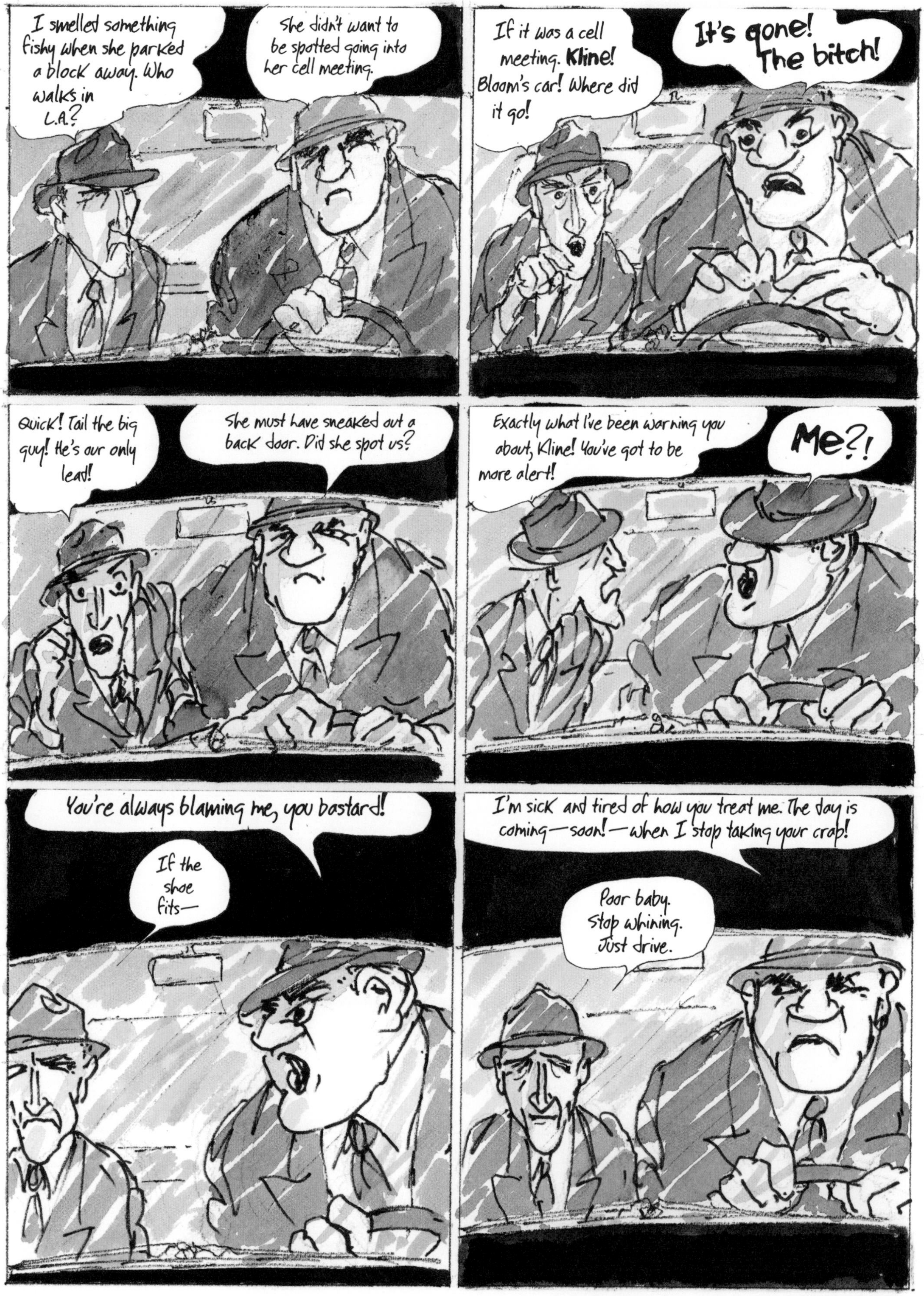

I smelled something fishy when she parked a block away. Who walks in L.A.?
She didn't want to be spotted going into her cell meeting.
If it was a cell meeting. **Kline!** Bloom's car! Where did it go!
It's gone! The bitch!
Quick! Tail the big guy! He's our only lead!
She must have sneaked out a back door. Did she spot us?
Exactly what I've been warning you about, Kline! You've got to be more alert!
Me?!
You're always blaming me, you bastard!
If the shoe fits—
I'm sick and tired of how you treat me. The day is coming—soon!—when I stop taking your crap!
Poor baby. Stop whining. Just drive.

Chapter Twenty: Bedroom II

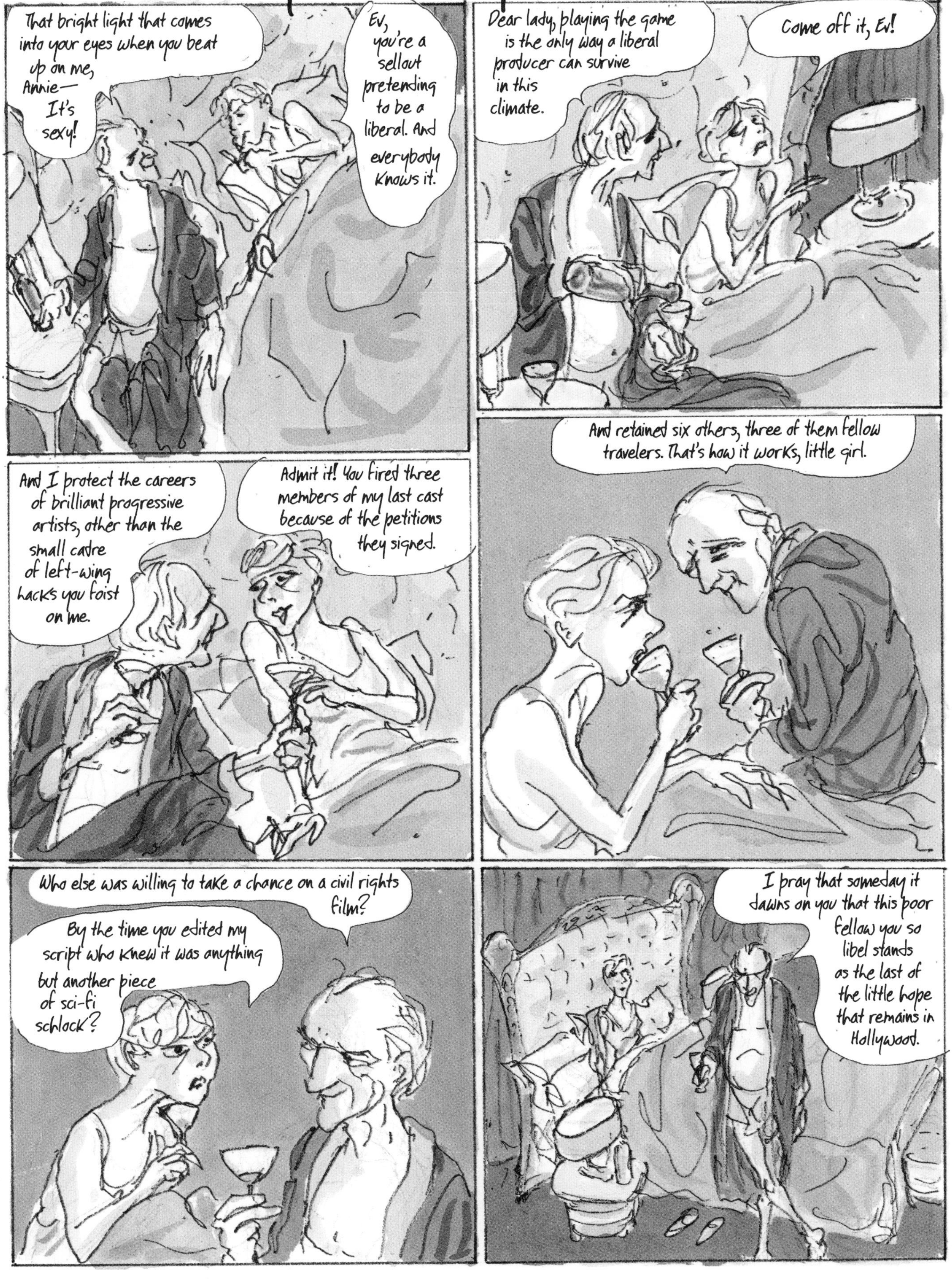

That bright light that comes into your eyes when you beat up on me, Annie— It's sexy!
Ev, you're a sellout pretending to be a liberal. And everybody knows it.
Dear lady, playing the game is the only way a liberal producer can survive in this climate.
Come off it, Ev!
And I protect the careers of brilliant progressive artists, other than the small cadre of left-wing hacks you foist on me.
Admit it! You fired three members of my last cast because of the petitions they signed.
And retained six others, three of them fellow travelers. That's how it works, little girl.
Who else was willing to take a chance on a civil rights film?
By the time you edited my script who knew it was anything but another piece of sci-fi schlock?
I pray that someday it dawns on you that this poor fellow you so libel stands as the last of the little hope that remains in Hollywood.

Chapter Twenty-One: Goldman and Mother

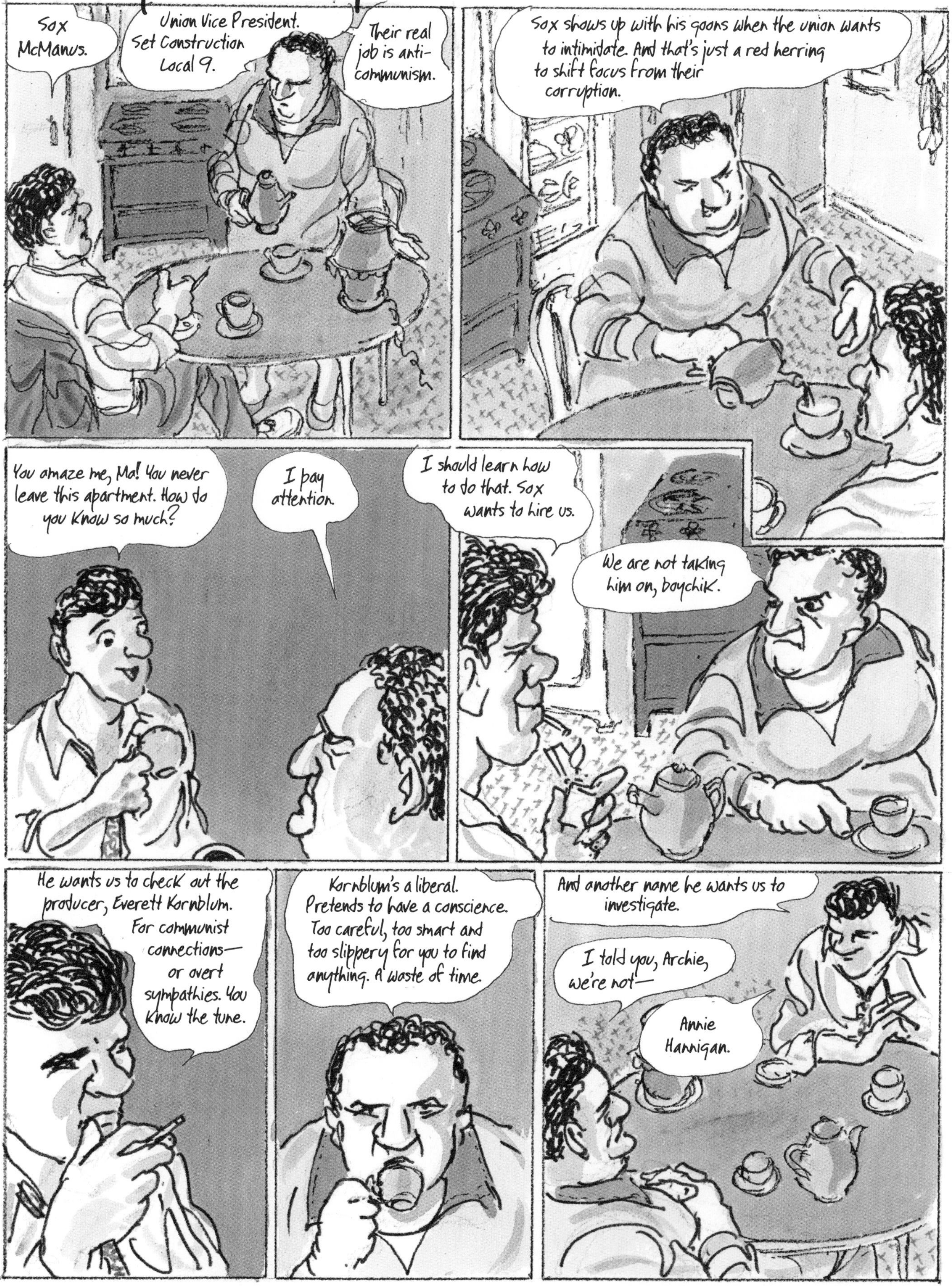

Sox McManus.
Union Vice President. Set Construction Local 9.
Their real job is anti-communism.
Sox shows up with his goons when the union wants to intimidate. And that's just a red herring to shift focus from their corruption.
You amaze me, Ma! You never leave this apartment. How do you know so much?
I pay attention.
I should learn how to do that. Sox wants to hire us.
We are not taking him on, boychik.
He wants us to check out the producer, Everett Kornblum. For communist connections— or overt sympathies. You know the tune.
Kornblum's a liberal. Pretends to have a conscience. Too careful, too smart and too slippery for you to find anything. A waste of time.
And another name he wants us to investigate.
I told you, Archie, we're not—
Annie Hannigan.

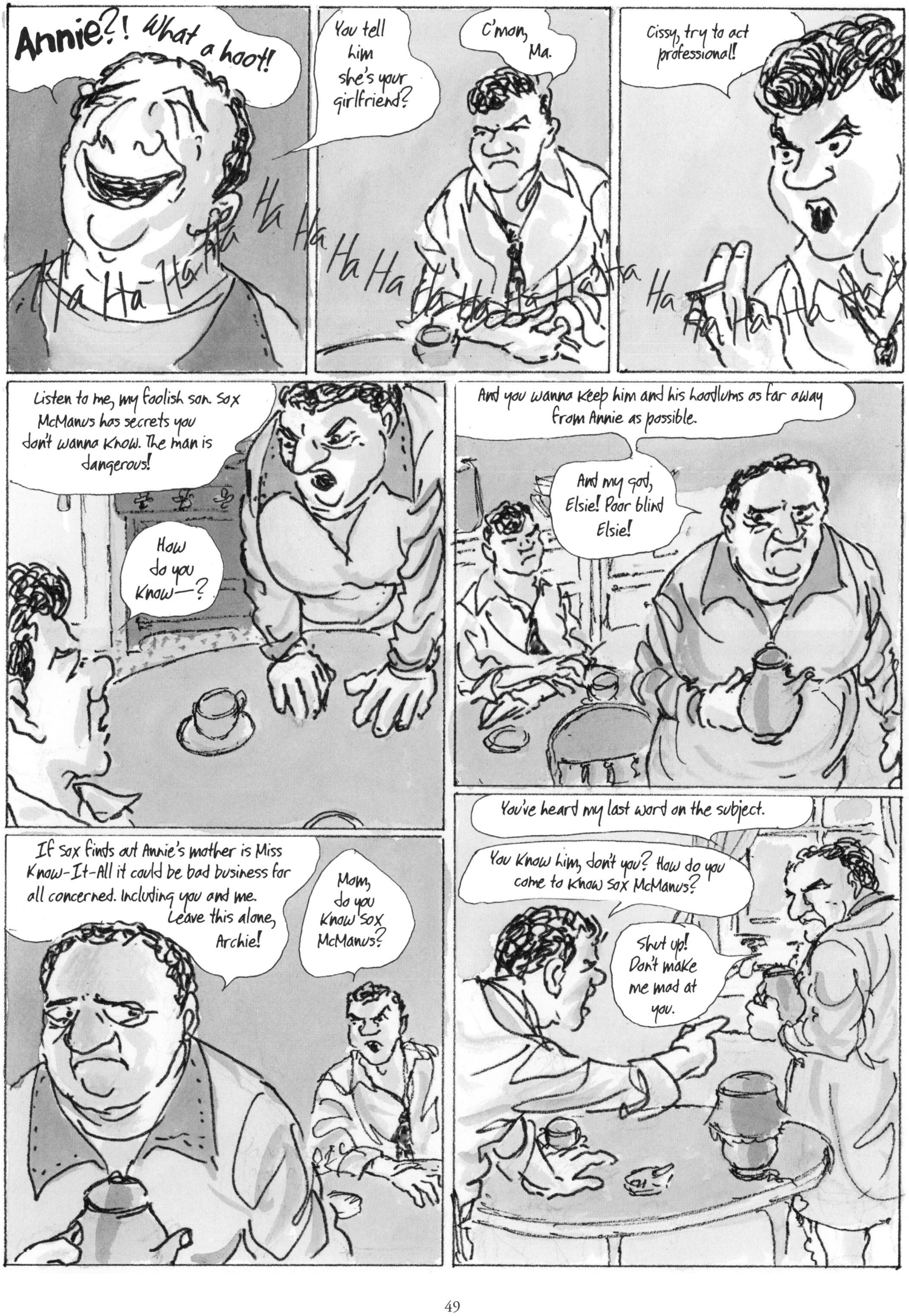

Annie?! What a hoot!
Ha Ha Ha Ha Ha Ha Ha Ha Ha Ha
You tell him she's your girlfriend?
C'mon, Ma.
Cissy, try to act professional!
Listen to me, my foolish son. Sox McManus has secrets you don't wanna know. The man is dangerous!
How do you know—?
And you wanna keep him and his hoodlums as far away from Annie as possible.
And my god, Elsie! Poor blind Elsie!
If Sox finds out Annie's mother is Miss Know-It-All it could be bad business for all concerned. Including you and me. Leave this alone, Archie!
Mom, do you know Sox McManus?
You've heard my last word on the subject.
You know him, don't you? How do you come to know Sox McManus?
Shut up! Don't make me mad at you.

Chapter Twenty-Two: A Disappearing Act

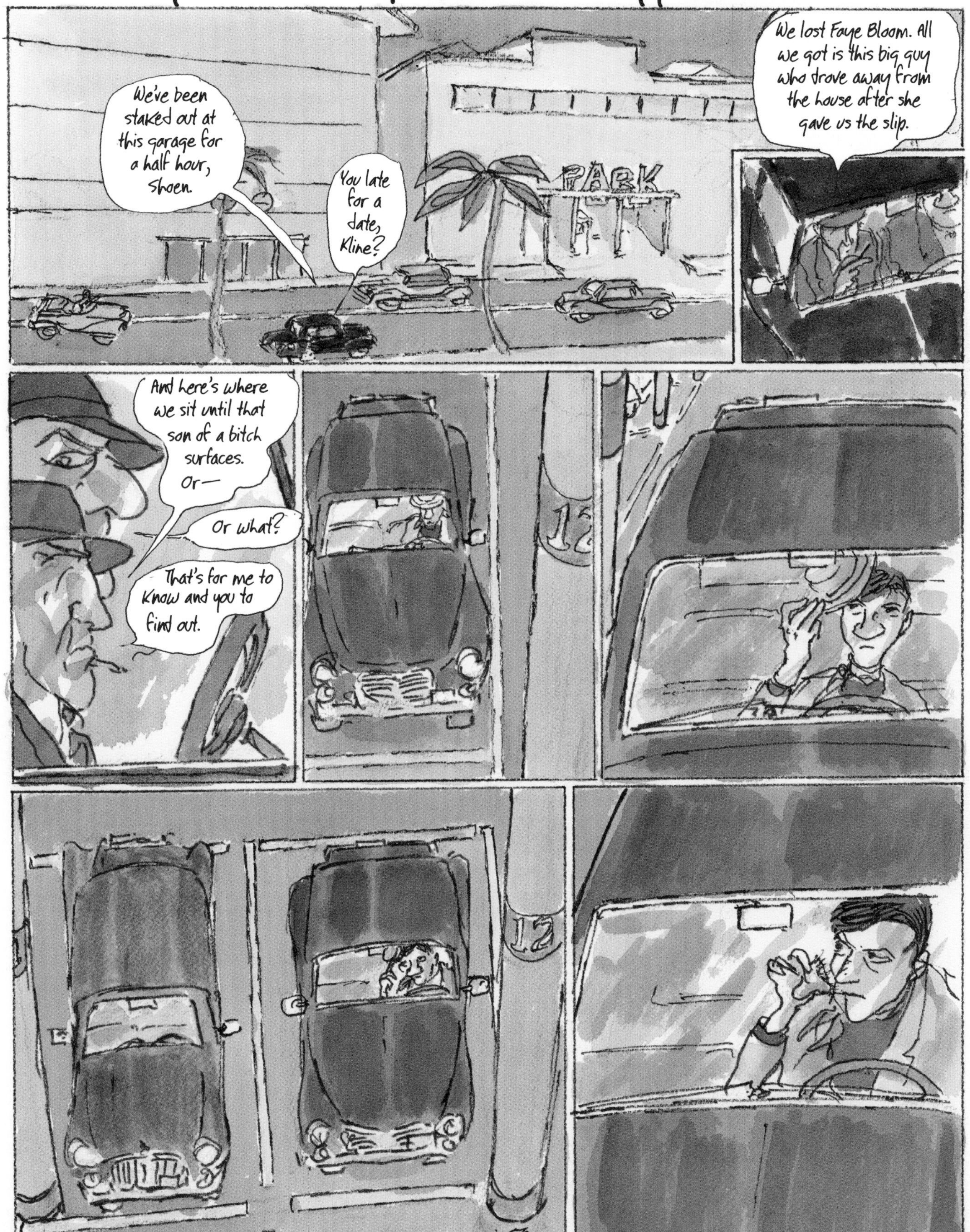

We've been staked out at this garage for a half hour, Shoen.
You late for a date, Kline?
PARK
We lost Faye Bloom. All we got is this big guy who drove away from the house after she gave us the slip.
And here's where we sit until that son of a bitch surfaces. Or—
Or what?
That's for me to know and you to find out.
12
12

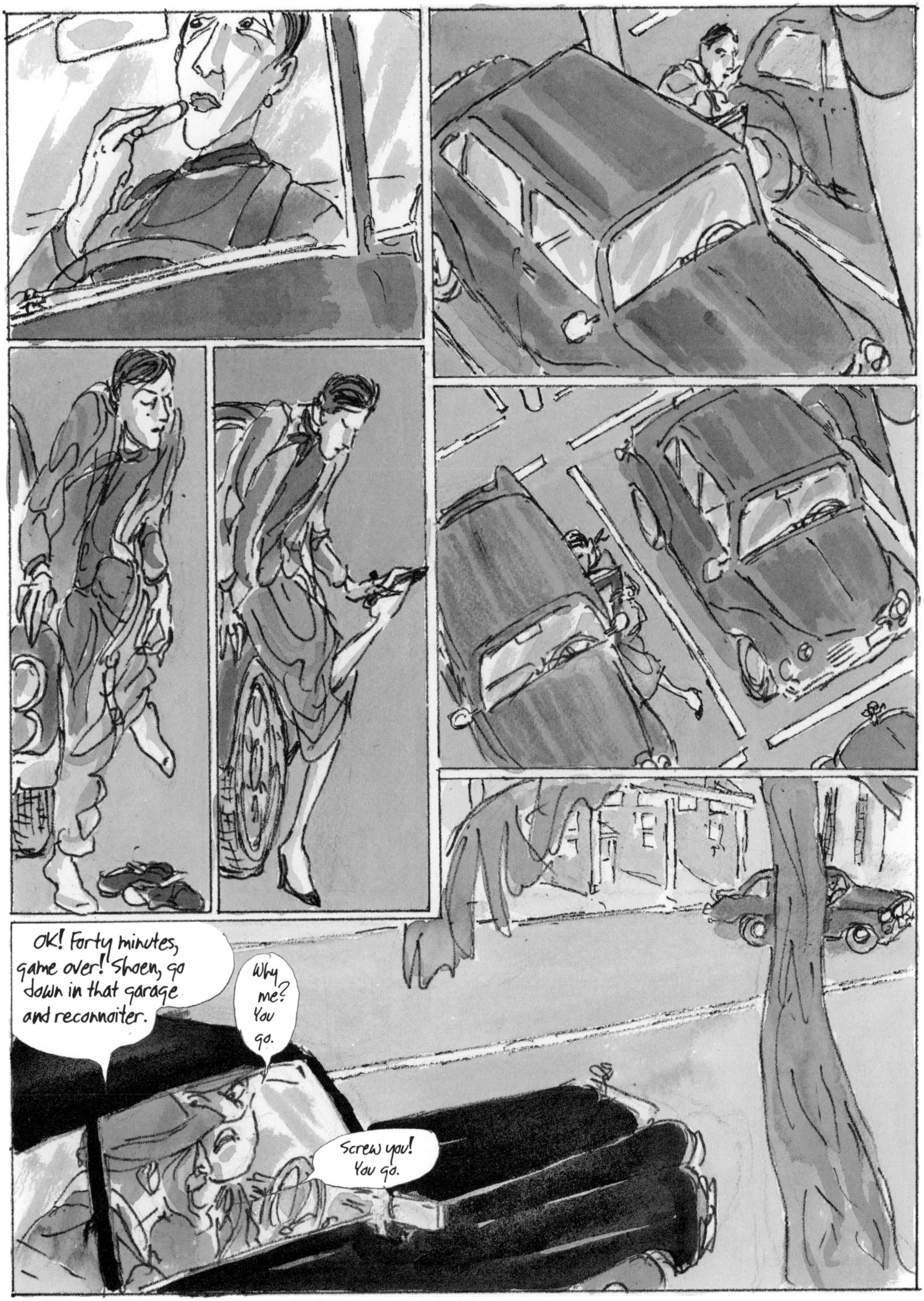

OK! Forty minutes, game over! Shoen, go down in that garage and reconnoiter.
Why me? You go.
Screw you! You go.

Chapter Twenty-Three: Beau and Beanie

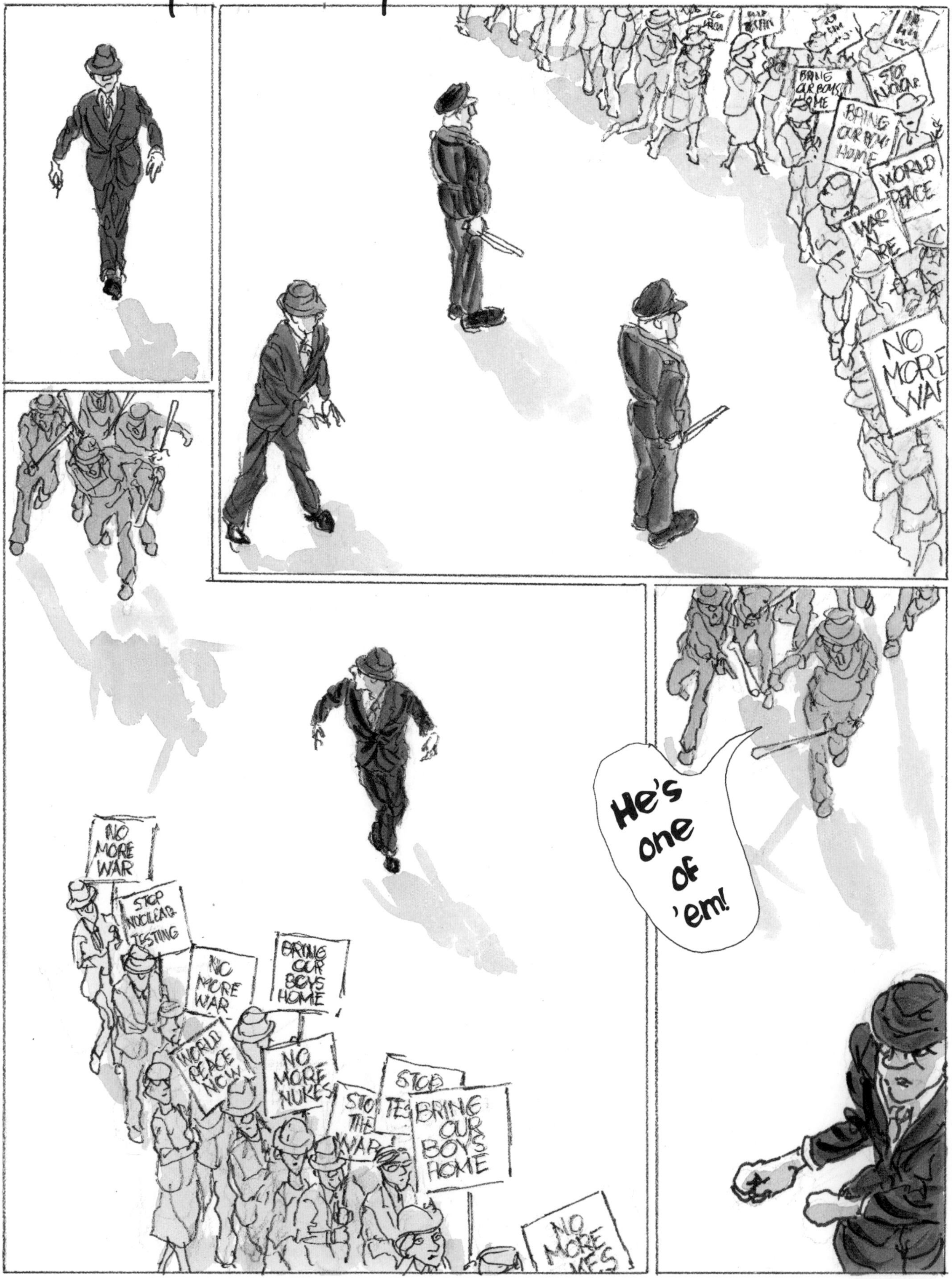
BRING OUR BOYS HOME
STOP NUCLEAR
BRING OUR BOYS HOME
WORLD PEACE
NO MORE WAR
He's one of 'em!
NO MORE WAR
STOP NUCLEAR TESTING
NO MORE WAR
BRING OUR BOYS HOME
WORLD PEACE NOW
NO MORE NUKES
BRING OUR BOYS HOME

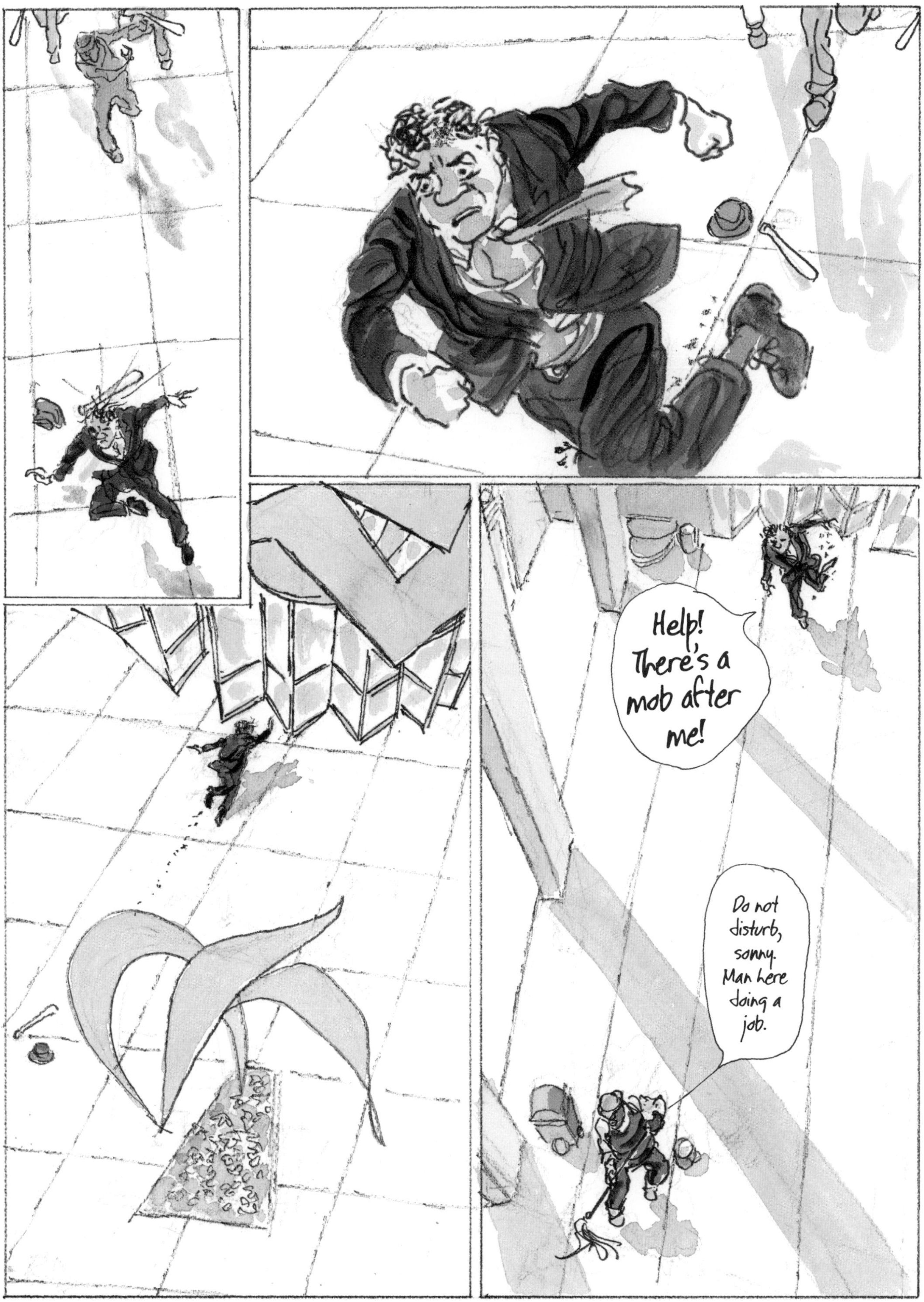
Help! There's a mob after me!
Do not disturb, sonny. Man here doing a job.

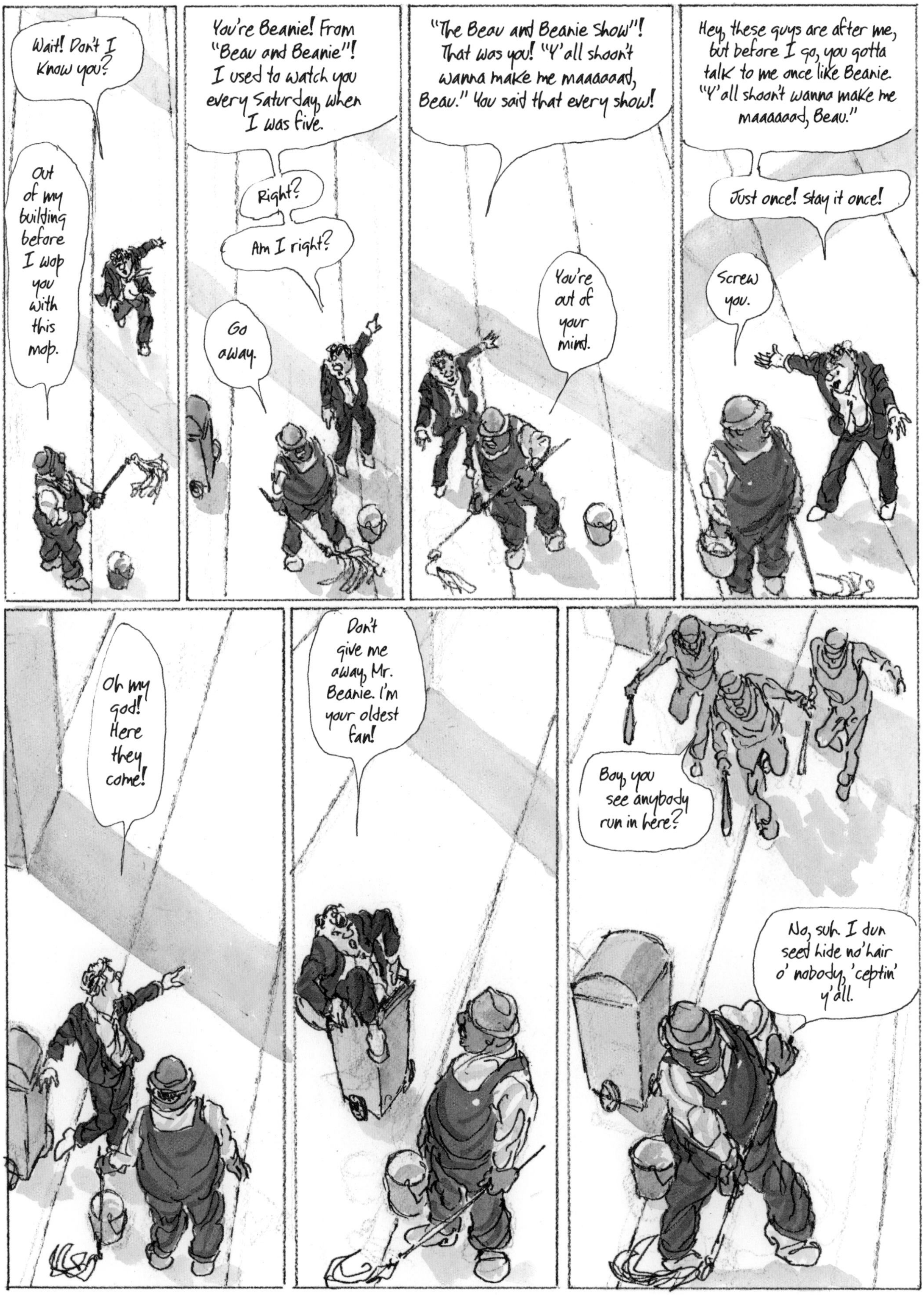

Wait! Don't I know you?
Out of my building before I wop you with this mop.
You're Beanie! From "Beau and Beanie"! I used to watch you every Saturday, when I was five.
Right?
Am I right?
Go away.
"The Beau and Beanie Show"! That was you! "Y'all shoon't wanna make me maaaaaad, Beau." You said that every show!
You're out of your mind.
Hey, these guys are after me, but before I go, you gotta talk to me once like Beanie. "Y'all shoon't wanna make me maaaaaad, Beau."
Just once! Stay it once!
Screw you.
Oh my god! Here they come!
Don't give me away, Mr. Beanie. I'm your oldest fan!
Boy, you see anybody run in here?
No, suh. I dun seed hide no'hair o' nobody, 'ceptin' y'all.

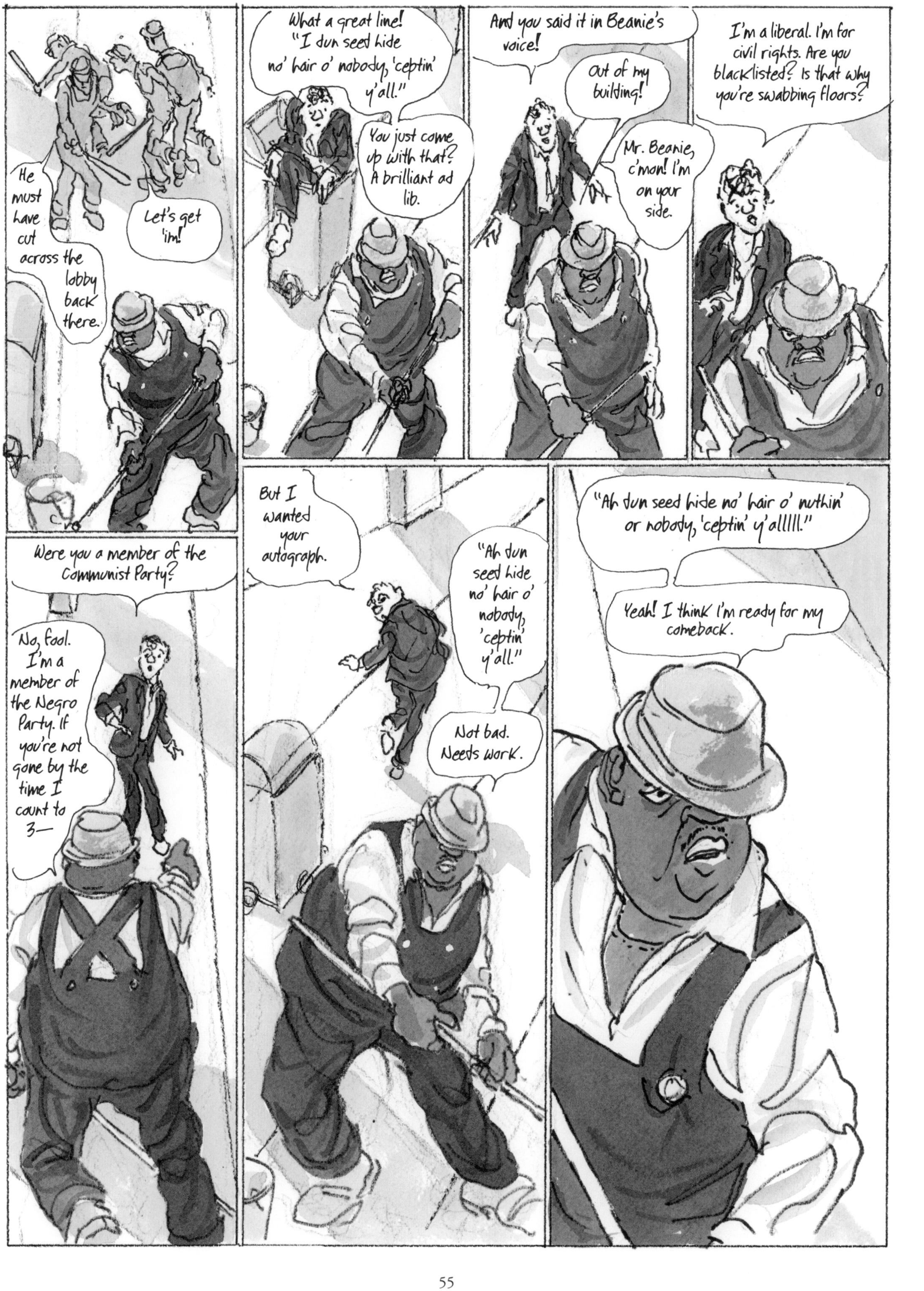
He must have cut across the lobby back there.
Let's get 'im!
What a great line! "I dun seed hide no' hair o' nobody, 'ceptin' y'all."
You just come up with that? A brilliant ad lib.
And you said it in Beanie's voice!
Out of my building!
Mr. Beanie, c'mon! I'm on your side.
I'm a liberal. I'm for civil rights. Are you blacklisted? Is that why you're swabbing floors?
Were you a member of the Communist Party?
No, fool. I'm a member of the Negro Party. If you're not gone by the time I count to 3—
But I wanted your autograph.
"Ah dun seed hide no' hair o' nobody, 'ceptin' y'all."
Not bad. Needs work.
"Ah dun seed hide no' hair o' nuthin' or nobody, 'ceptin' y'alllll."
Yeah! I think I'm ready for my comeback.

Chapter Twenty-Four: Bedroom III

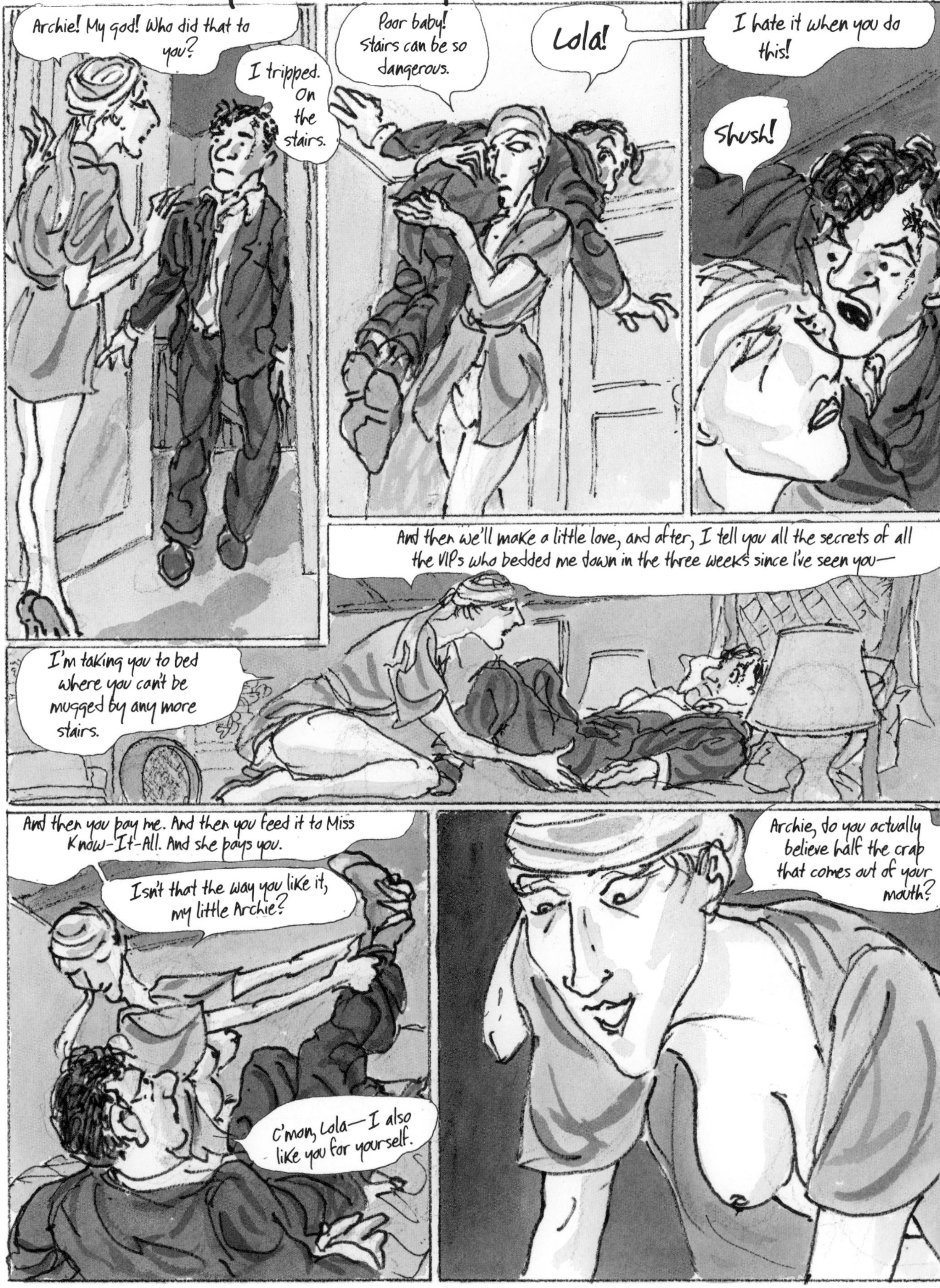

Archie! My god! Who did that to you?
I tripped. On the stairs.
Poor baby! Stairs can be so dangerous.
Lola!
I hate it when you do this!
Shush!
And then we'll make a little love, and after, I tell you all the secrets of all the VIPs who bedded me down in the three weeks since I've seen you—
I'm taking you to bed where you can't be mugged by any more stairs.
And then you pay me. And then you feed it to Miss Know-It-All. And she pays you.
Isn't that the way you like it, my little Archie?
C'mon, Lola—I also like you for yourself.
Archie, do you actually believe half the crap that comes out of your mouth?

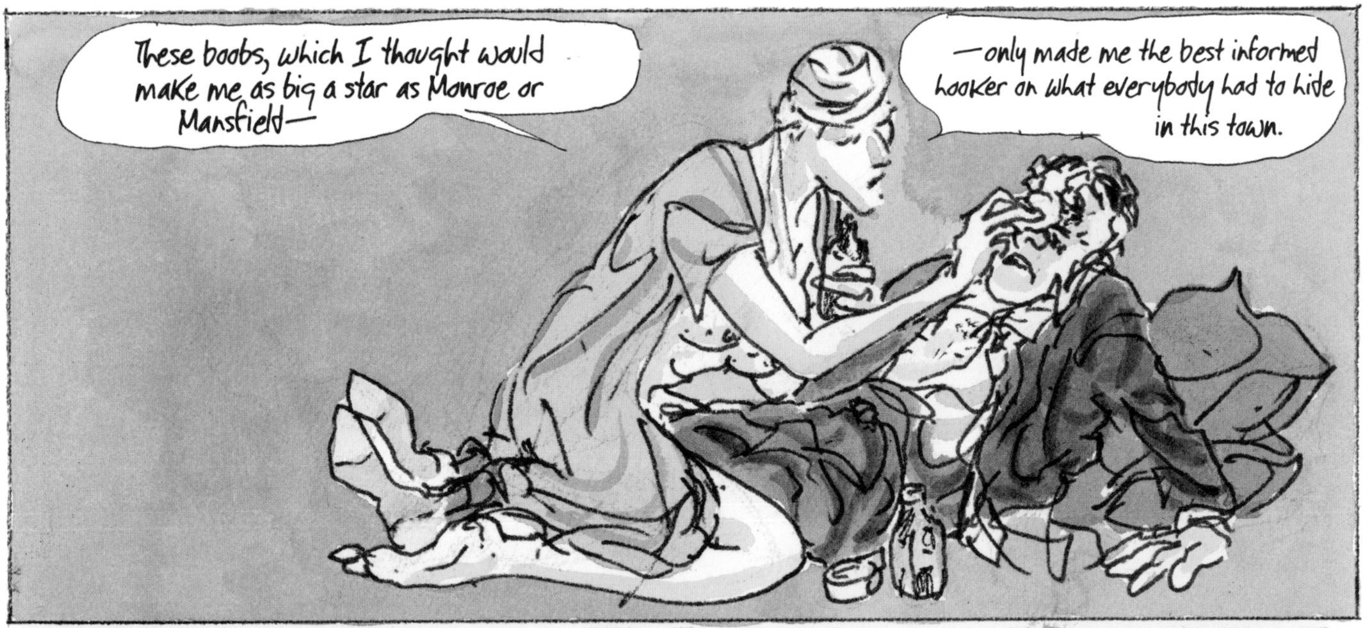
These boobs, which I thought would make me as big a star as Monroe or Mansfield—
—only made me the best informed hooker on what everybody had to hide in this town.

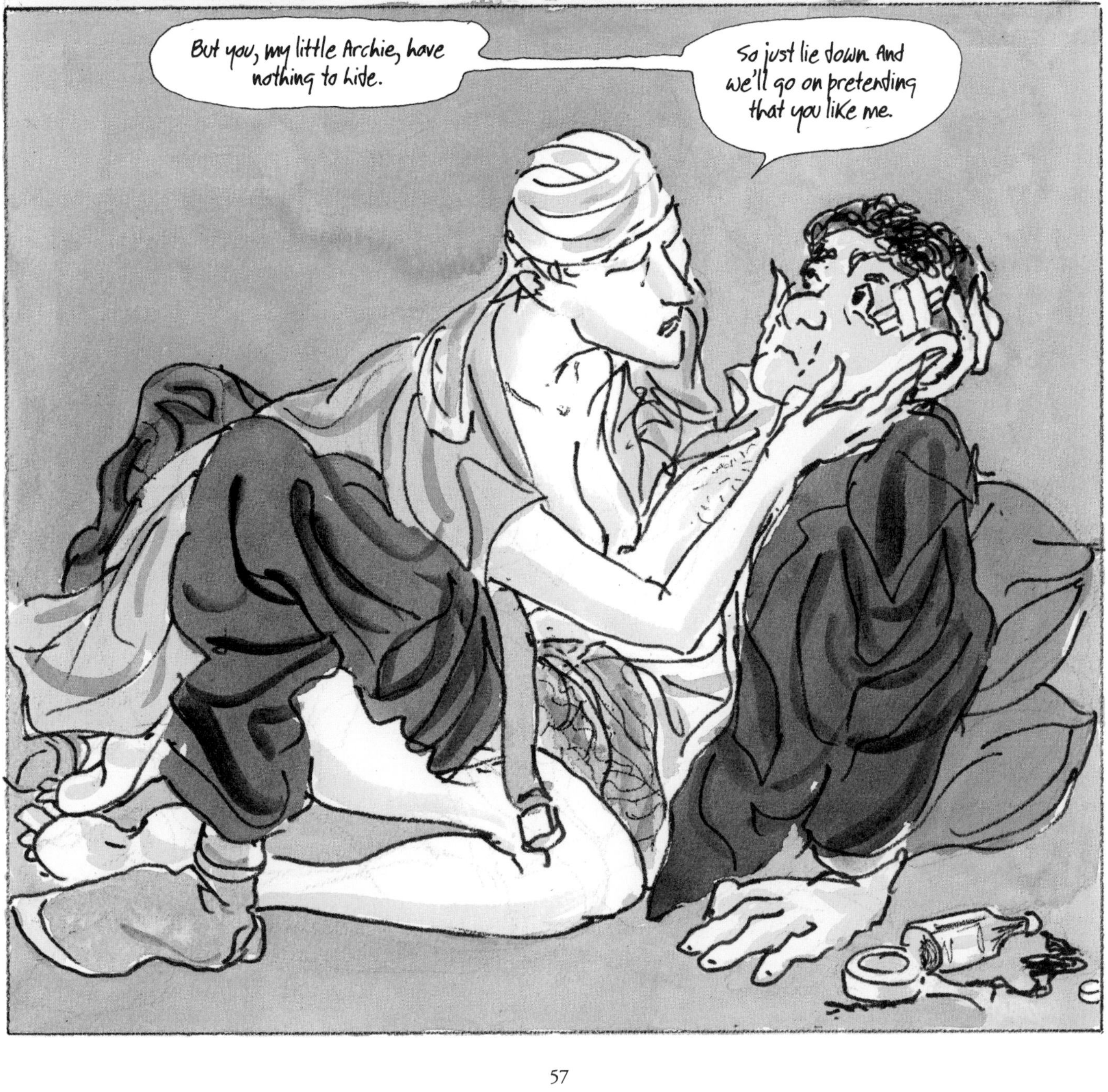
But you, my little Archie, have nothing to hide.
So just lie down. And we'll go on pretending that you like me.

Chapter Twenty-Five: Story Conference

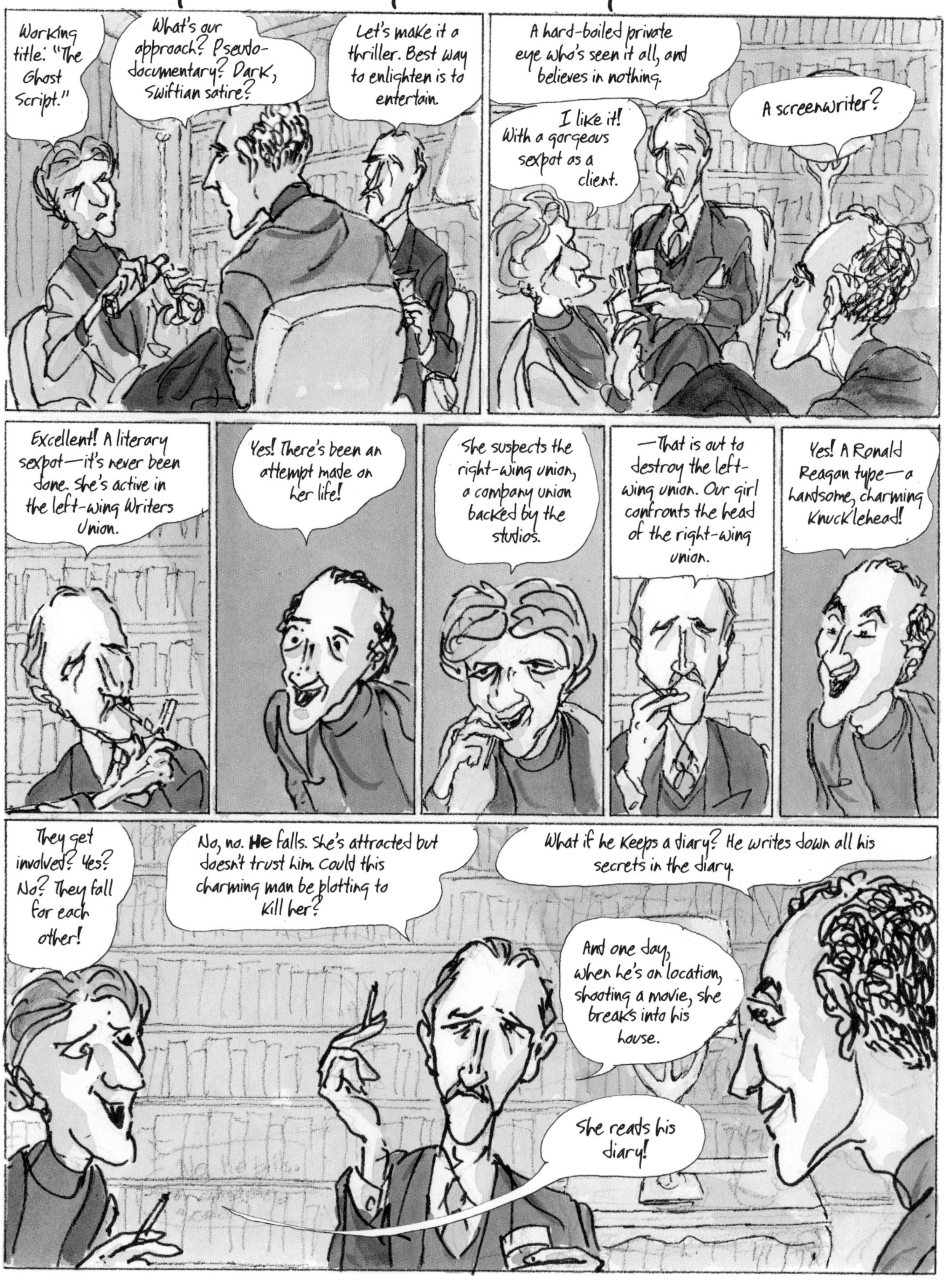

Working title: "The Ghost Script."
What's our approach? Pseudo-documentary? Dark, Swiftian satire?
Let's make it a thriller. Best way to enlighten is to entertain.
A hard-boiled private eye who's seen it all, and believes in nothing.
I like it! With a gorgeous sexpot as a client.
A screenwriter?
Excellent! A literary sexpot—it's never been done. She's active in the left-wing Writers Union.
Yes! There's been an attempt made on her life!
She suspects the right-wing union, a company union backed by the studios.
—That is out to destroy the left-wing union. Our girl confronts the head of the right-wing union.
Yes! A Ronald Reagan type—a handsome, charming Knucklehead!
They get involved? Yes? No? They fall for each other!
No, no. **He** falls. She's attracted but doesn't trust him. Could this charming man be plotting to kill her?
What if he Keeps a diary? He writes down all his secrets in the diary.
And one day, when he's on location, shooting a movie, she breaks into his house.
She reads his diary!

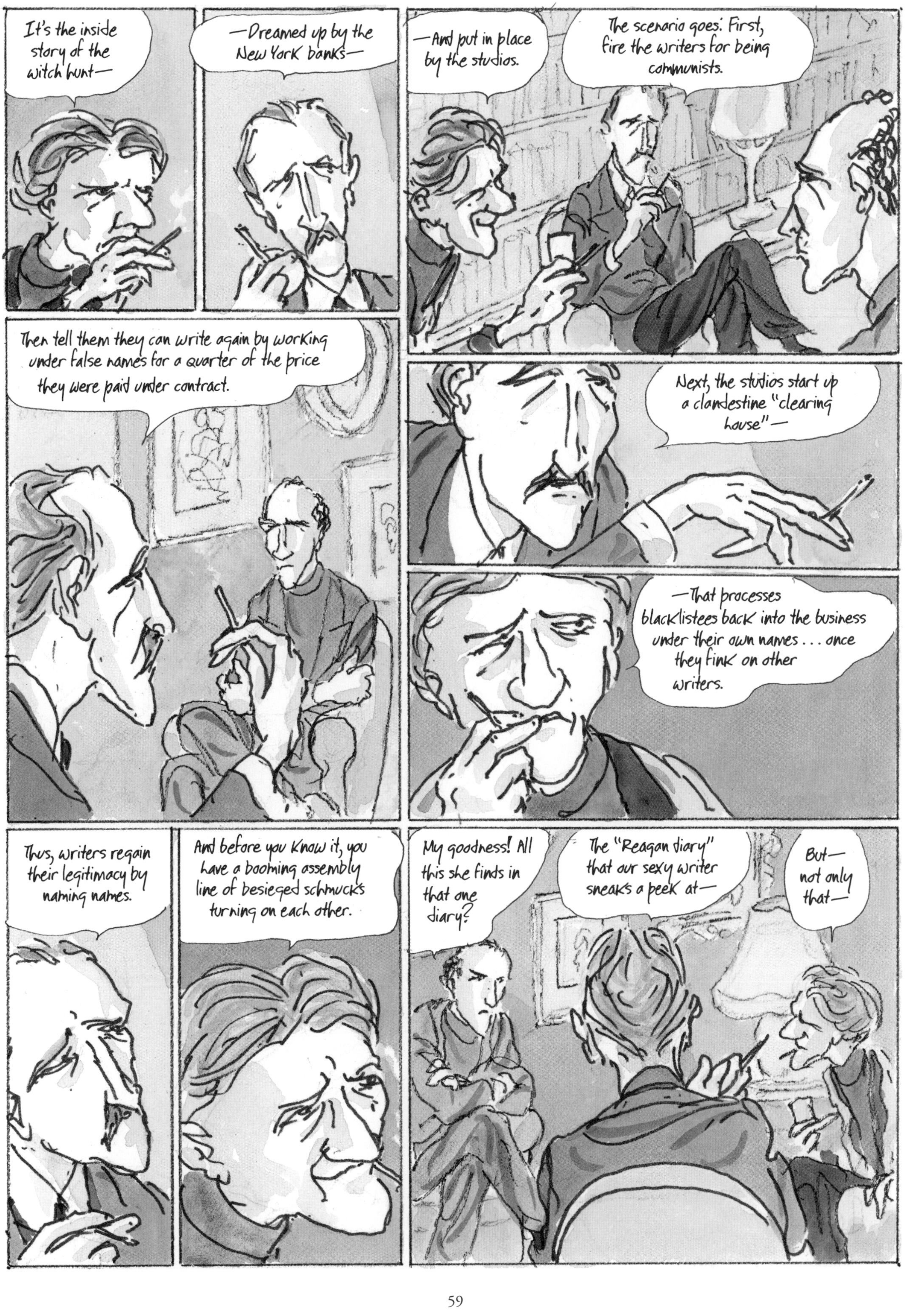
It's the inside story of the witch hunt—
—Dreamed up by the New York banks—
—And put in place by the studios.
The scenario goes: First, fire the writers for being communists.
Then tell them they can write again by working under false names for a quarter of the price they were paid under contract.
Next, the studios start up a clandestine "clearing house"—
—That processes blacklistees back into the business under their own names . . . once they fink on other writers.
Thus, writers regain their legitimacy by naming names.
And before you know it, you have a booming assembly line of besieged schmucks turning on each other.
My goodness! All this she finds in that one diary?
The "Reagan diary" that our sexy writer sneaks a peek at—
But— not only that—

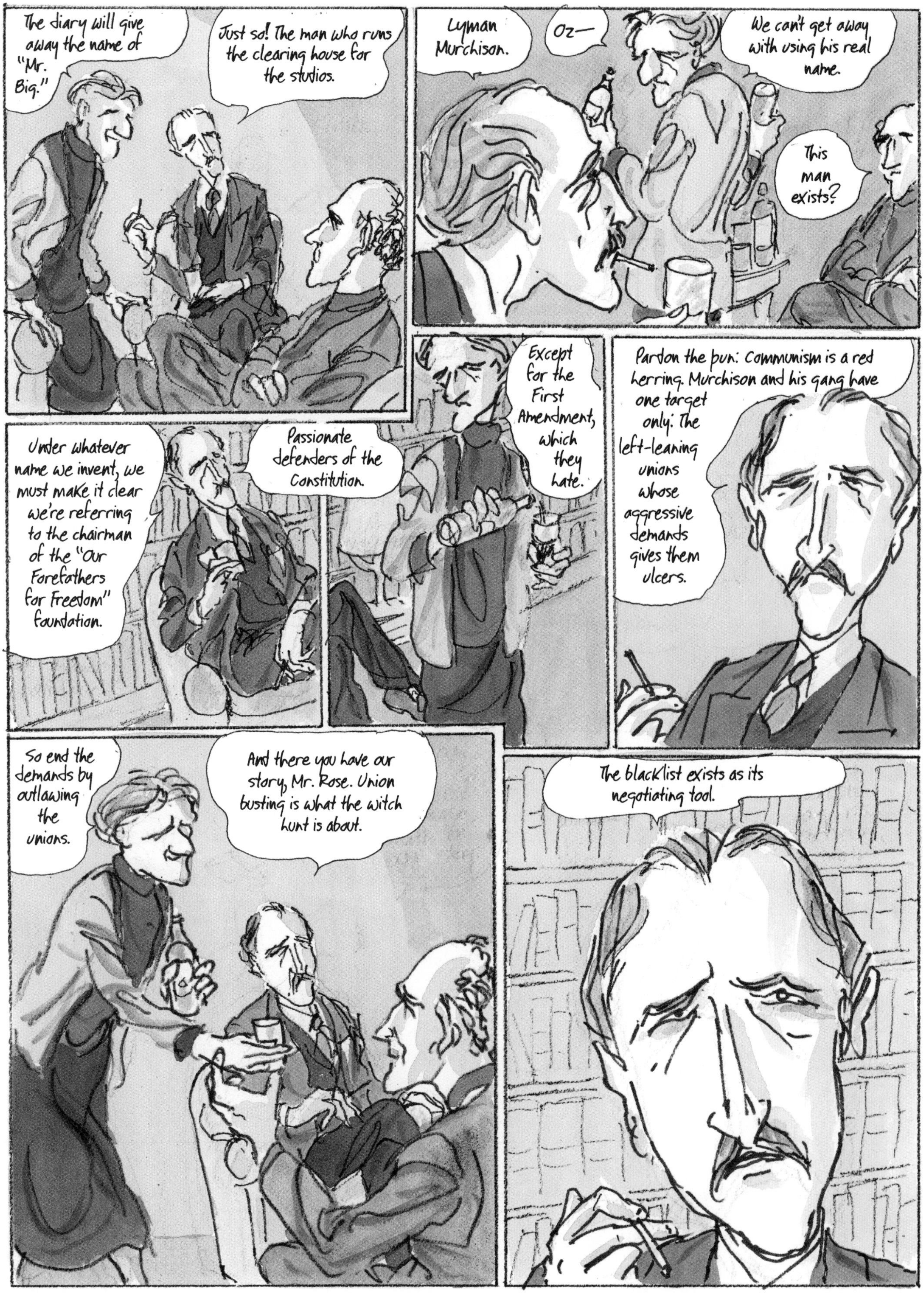
The diary will give away the name of "Mr. Big."
Just so! The man who runs the clearing house for the studios.
Lyman Murchison.
Oz—
We can't get away with using his real name.
This man exists?
Under whatever name we invent, we must make it clear we're referring to the chairman of the "Our Forefathers for Freedom" foundation.
Passionate defenders of the Constitution.
Except for the First Amendment, which they hate.
Pardon the pun: Communism is a red herring. Murchison and his gang have one target only: The left-leaning unions whose aggressive demands gives them ulcers.
So end the demands by outlawing the unions.
And there you have our story, Mr. Rose. Union busting is what the witch hunt is about.
The blacklist exists as its negotiating tool.

Chapter Twenty-Six: Bedroom III, Part II

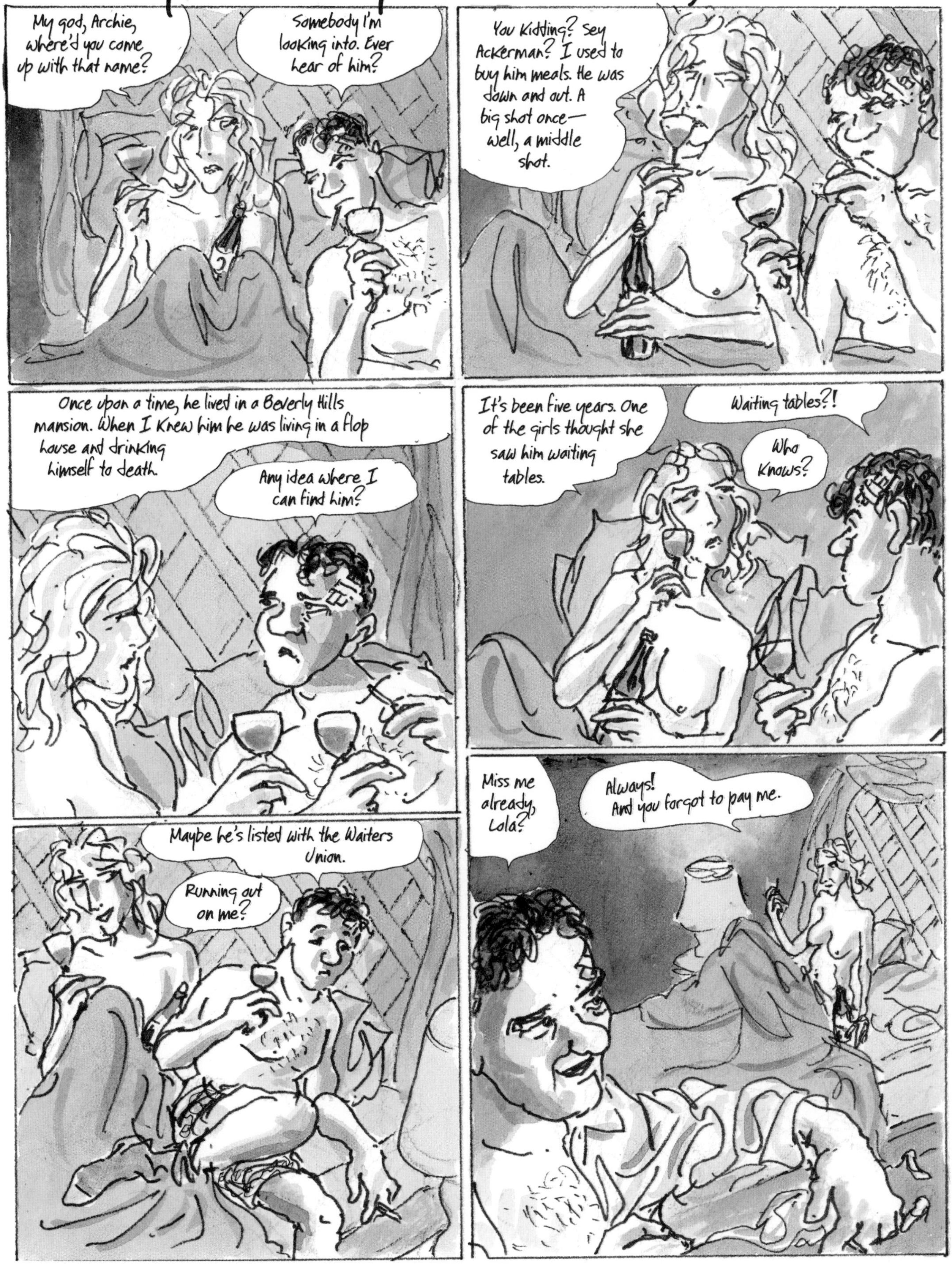
My god, Archie, where'd you come up with that name?
Somebody I'm looking into. Ever hear of him?
You kidding? Sey Ackerman? I used to buy him meals. He was down and out. A big shot once— well, a middle shot.
Once upon a time, he lived in a Beverly Hills mansion. When I knew him he was living in a flop house and drinking himself to death.
Any idea where I can find him?
It's been five years. One of the girls thought she saw him waiting tables.
Waiting tables?!
Who knows?
Maybe he's listed with the Waiters Union.
Running out on me?
Miss me already, Lola?
Always! And you forgot to pay me.

Chapter Twenty-Seven: Flashback—Beverly Hills, 1931

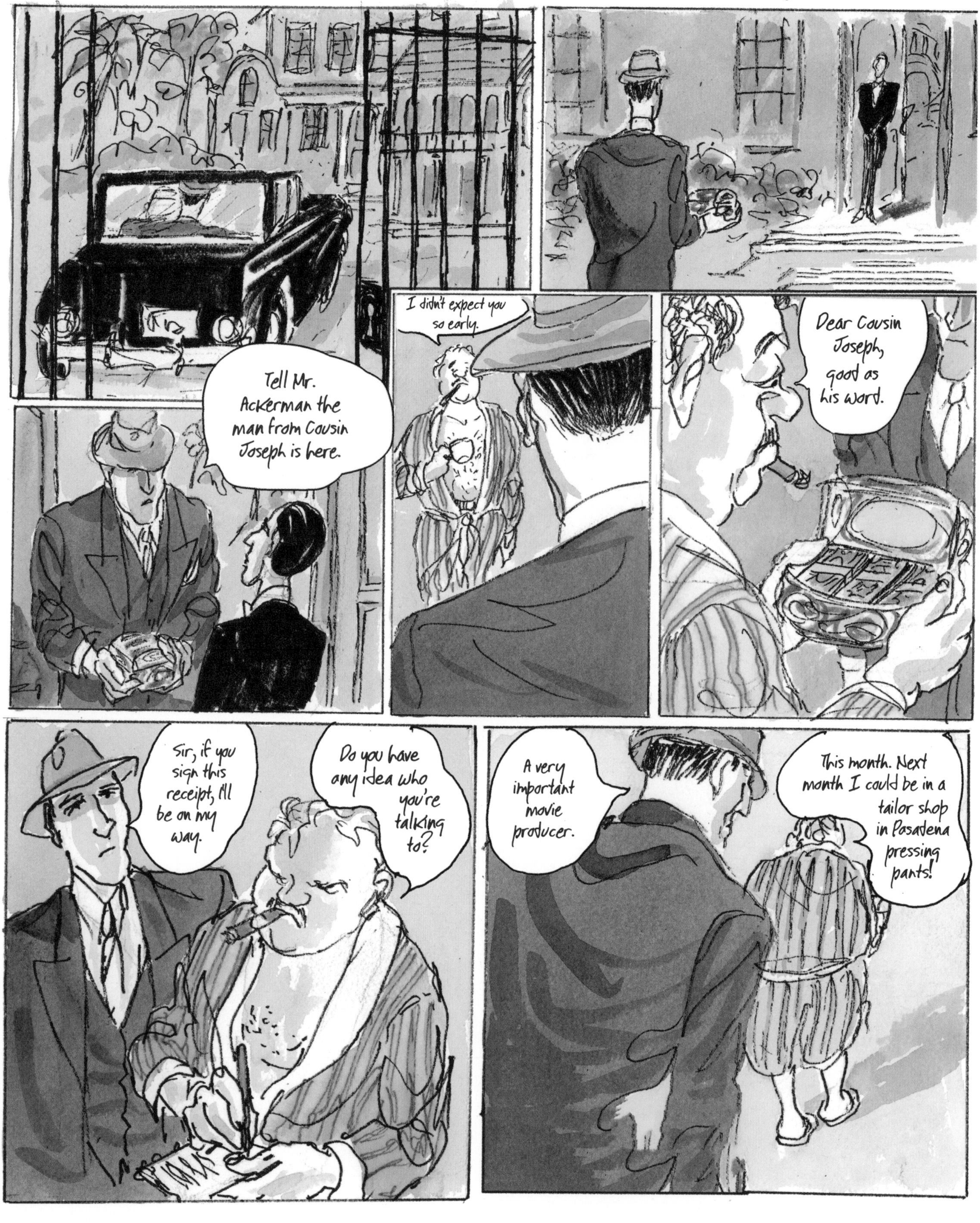
Tell Mr. Ackerman the man from Cousin Joseph is here.
I didn't expect you so early.
Dear Cousin Joseph, good as his word.
Sir, if you sign this receipt, I'll be on my way.
Do you have any idea who you're talking to?
A very important movie producer.
This month. Next month I could be in a tailor shop in Pasadena pressing pants!

Chapter Twenty-Eight: The Waiter

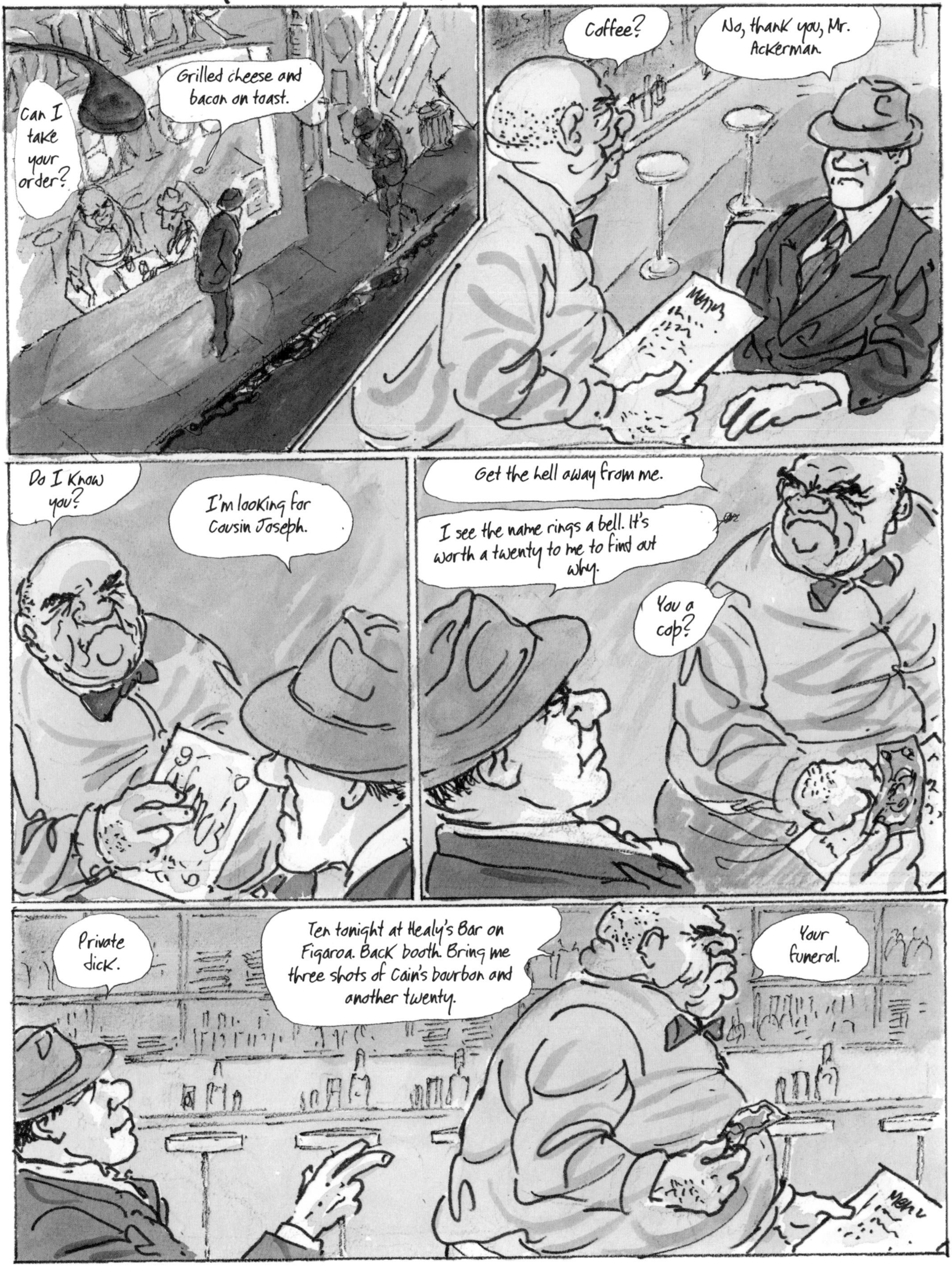

Can I take your order?
Grilled cheese and bacon on toast.
Coffee?
No, thank you, Mr. Ackerman.
Do I know you?
I'm looking for Cousin Joseph.
Get the hell away from me.
I see the name rings a bell. It's worth a twenty to me to find out why.
You a cop?
Private dick.
Ten tonight at Healy's Bar on Figaroa. Back booth. Bring me three shots of Cain's bourbon and another twenty.
Your funeral.

Chapter Twenty-Nine: Ackerman's Complaint

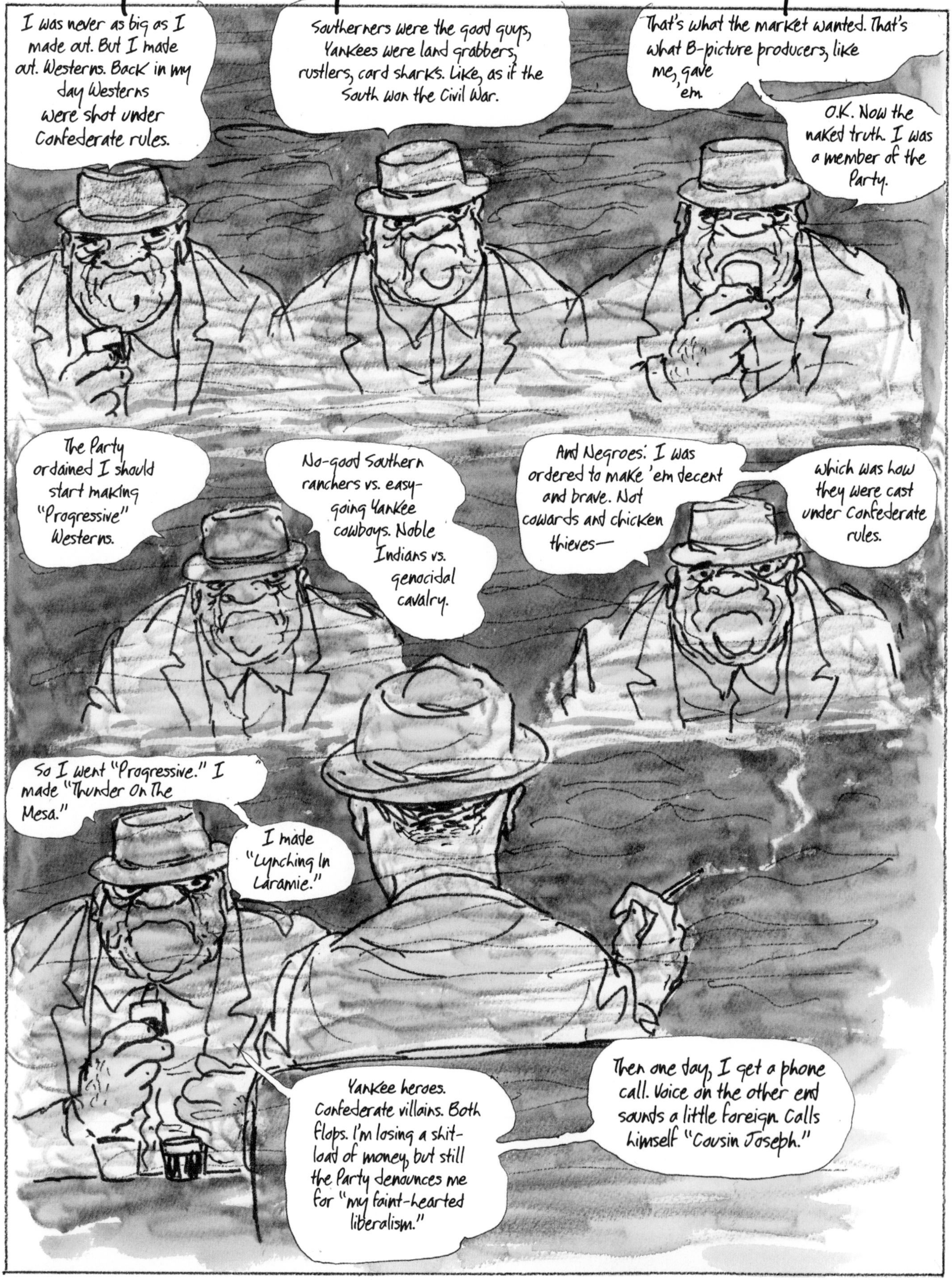

I was never as big as I made out. But I made out. Westerns. Back in my day Westerns were shot under Confederate rules.
Southerners were the good guys, Yankees were land grabbers, rustlers, card sharks. Like, as if the South won the Civil War.
That's what the market wanted. That's what B-picture producers, like me, gave 'em.
O.K. Now the naked truth. I was a member of the Party.
The Party ordained I should start making "Progressive" Westerns.
No-good Southern ranchers vs. easy-going Yankee cowboys. Noble Indians vs. genocidal cavalry.
And Negroes: I was ordered to make 'em decent and brave. Not cowards and chicken thieves—
which was how they were cast under Confederate rules.
So I went "Progressive." I made "Thunder On The Mesa."
I made "Lynching In Laramie."
Yankee heroes. Confederate villains. Both flops. I'm losing a shit-load of money, but still the Party denounces me for "my faint-hearted liberalism."
Then one day, I get a phone call. Voice on the other end sounds a little foreign. Calls himself "Cousin Joseph."

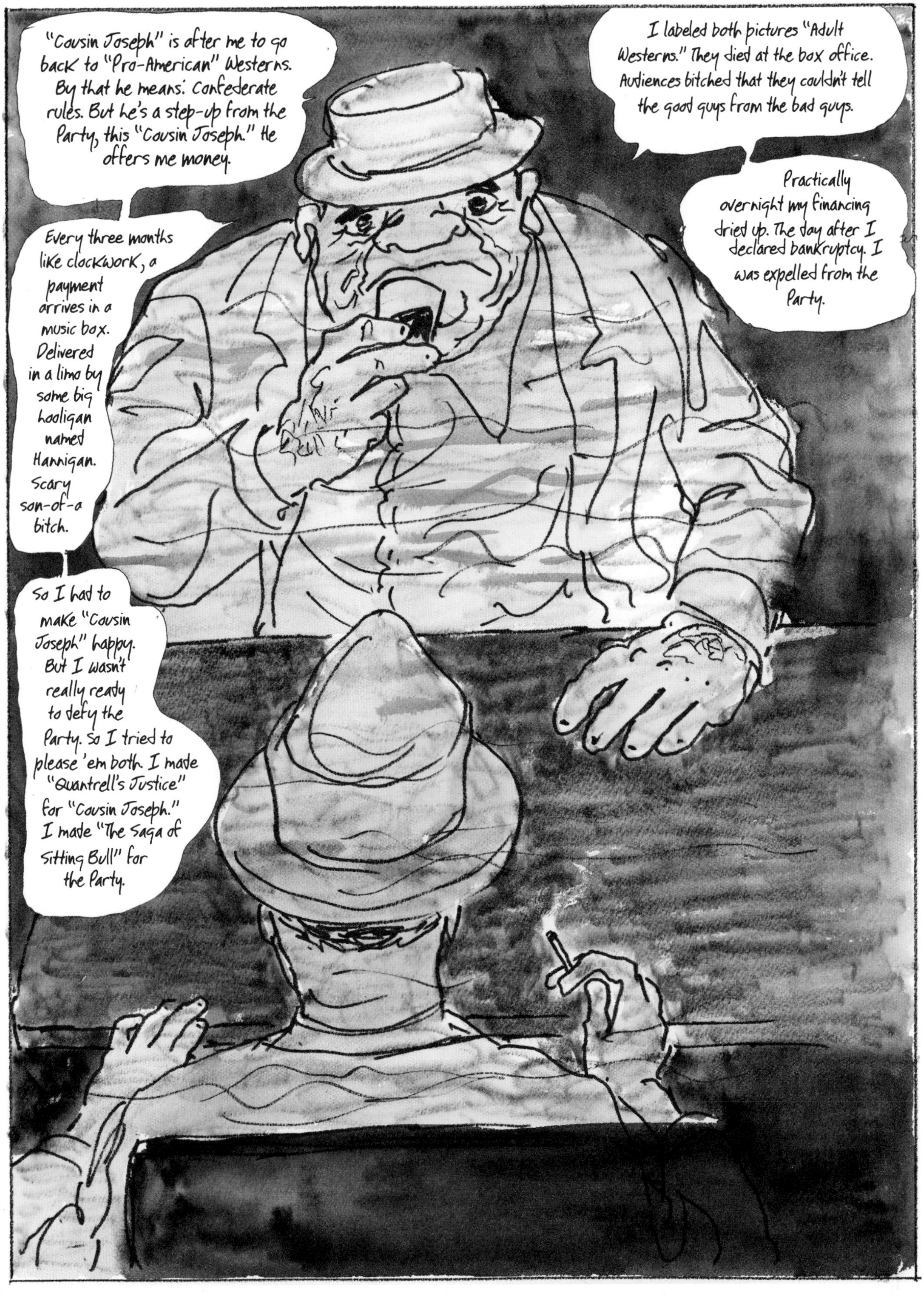
"Cousin Joseph" is after me to go back to "Pro-American" Westerns. By that he means: Confederate rules. But he's a step-up from the Party, this "Cousin Joseph." He offers me money.
Every three months like clockwork, a payment arrives in a music box. Delivered in a limo by some big hooligan named Hannigan. Scary son-of-a bitch.
So I had to make "Cousin Joseph" happy. But I wasn't really ready to defy the Party. So I tried to please 'em both. I made "Quantrell's Justice" for "Cousin Joseph." I made "The Saga of Sitting Bull" for the Party.
I labeled both pictures "Adult Westerns." They died at the box office. Audiences bitched that they couldn't tell the good guys from the bad guys.
Practically overnight my financing dried up. The day after I declared bankruptcy, I was expelled from the Party.

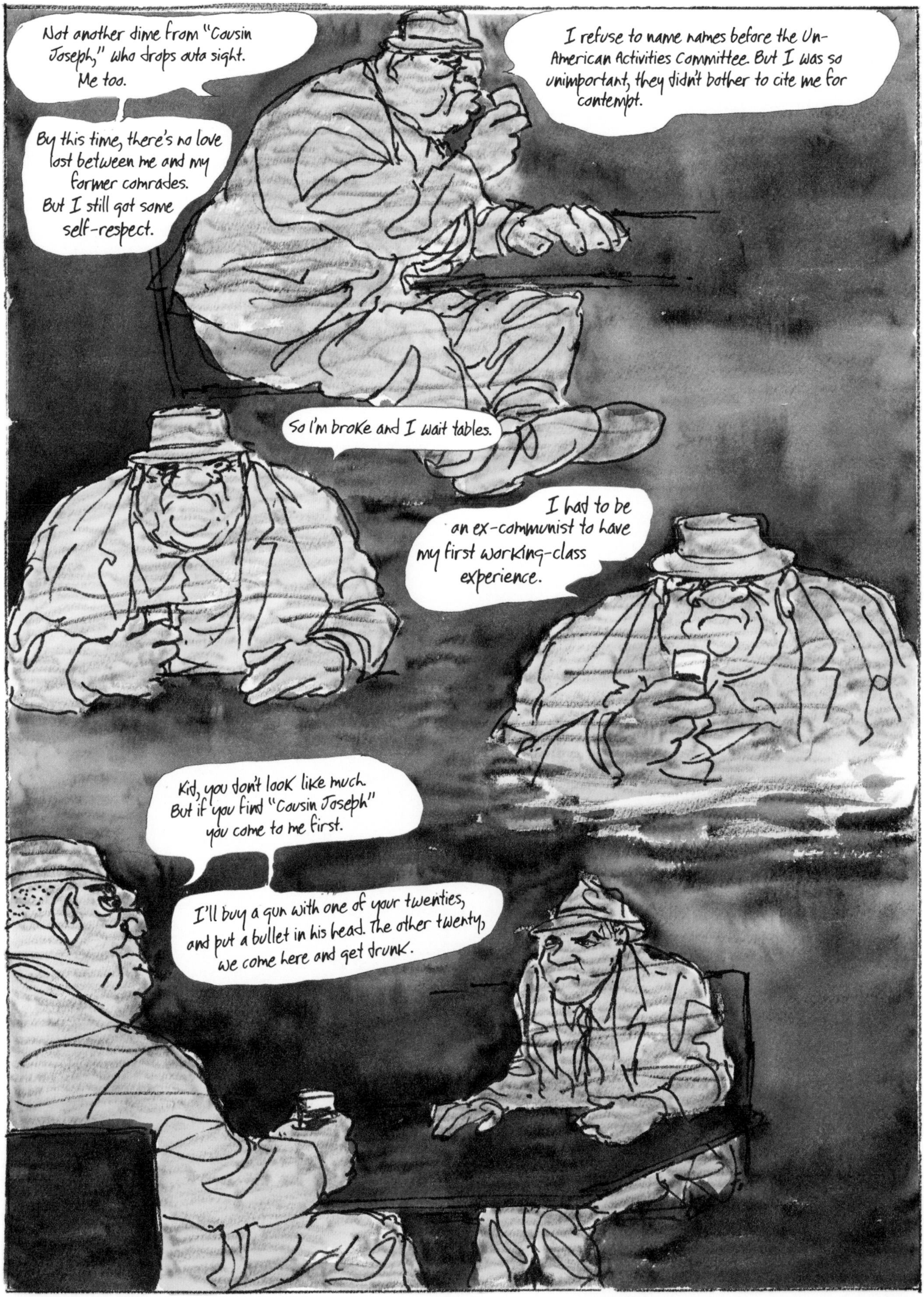
Not another dime from "Cousin Joseph," who drops outa sight. Me too.
I refuse to name names before the Un-American Activities Committee. But I was so unimportant, they didn't bother to cite me for contempt.
By this time, there's no love lost between me and my former comrades. But I still got some self-respect.
So I'm broke and I wait tables.
I had to be an ex-communist to have my first working-class experience.
Kid, you don't look like much. But if you find "Cousin Joseph" you come to me first.
I'll buy a gun with one of your twenties, and put a bullet in his head. The other twenty, we come here and get drunk.

Chapter Thirty: Mr. Elliot

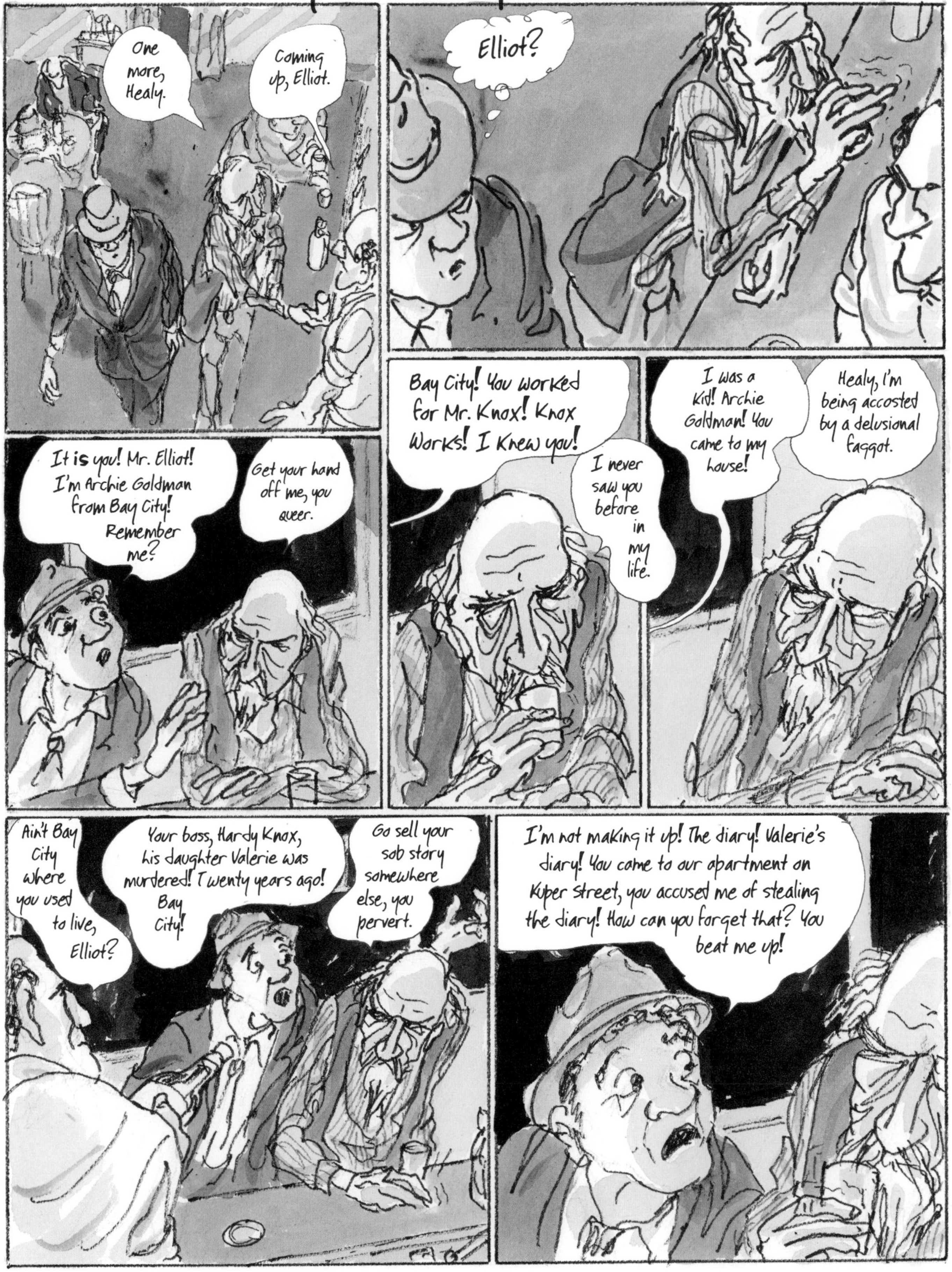

One more, Healy.
Coming up, Elliot.
Elliot?
It is you! Mr. Elliot! I'm Archie Goldman from Bay City! Remember me?
Get your hand off me, you queer.
Bay City! You worked for Mr. Knox! Knox Works! I knew you!
I never saw you before in my life.
I was a kid! Archie Goldman! You came to my house!
Healy, I'm being accosted by a delusional faggot.
Ain't Bay City where you used to live, Elliot?
Your boss, Hardy Knox, his daughter Valerie was murdered! Twenty years ago! Bay City!
Go sell your sob story somewhere else, you pervert.
I'm not making it up! The diary! Valerie's diary! You came to our apartment on Kuper Street, you accused me of stealing the diary! How can you forget that? You beat me up!

Chapter Thirty-One: Flashback—Bay City, 1931

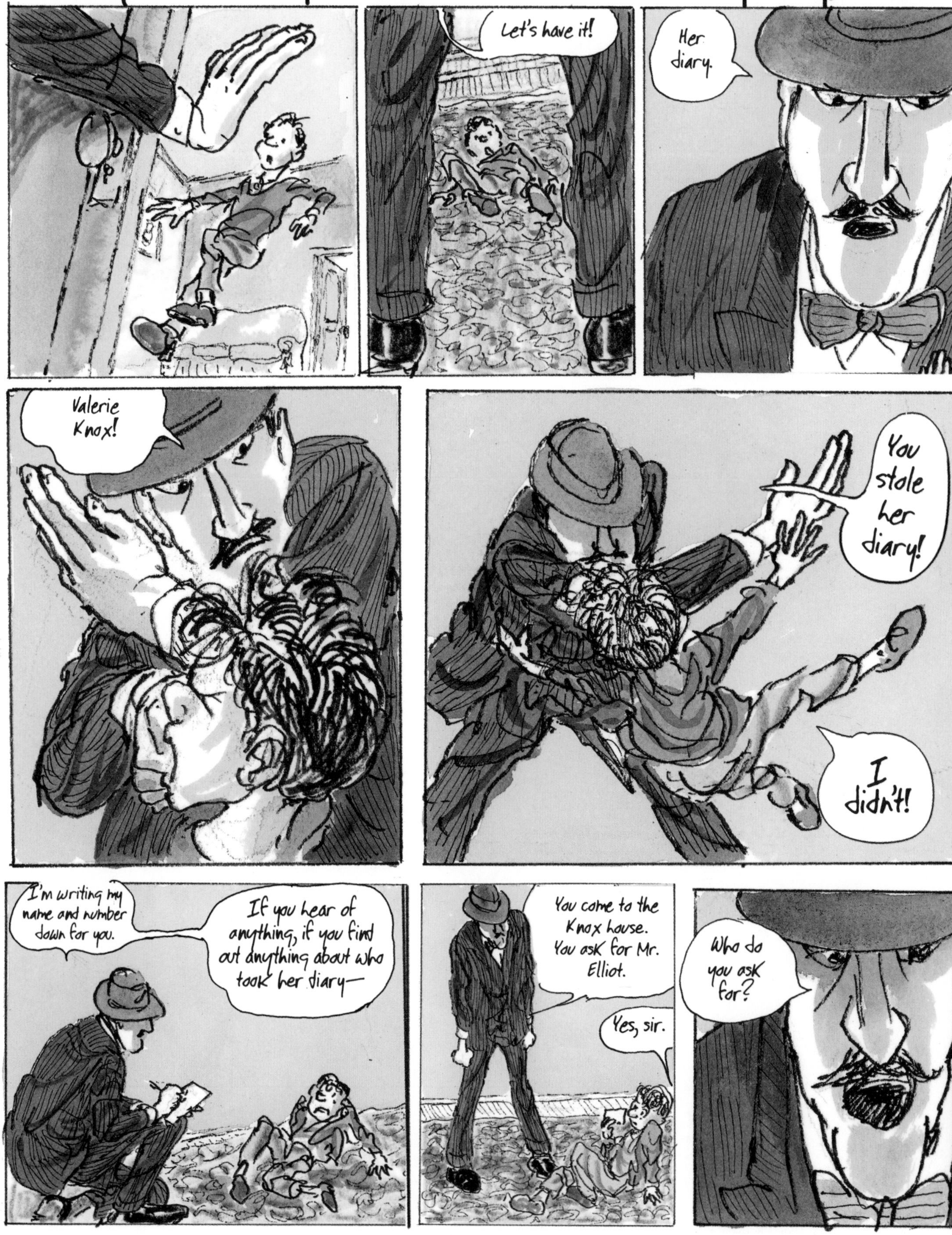
Let's have it!
Her diary.
Valerie Knox!
You stole her diary!
I didn't!
I'm writing my name and number down for you.
If you hear of anything, if you find out anything about who took her diary—
You come to the Knox house. You ask for Mr. Elliot.
Yes, sir.
Who do you ask for?

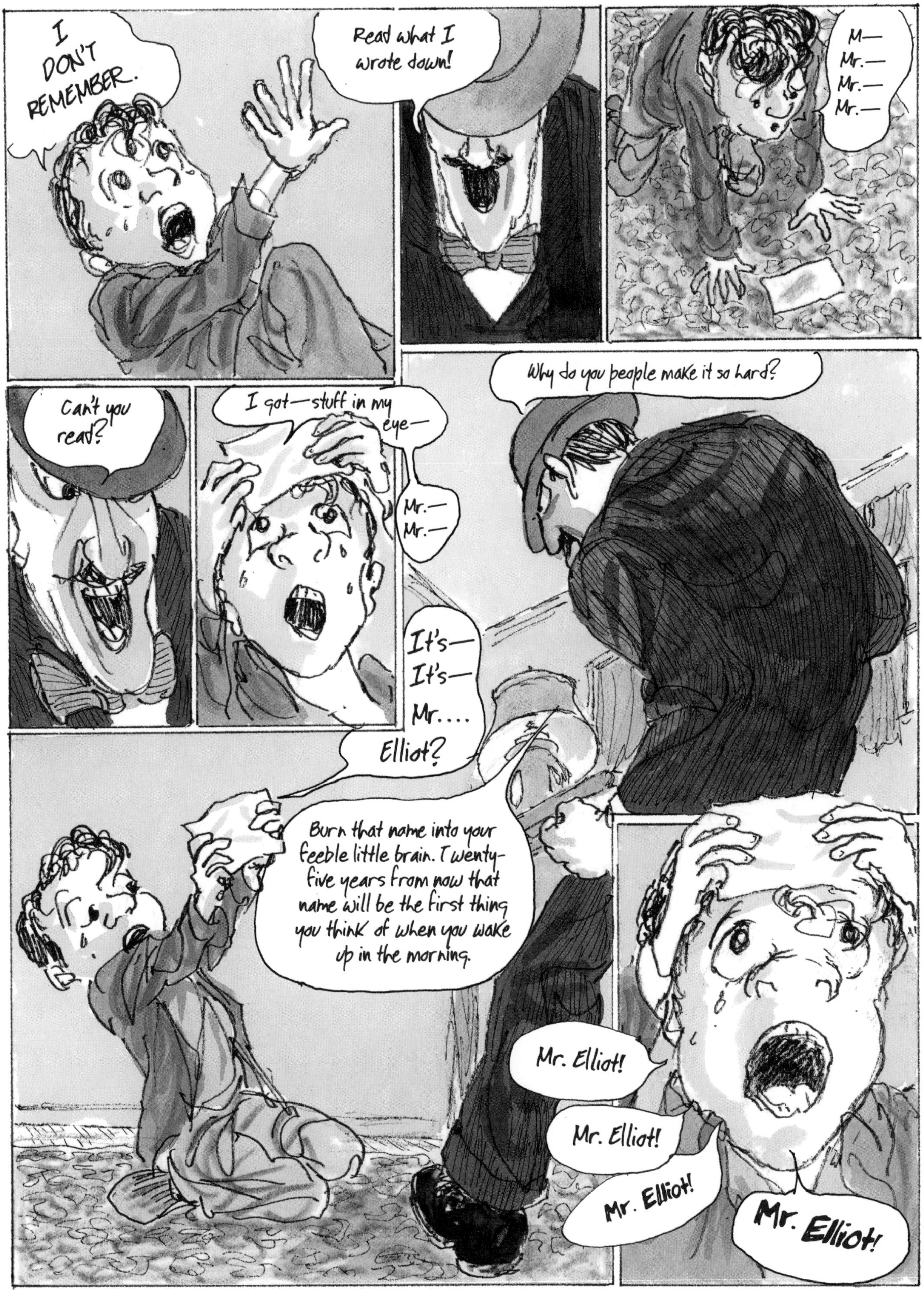
I DON'T REMEMBER.
Read what I wrote down!
M—
Mr.—
Mr.—
Mr.—
Why do you people make it so hard?
Can't you read?
I got—stuff in my eye—
Mr.—
Mr.—
It's—
It's—
Mr....
Elliot?
Burn that name into your feeble little brain. Twenty-five years from now that name will be the first thing you think of when you wake up in the morning.
Mr. Elliot!
Mr. Elliot!
Mr. Elliot!
Mr. Elliot!

Chapter Thirty-Two: Mr. Elliot, Part II

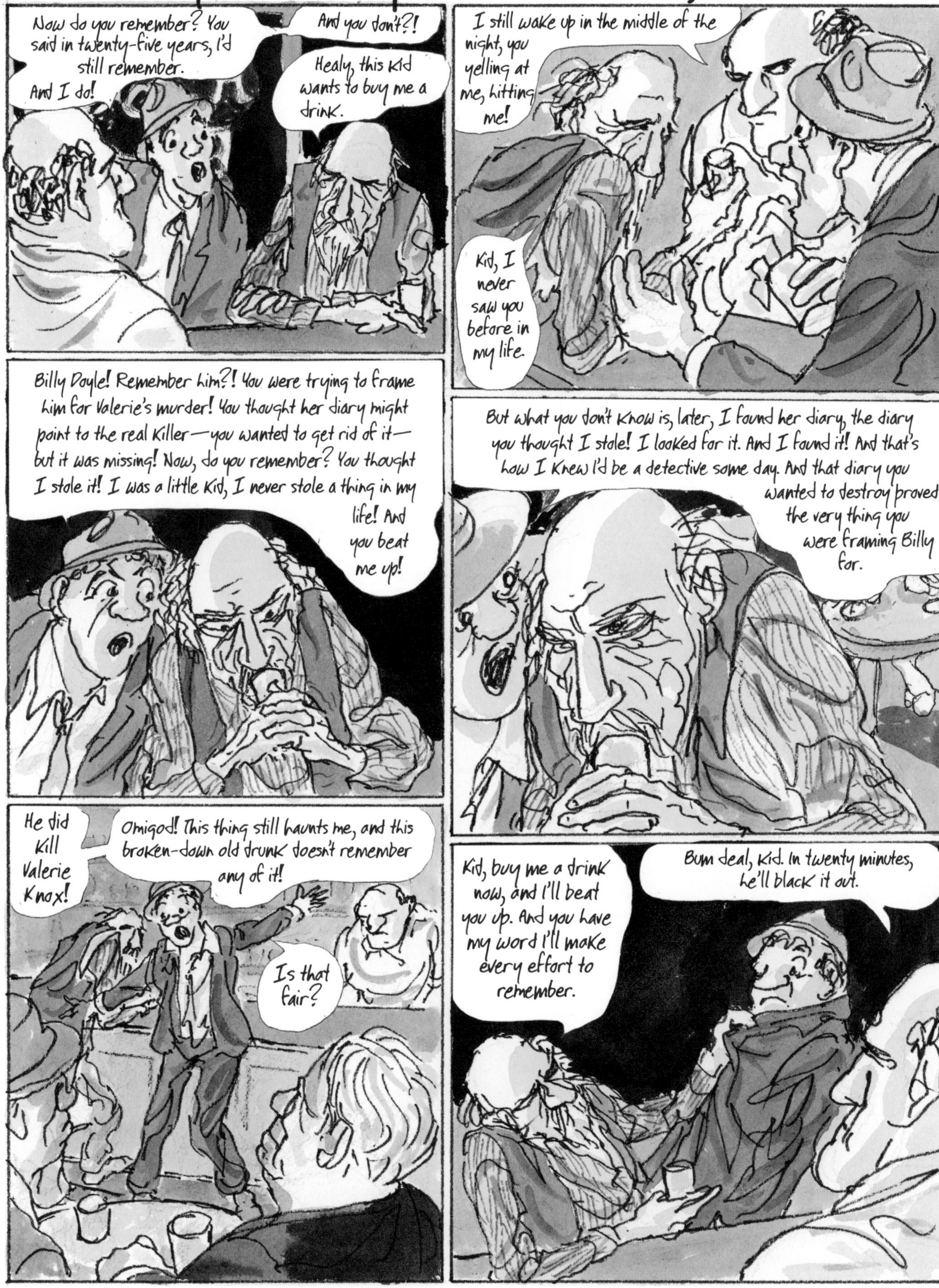
Now do you remember? You said in twenty-five years, I'd still remember.
And I do!
And you don't?!
Healy, this kid wants to buy me a drink.
I still wake up in the middle of the night, you yelling at me, hitting me!
Kid, I never saw you before in my life.
Billy Doyle! Remember him?! You were trying to frame him for Valerie's murder! You thought her diary might point to the real killer—you wanted to get rid of it—but it was missing! Now, do you remember? You thought I stole it! I was a little kid, I never stole a thing in my life! And you beat me up!
But what you don't know is, later, I found her diary, the diary you thought I stole! I looked for it. And I found it! And that's how I knew I'd be a detective some day. And that diary you wanted to destroy proved the very thing you were framing Billy for.
He did kill Valerie Knox!
Omigod! This thing still haunts me, and this broken-down old drunk doesn't remember any of it!
Is that fair?
Kid, buy me a drink now, and I'll beat you up. And you have my word I'll make every effort to remember.
Bum deal, kid. In twenty minutes, he'll black it out.

Chapter Thirty-Three: Self-Loathing

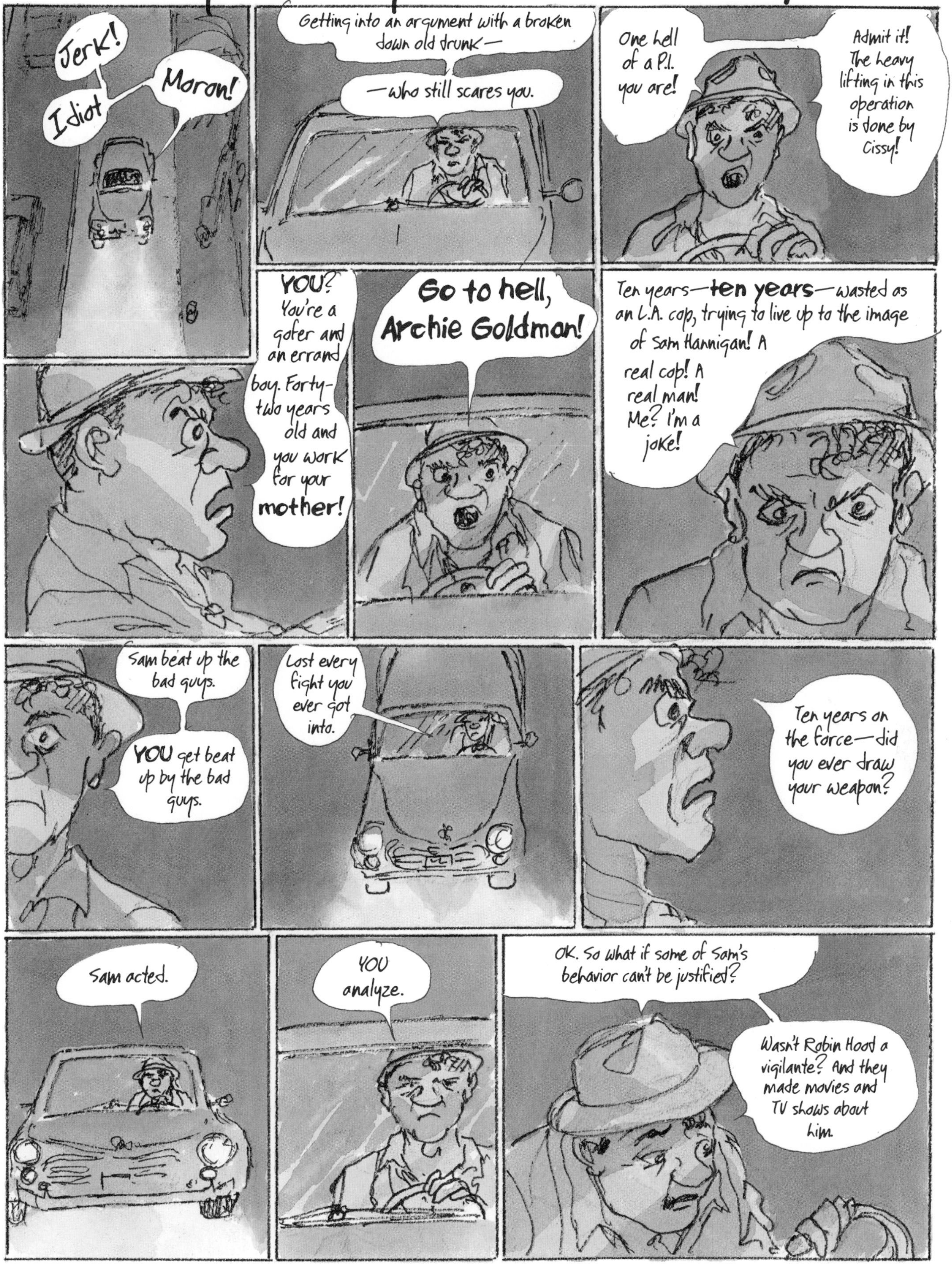
Jerk!
Idiot
Moron!
Getting into an argument with a broken down old drunk—
—who still scares you.
One hell of a P.I. you are!
Admit it! The heavy lifting in this operation is done by Cissy!
YOU? You're a gofer and an errand boy. Forty-two years old and you work for your mother!
Go to hell, Archie Goldman!
Ten years—ten years—wasted as an L.A. cop, trying to live up to the image of Sam Hannigan! A real cop! A real man! Me? I'm a joke!
Sam beat up the bad guys.
YOU get beat up by the bad guys.
Lost every fight you ever got into.
Ten years on the force—did you ever draw your weapon?
Sam acted.
YOU analyze.
OK. So what if some of Sam's behavior can't be justified?
Wasn't Robin Hood a vigilante? And they made movies and TV shows about him.

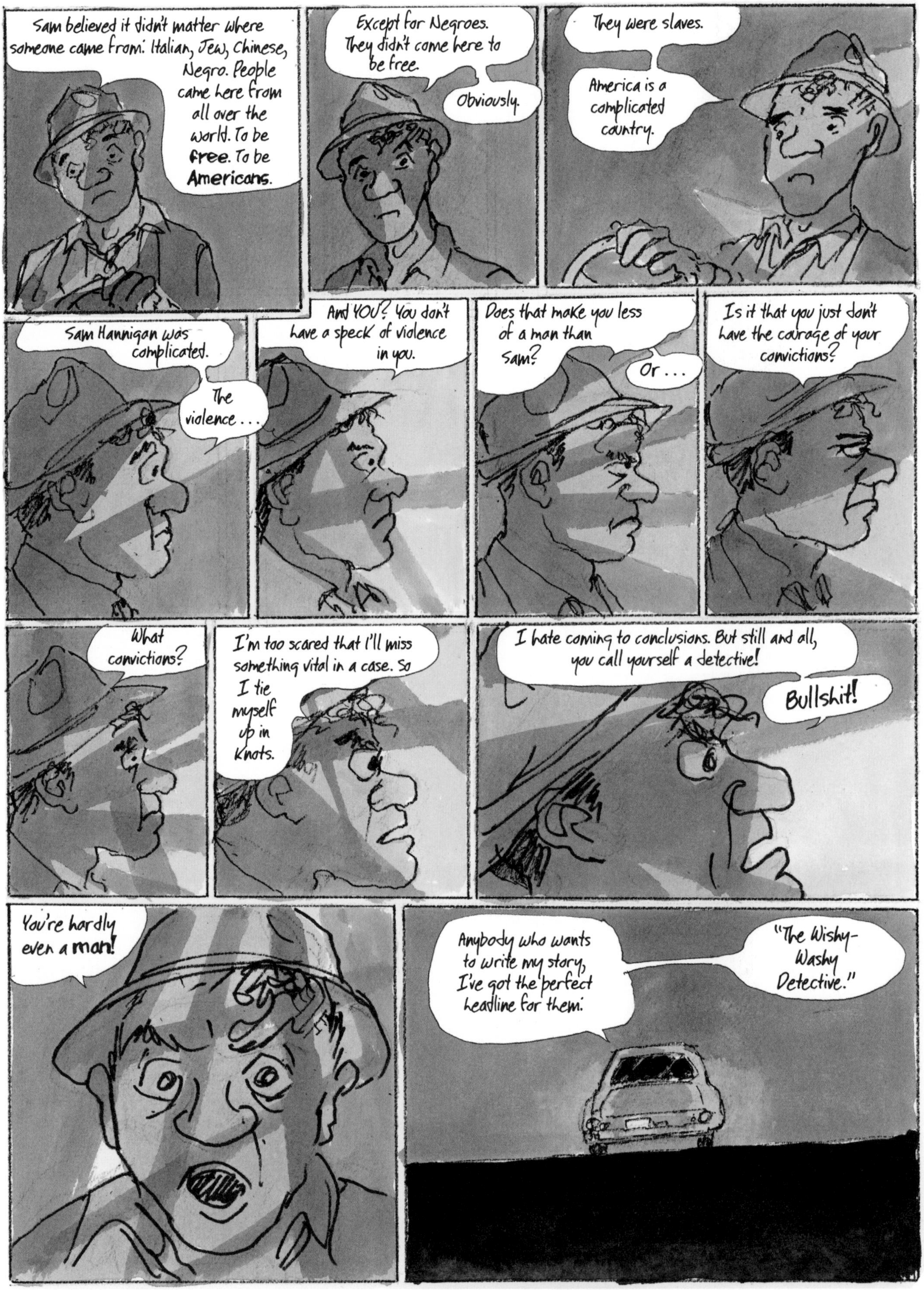
Sam believed it didn't matter where someone came from: Italian, Jew, Chinese, Negro. People came here from all over the world. To be **free**. To be **Americans**.
Except for Negroes. They didn't come here to be free.
Obviously.
They were slaves.
America is a complicated country.
Sam Hannigan was complicated.
The violence . . .
And YOU? You don't have a speck of violence in you.
Does that make you less of a man than Sam?
Or . . .
Is it that you just don't have the courage of your convictions?
What convictions?
I'm too scared that I'll miss something vital in a case. So I tie myself up in knots.
I hate coming to conclusions. But still and all, you call yourself a detective!
Bullshit!
You're hardly even a **man**!
Anybody who wants to write my story, I've got the perfect headline for them:
"The Wishy-Washy Detective."

Chapter Thirty-Four: Bedroom IV

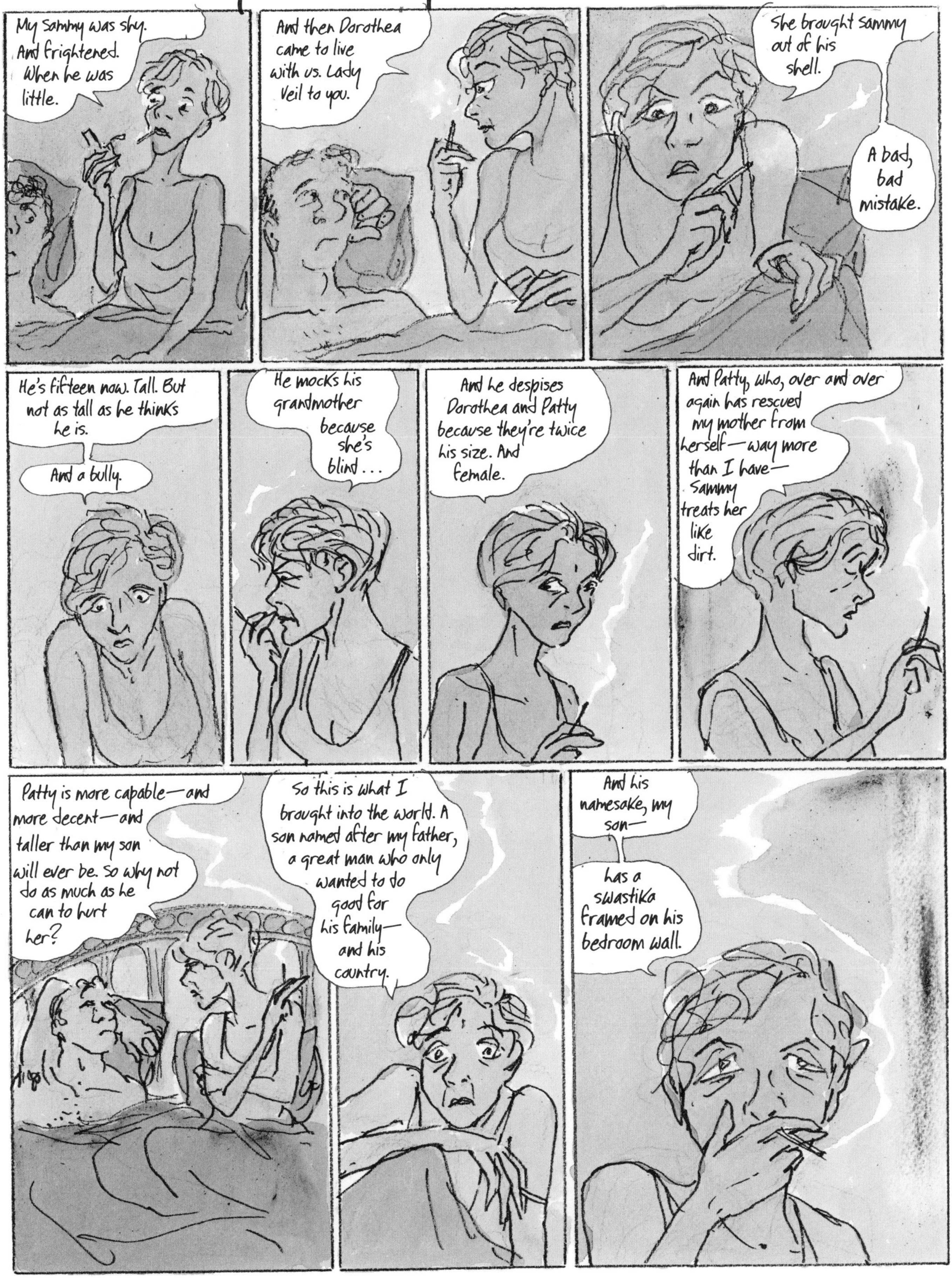
My Sammy was shy. And frightened. When he was little.
And then Dorothea came to live with us. Lady Veil to you.
She brought Sammy out of his shell.
A bad, bad mistake.
He's fifteen now. Tall. But not as tall as he thinks he is.
And a bully.
He mocks his grandmother because she's blind . . .
And he despises Dorothea and Patty because they're twice his size. And female.
And Patty, who, over and over again has rescued my mother from herself—way more than I have—Sammy treats her like dirt.
Patty is more capable—and more decent—and taller than my son will ever be. So why not do as much as he can to hurt her?
So this is what I brought into the world. A son named after my father, a great man who only wanted to do good for his family—and his country.
And his namesake, my son—
has a swastika framed on his bedroom wall.

Chapter Thirty-Five: Orville

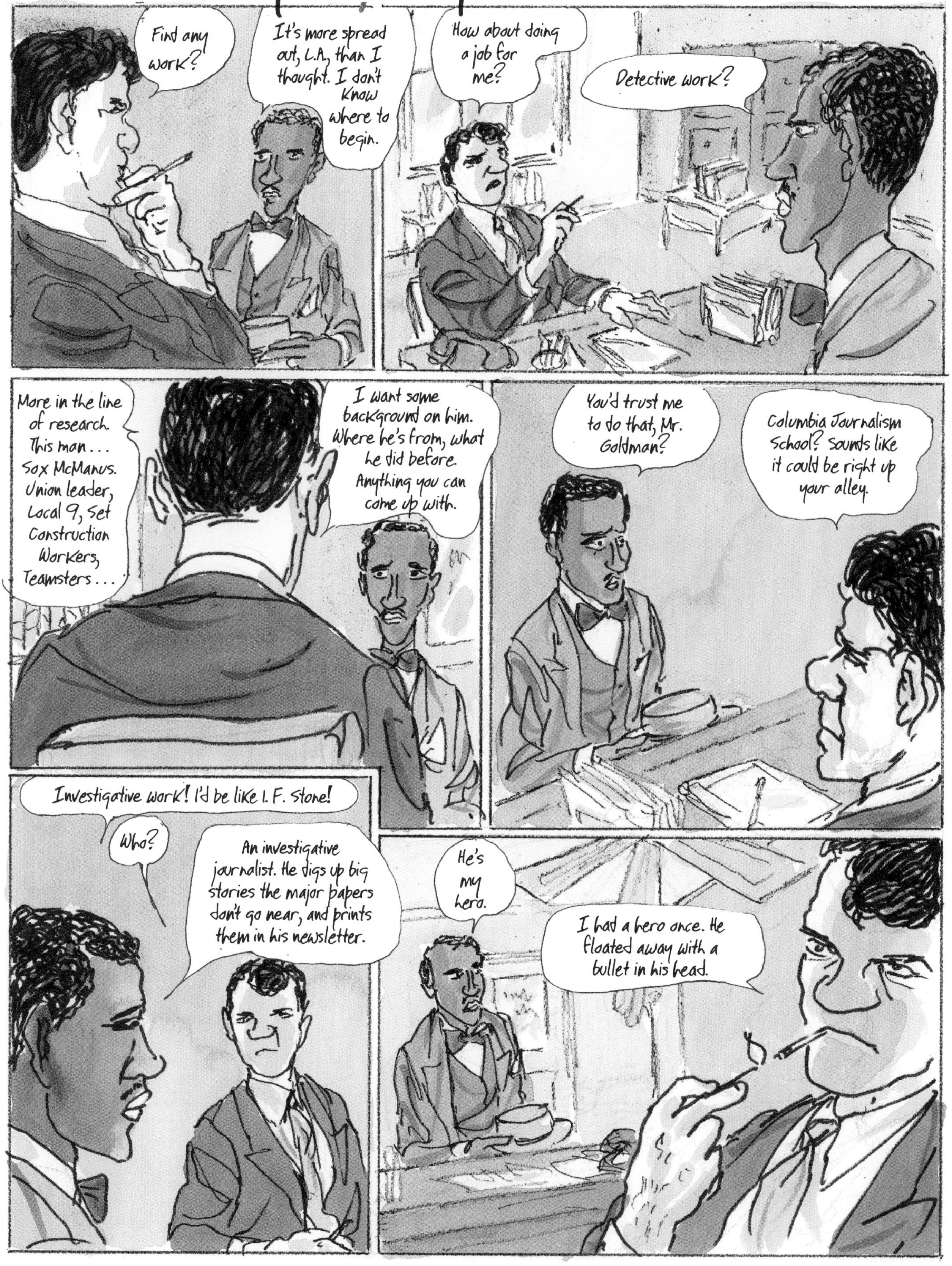

Find any work?
It's more spread out, L.A., than I thought. I don't know where to begin.
How about doing a job for me?
Detective work?
More in the line of research. This man . . . Sox McManus. Union leader, Local 9, Set Construction Workers, Teamsters . . .
I want some background on him. Where he's from, what he did before. Anything you can come up with.
You'd trust me to do that, Mr. Goldman?
Columbia Journalism School? Sounds like it could be right up your alley.
Investigative work! I'd be like I. F. Stone!
Who?
An investigative journalist. He digs up big stories the major papers don't go near, and prints them in his newsletter.
He's my hero.
I had a hero once. He floated away with a bullet in his head.

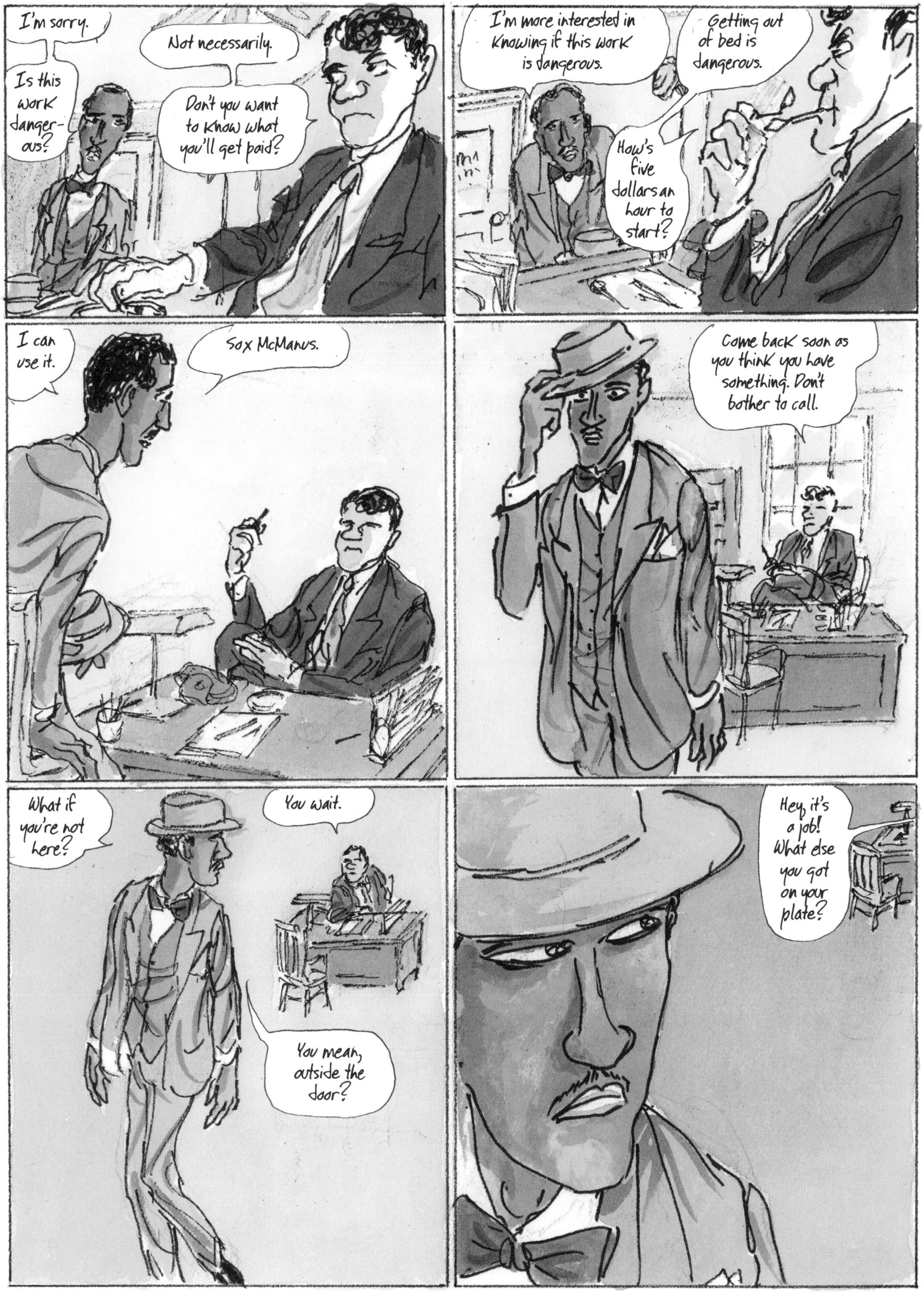
I'm sorry.
Is this work danger-ous?
Not necessarily.
Don't you want to know what you'll get paid?
I'm more interested in knowing if this work is dangerous.
Getting out of bed is dangerous.
How's five dollars an hour to start?
I can use it.
Sox McManus.
Come back soon as you think you have something. Don't bother to call.
What if you're not here?
You wait.
You mean, outside the door?
Hey, it's a job! What else you got on your plate?

Chapter Thirty-Six: The Collective

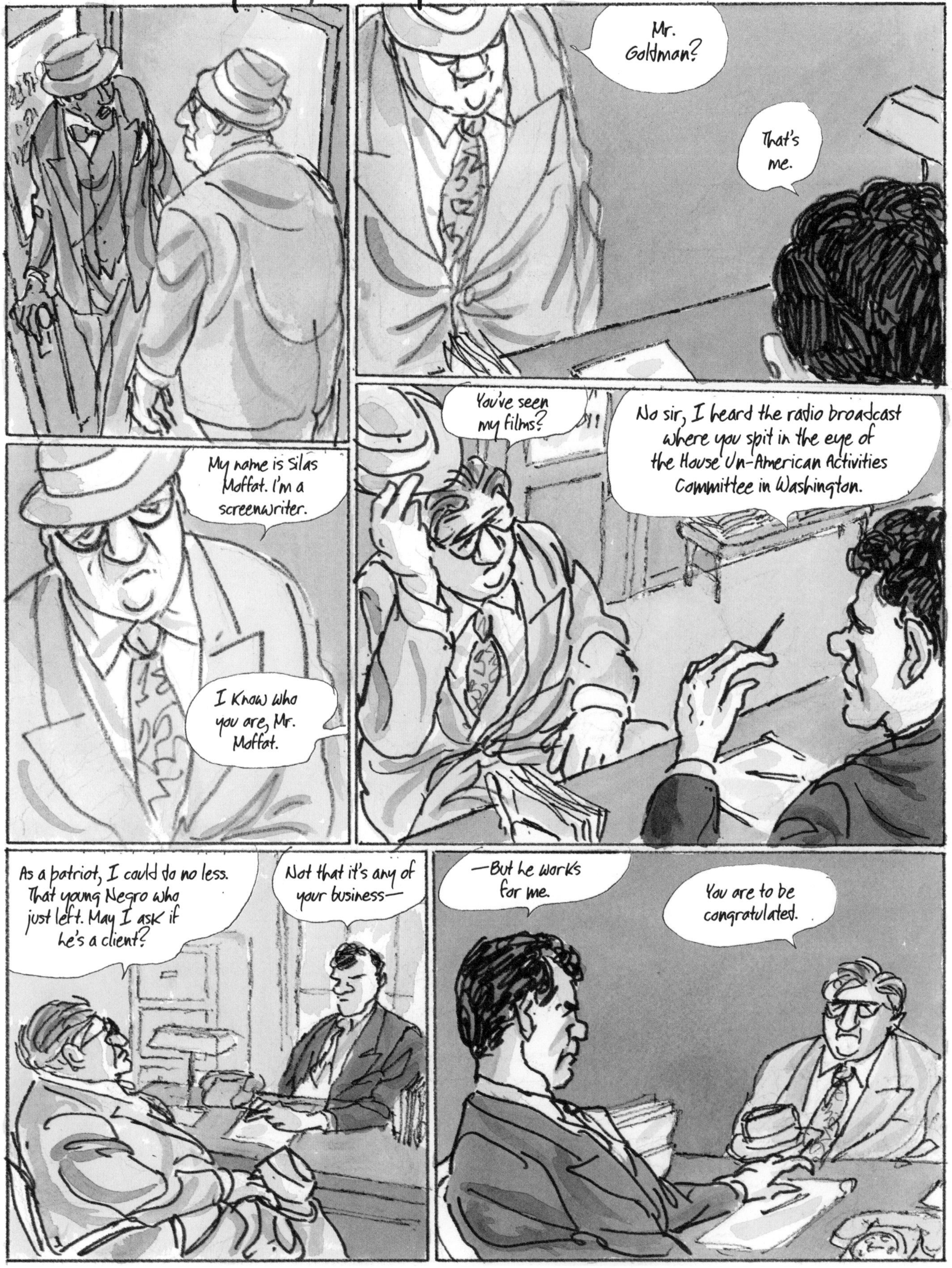
Mr. Goldman?
That's me.
My name is Silas Moffat. I'm a screenwriter.
I know who you are, Mr. Moffat.
You've seen my films?
No sir, I heard the radio broadcast where you spit in the eye of the House Un-American Activities Committee in Washington.
As a patriot, I could do no less. That young Negro who just left. May I ask if he's a client?
Not that it's any of your business—
—But he works for me.
You are to be congratulated.

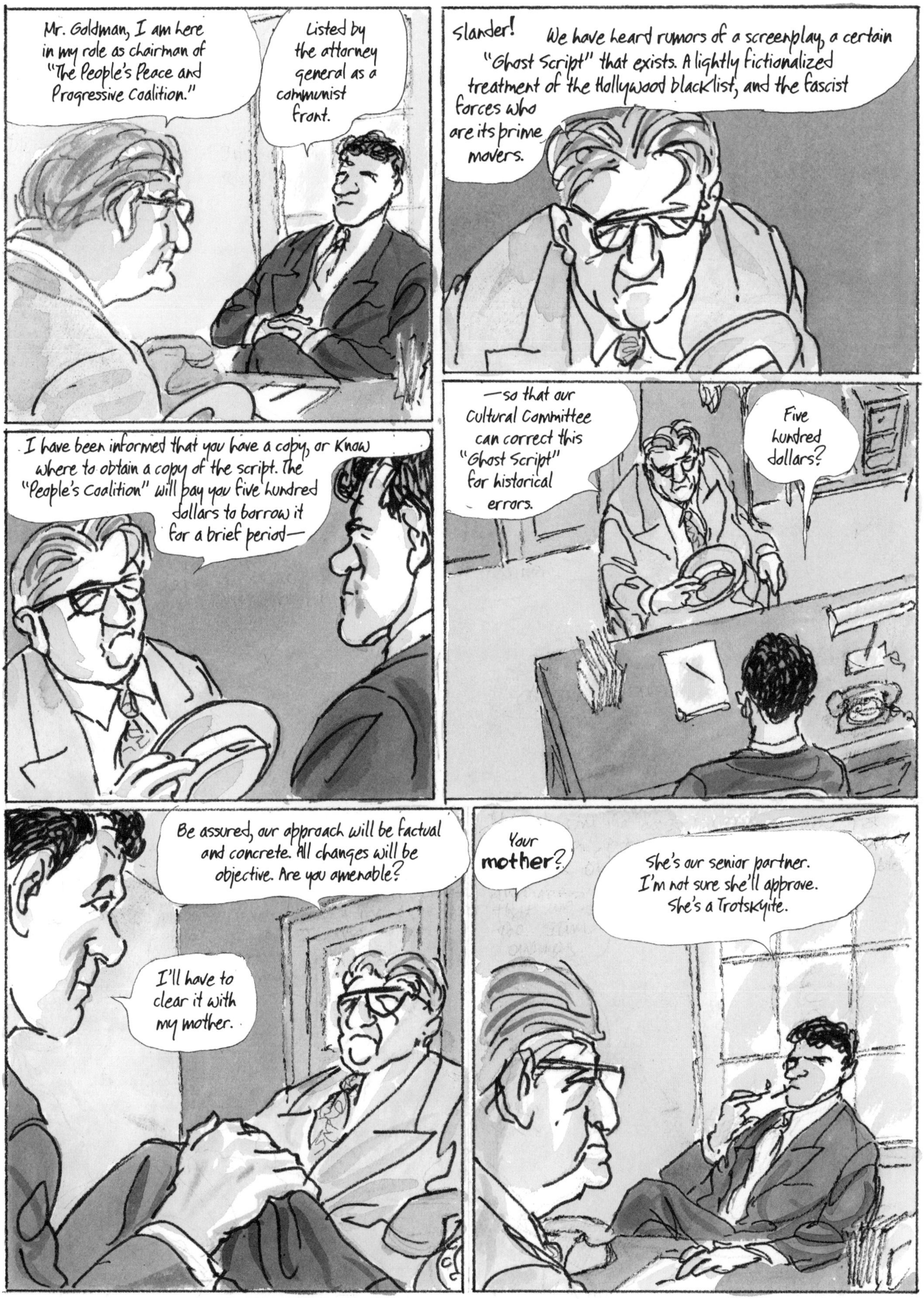
Mr. Goldman, I am here in my role as chairman of "The People's Peace and Progressive Coalition."
Listed by the attorney general as a communist front.
Slander!
We have heard rumors of a screenplay, a certain "Ghost Script" that exists. A lightly fictionalized treatment of the Hollywood blacklist, and the fascist forces who are its prime movers.
I have been informed that you have a copy, or know where to obtain a copy of the script. The "People's Coalition" will pay you five hundred dollars to borrow it for a brief period—
—so that our Cultural Committee can correct this "Ghost Script" for historical errors.
Five hundred dollars?
Be assured, our approach will be factual and concrete. All changes will be objective. Are you amenable?
I'll have to clear it with my mother.
Your **mother**?
She's our senior partner. I'm not sure she'll approve. She's a Trotskyite.

Chapter Thirty-Seven: The Spooks II

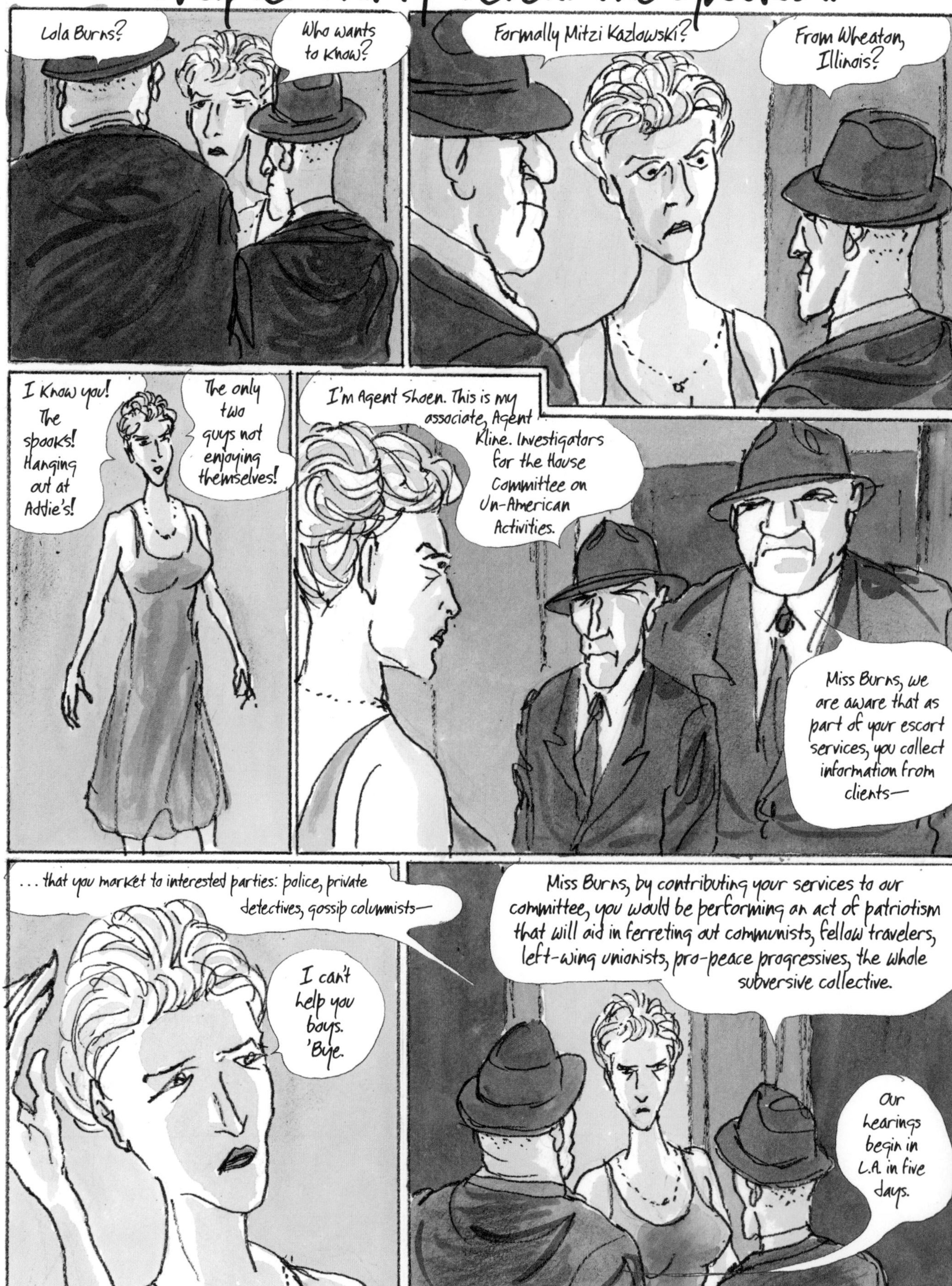

Lola Burns?
Who wants to know?
Formally Mitzi Kazlowski?
From Wheaton, Illinois?
I know you! The spooks! Hanging out at Addie's!
The only two guys not enjoying themselves!
I'm Agent Shoen. This is my associate, Agent Kline. Investigators for the House Committee on Un-American Activities.
Miss Burns, we are aware that as part of your escort services, you collect information from clients—
... that you market to interested parties: police, private detectives, gossip columnists—
I can't help you boys. 'Bye.
Miss Burns, by contributing your services to our committee, you would be performing an act of patriotism that will aid in ferreting out communists, fellow travelers, left-wing unionists, pro-peace progressives, the whole subversive collective.
Our hearings begin in L.A. in five days.

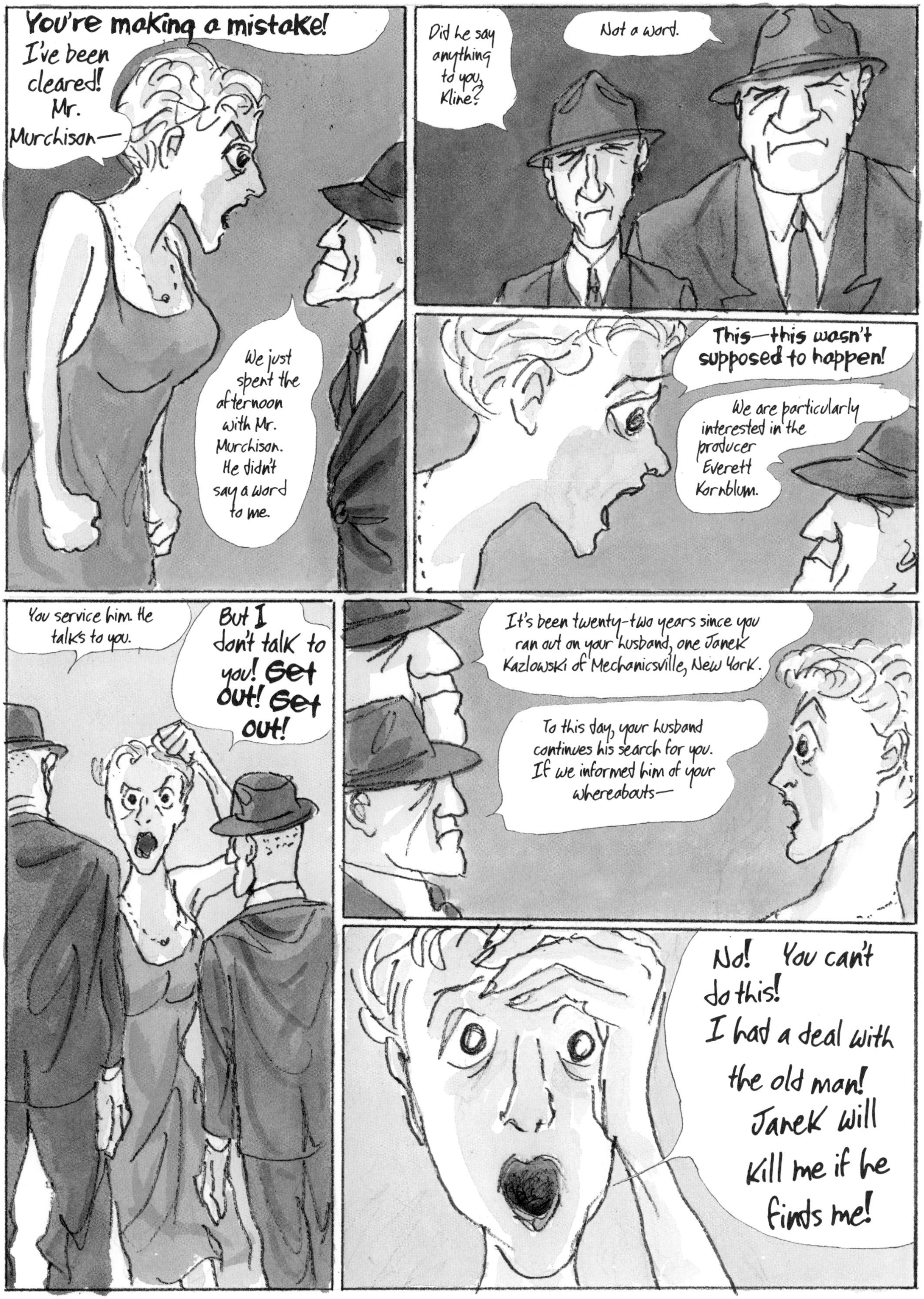

You're making a mistake! I've been cleared! Mr. Murchison—
We just spent the afternoon with Mr. Murchison. He didn't say a word to me.
Did he say anything to you, Kline?
Not a word.
This—this wasn't supposed to happen!
We are particularly interested in the producer Everett Kornblum.
You service him. He talks to you.
But I don't talk to you! Get out! Get out!
It's been twenty-two years since you ran out on your husband, one Janek Kazlowski of Mechanicsville, New York.
To this day, your husband continues his search for you. If we informed him of your whereabouts—
No! You can't do this! I had a deal with the old man! Janek will kill me if he finds me!

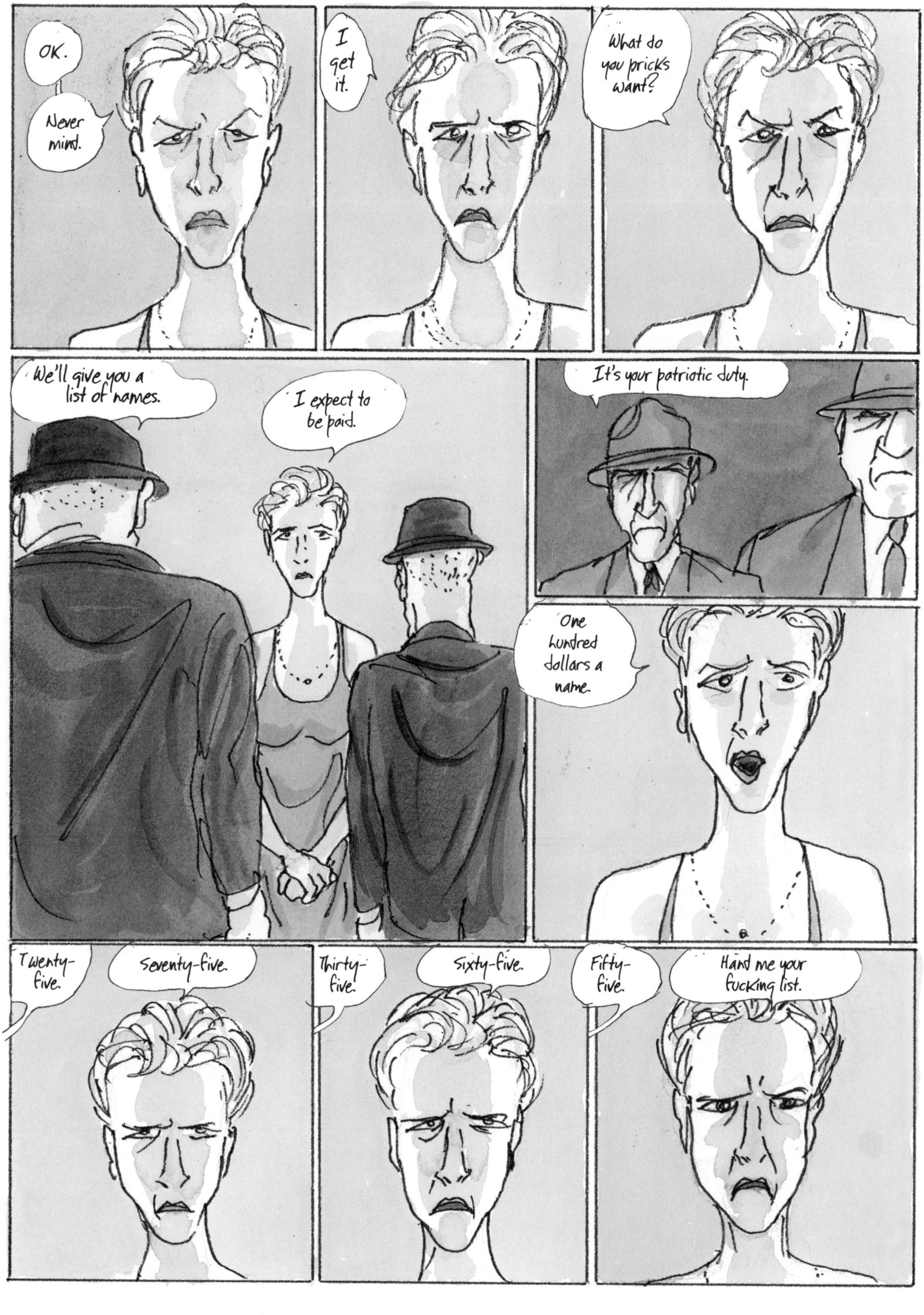
OK.
Never mind.
I get it.
What do you pricks want?
We'll give you a list of names.
I expect to be paid.
It's your patriotic duty.
One hundred dollars a name.
Twenty-five.
Seventy-five.
Thirty-five.
Sixty-five.
Fifty-five.
Hand me your fucking list.

Chapter Thirty-Eight: Story Conference II

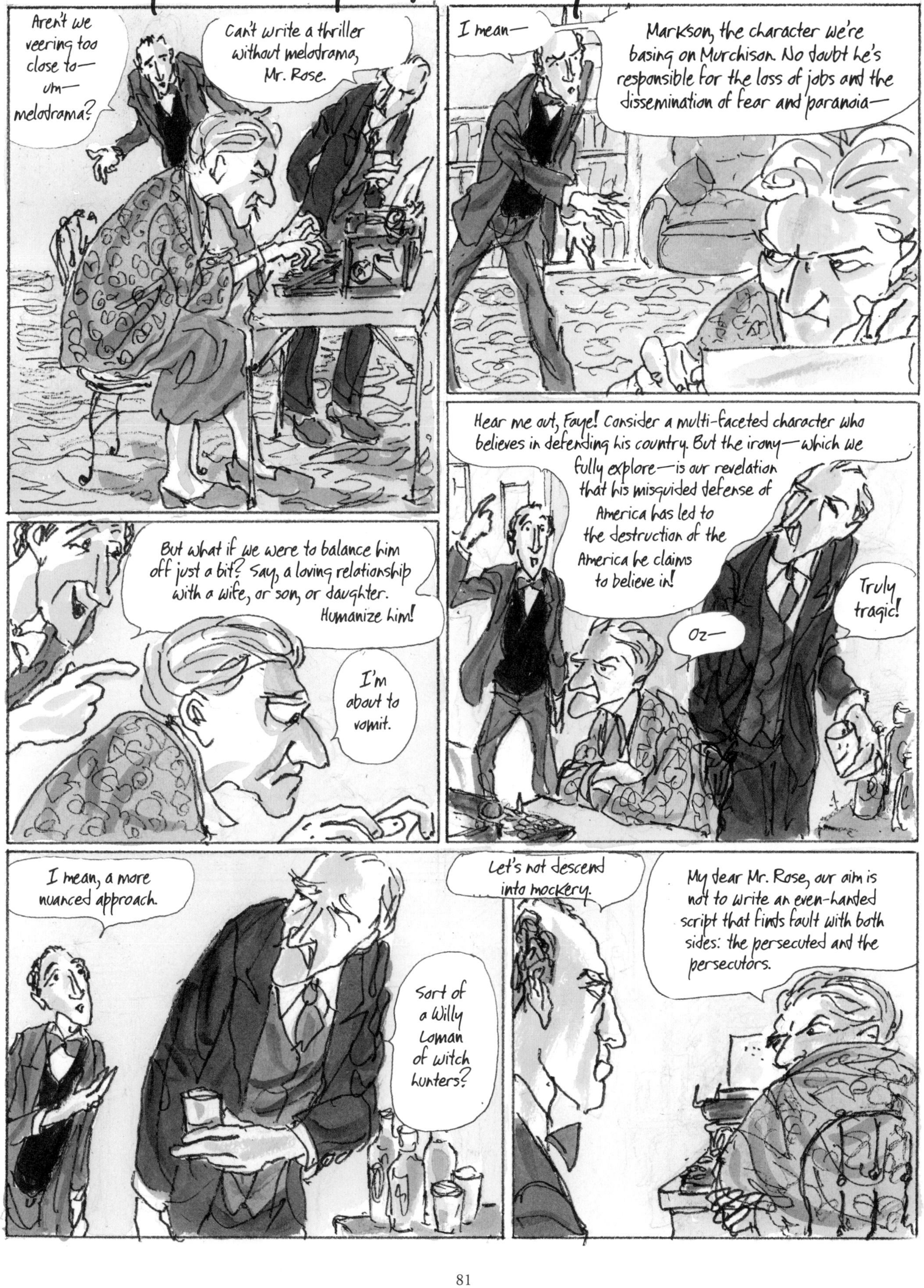

Aren't we veering too close to— um— melodrama?
Can't write a thriller without melodrama, Mr. Rose.
I mean—
Markson, the character we're basing on Murchison. No doubt he's responsible for the loss of jobs and the dissemination of fear and paranoia—
But what if we were to balance him off just a bit? Say, a loving relationship with a wife, or son, or daughter. Humanize him!
I'm about to vomit.
Hear me out, Faye! Consider a multi-faceted character who believes in defending his country. But the irony—which we fully explore—is our revelation that his misguided defense of America has led to the destruction of the America he claims to believe in!
Oz—
Truly tragic!
I mean, a more nuanced approach.
Sort of a Willy Loman of witch hunters?
Let's not descend into mockery.
My dear Mr. Rose, our aim is not to write an even-handed script that finds fault with both sides: the persecuted and the persecutors.

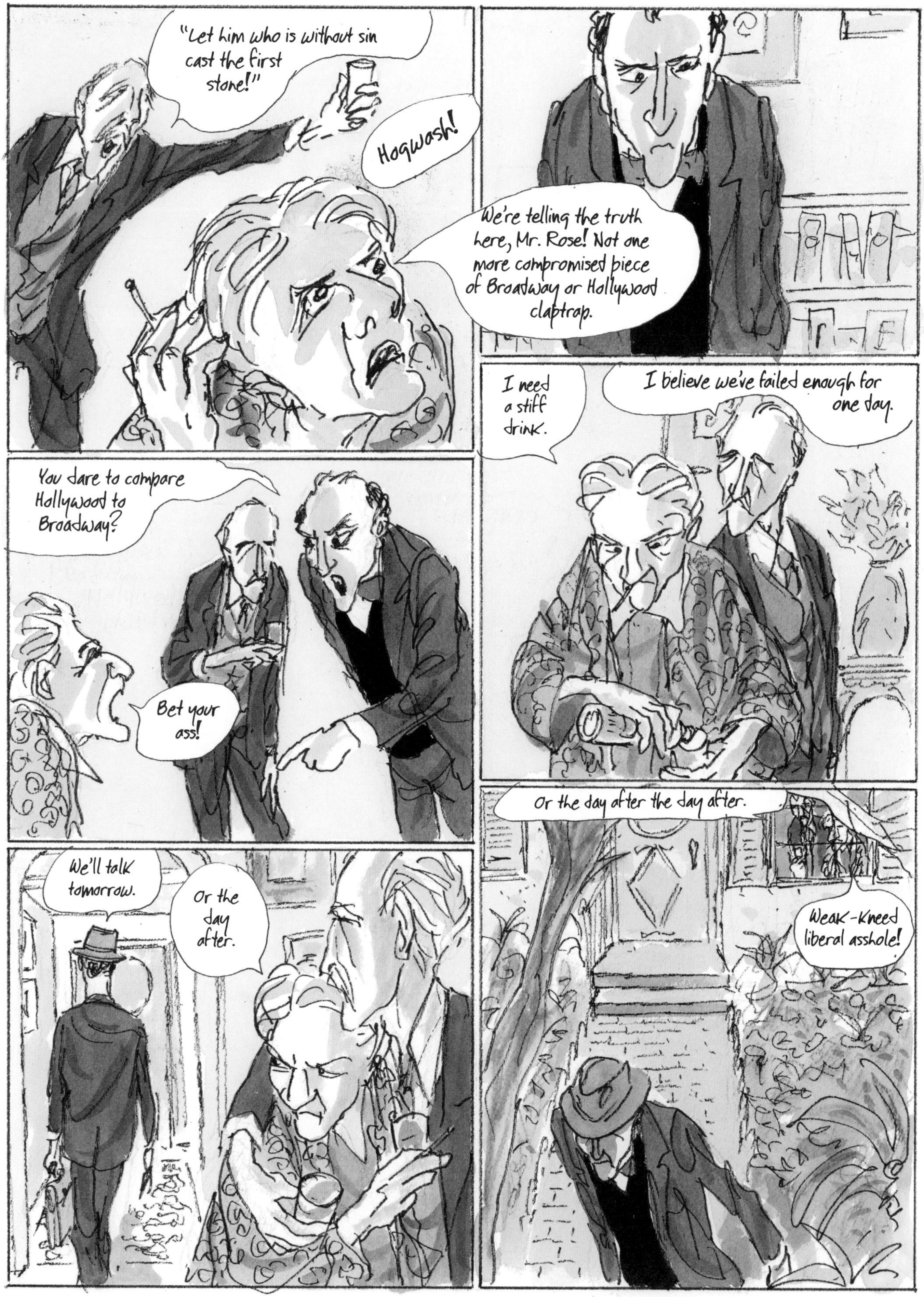
"Let him who is without sin cast the first stone!"
Hogwash!
We're telling the truth here, Mr. Rose! Not one more compromised piece of Broadway or Hollywood claptrap.
You dare to compare Hollywood to Broadway?
Bet your ass!
I need a stiff drink.
I believe we've failed enough for one day.
We'll talk tomorrow.
Or the day after.
Or the day after the day after.
Weak-kneed liberal asshole!

Chapter Thirty-Nine: Out of Step

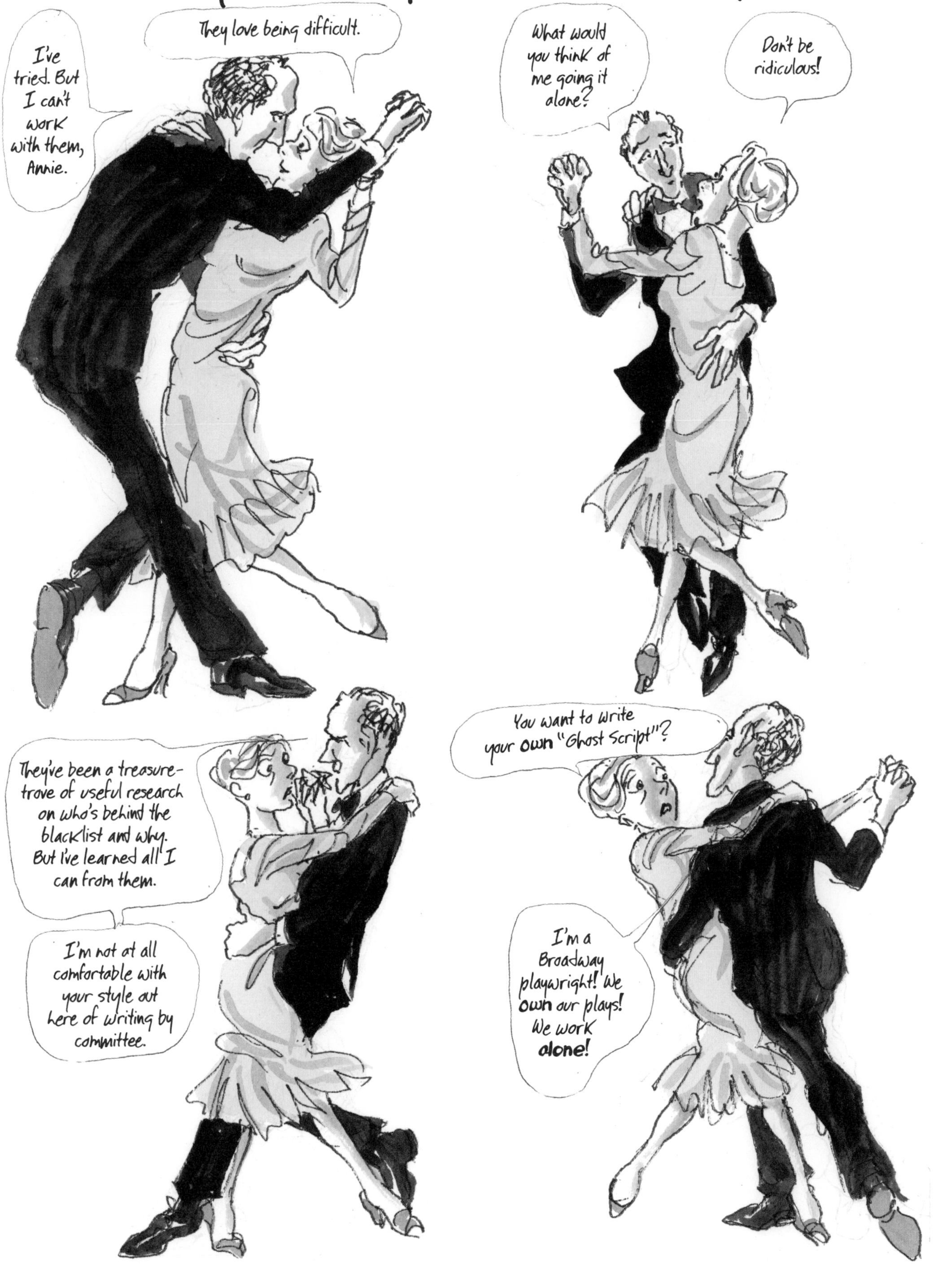
They love being difficult.
I've tried. But I can't work with them, Annie.
What would you think of me going it alone?
Don't be ridiculous!
They've been a treasure-trove of useful research on who's behind the blacklist and why. But I've learned all I can from them.
I'm not at all comfortable with your style out here of writing by committee.
You want to write your **own** "Ghost Script"?
I'm a Broadway playwright! We **own** our plays! We work **alone!**

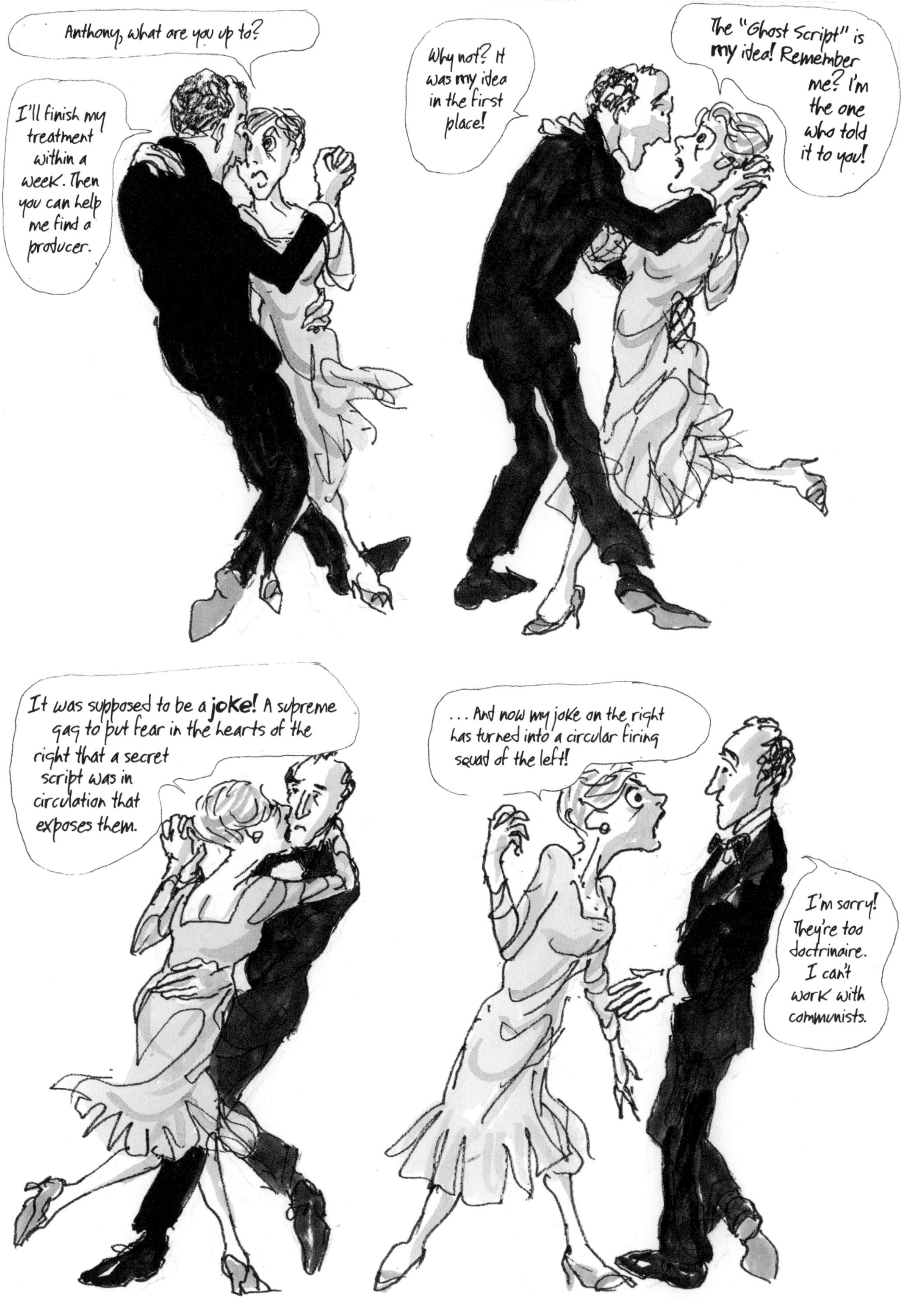
Anthony, what are you up to?
I'll finish my treatment within a week. Then you can help me find a producer.
Why not? It was my idea in the first place!
The "Ghost Script" is my idea! Remember me? I'm the one who told it to you!
It was supposed to be a joke! A supreme gag to put fear in the hearts of the right that a secret script was in circulation that exposes them.
... And now my joke on the right has turned into a circular firing squad of the left!
I'm sorry! They're too doctrinaire. I can't work with communists.

Chapter Forty: The Front

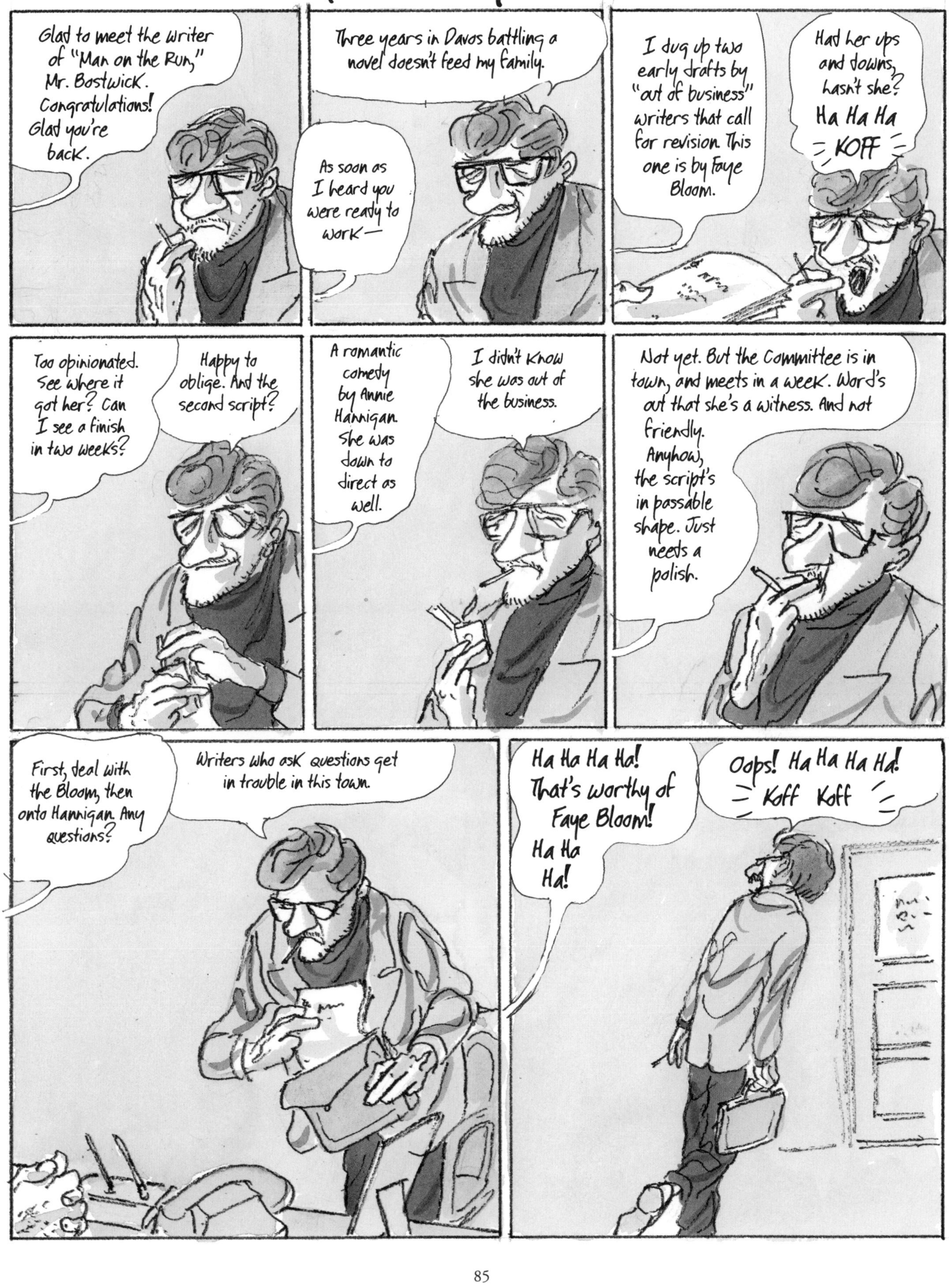

Glad to meet the writer of "Man on the Run," Mr. Bostwick. Congratulations! Glad you're back.
Three years in Davos battling a novel doesn't feed my family.
As soon as I heard you were ready to work—
I dug up two early drafts by "out of business" writers that call for revision. This one is by Faye Bloom.
Had her ups and downs, hasn't she? Ha Ha Ha
KOFF
Too opinionated. See where it got her? Can I see a finish in two weeks?
Happy to oblige. And the second script?
A romantic comedy by Annie Hannigan. She was down to direct as well.
I didn't know she was out of the business.
Not yet. But the Committee is in town, and meets in a week. Word's out that she's a witness. And not friendly. Anyhow, the script's in passable shape. Just needs a polish.
First, deal with the Bloom, then onto Hannigan. Any questions?
Writers who ask questions get in trouble in this town.
Ha Ha Ha Ha! That's worthy of Faye Bloom! Ha Ha Ha!
Oops! Ha Ha Ha Ha!
Koff Koff

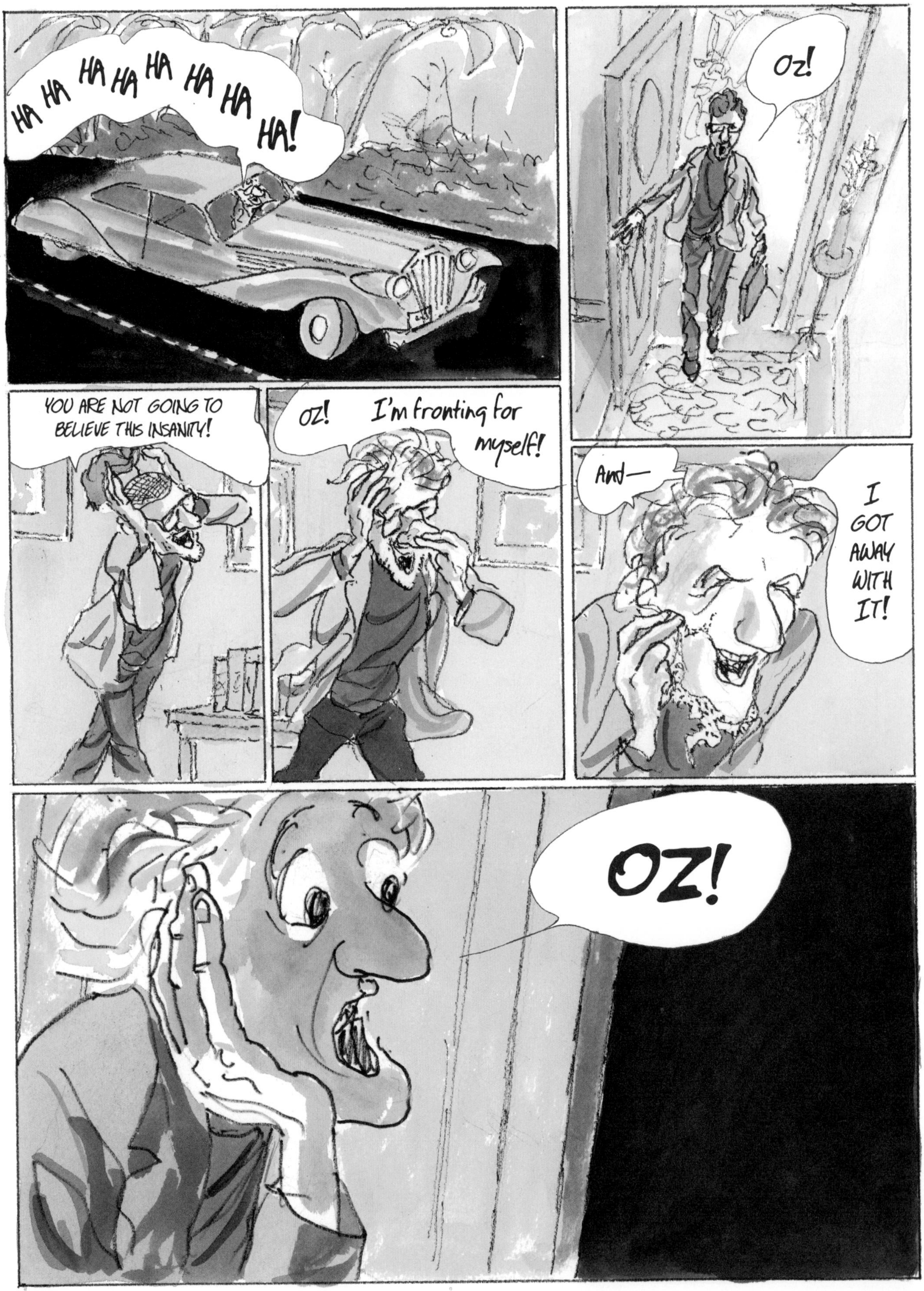
HA HA HA HA HA HA HA HA HA!
Oz!
YOU ARE NOT GOING TO BELIEVE THIS INSANITY!
OZ! I'm fronting for myself!
And—
I GOT AWAY WITH IT!
OZ!

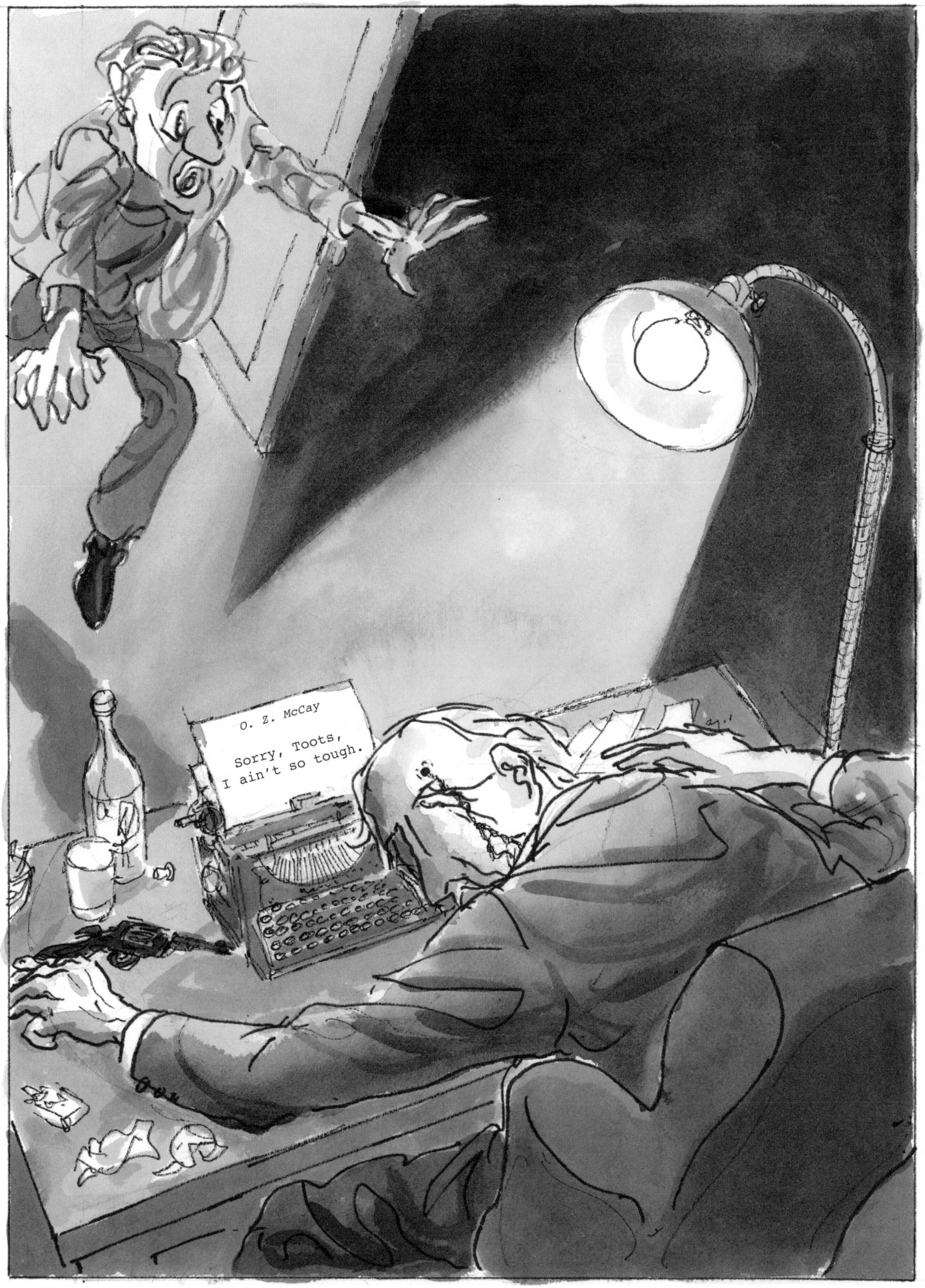
O. Z. McCay
Sorry, Toots,
I ain't so tough.

Part Two:
The Wishy-Washy Detective

Chapter Forty-One: Flashback—Bay City Docks, 1931

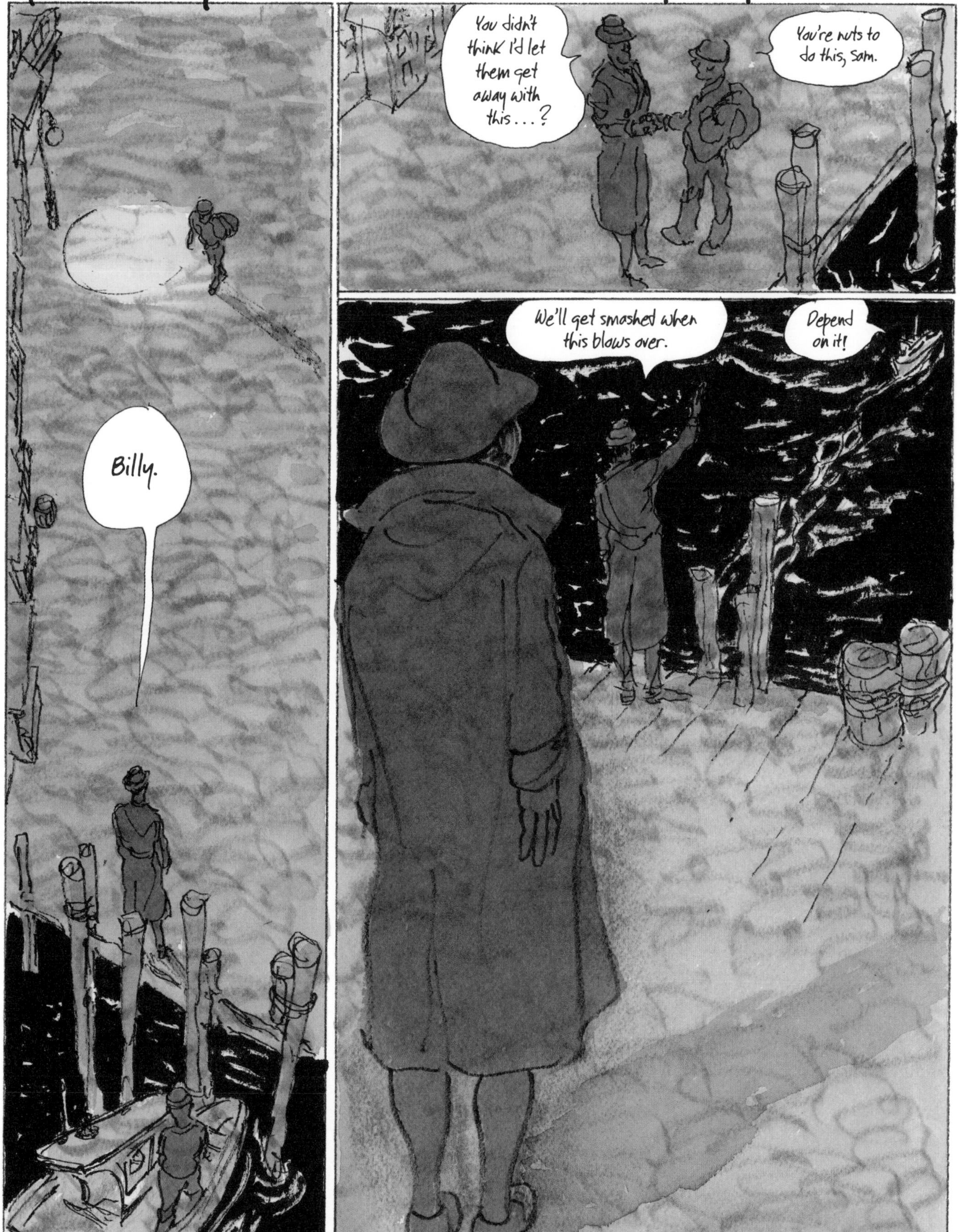
Billy.
You didn't think I'd let them get away with this...?
You're nuts to do this, Sam.
We'll get smashed when this blows over.
Depend on it!

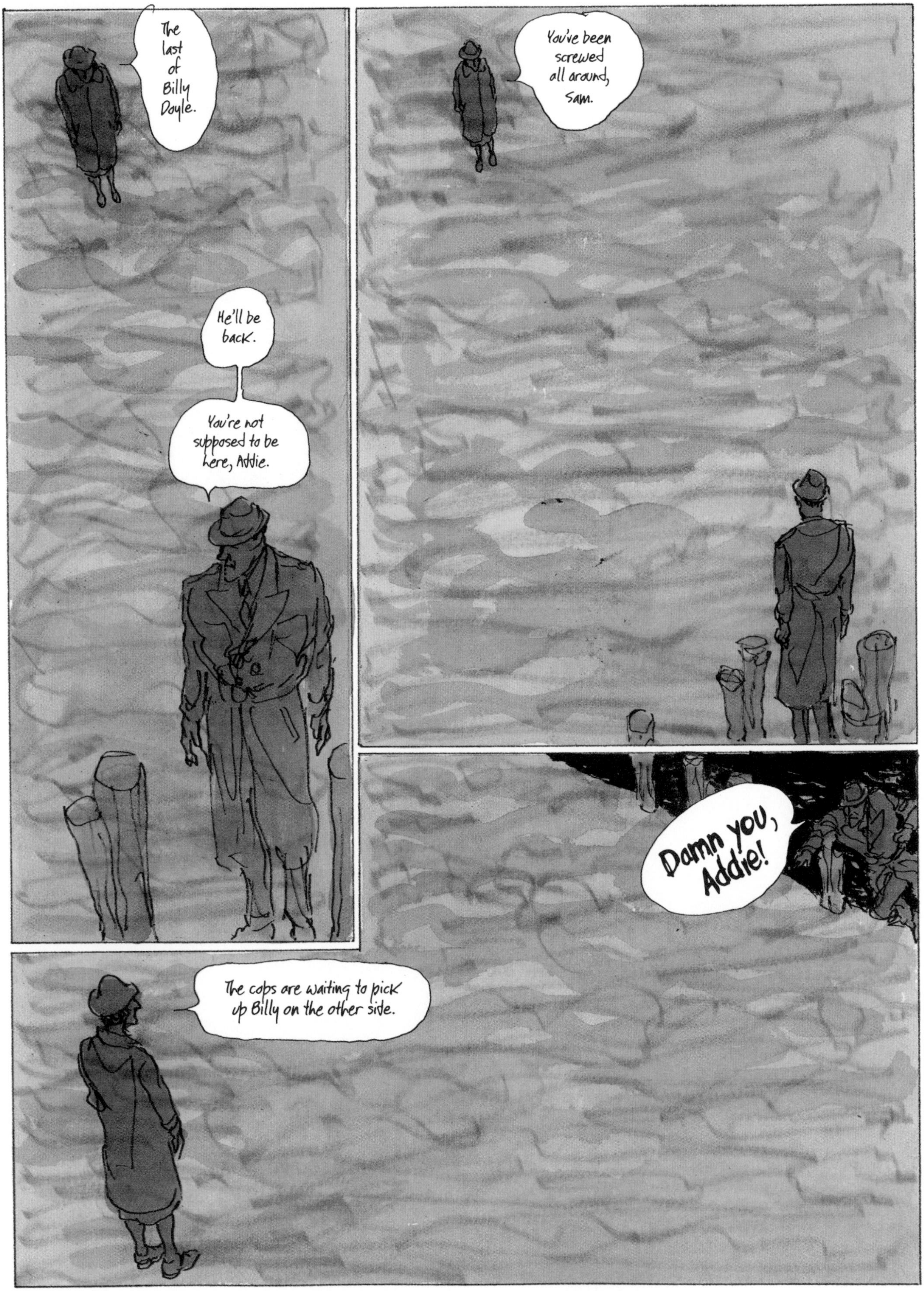
The last of Billy Doyle.
You've been screwed all around, Sam.
He'll be back.
You're not supposed to be here, Addie.
Damn you, Addie!
The cops are waiting to pick up Billy on the other side.

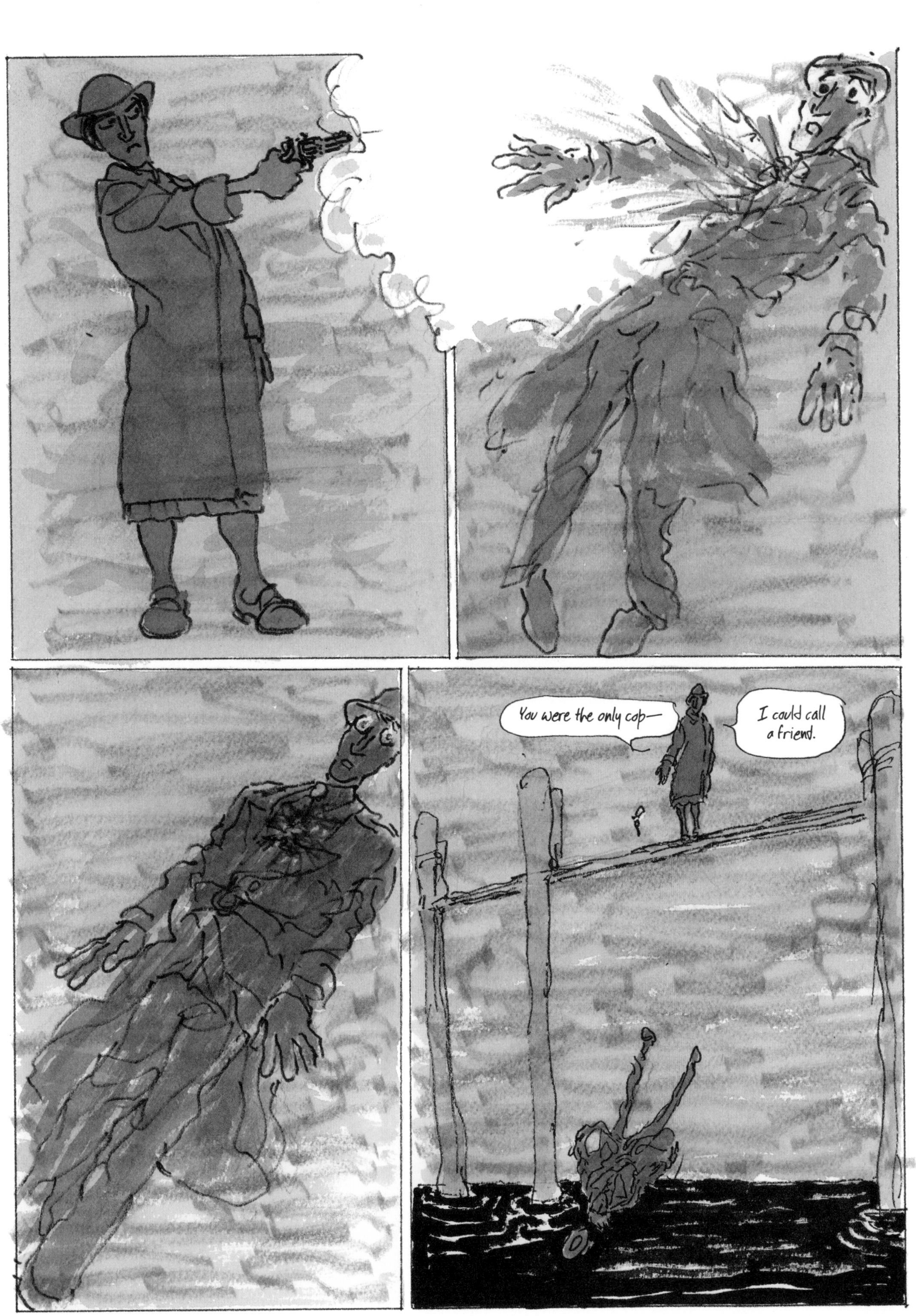
You were the only cop—
I could call a friend.

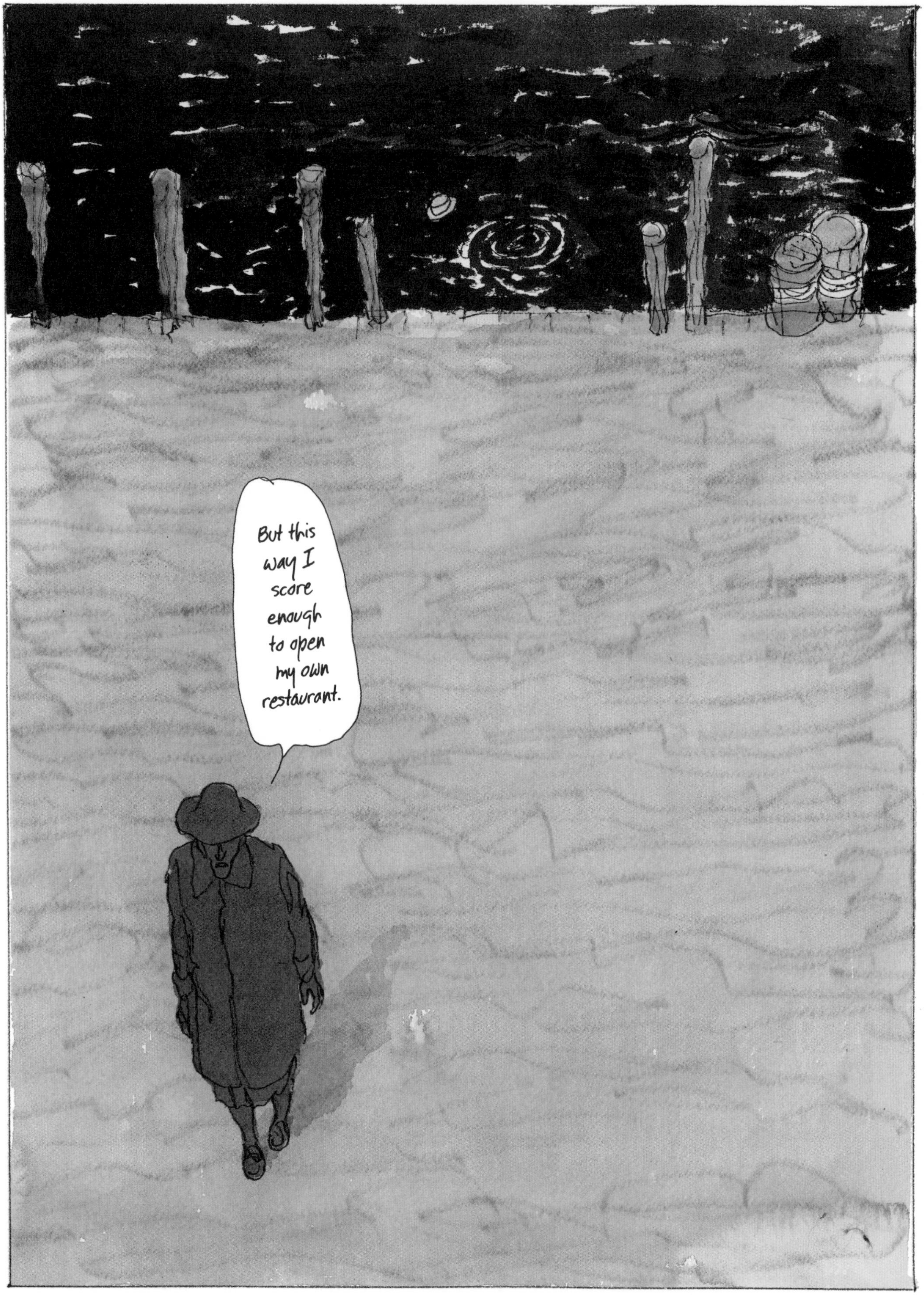
But this way I score enough to open my own restaurant.

Chapter Forty-Two: Old Times

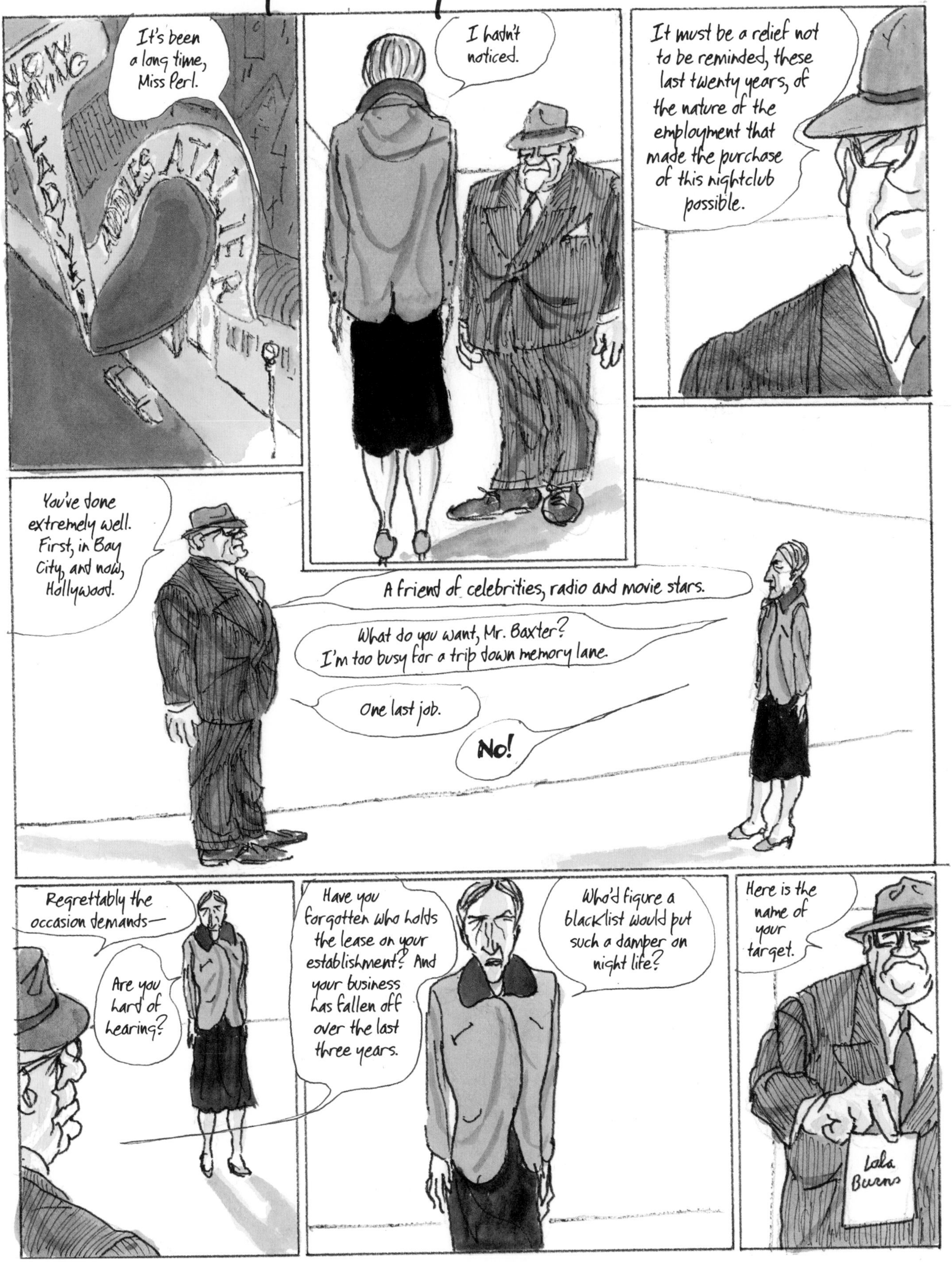
NOW PLAYING
It's been a long time, Miss Perl.
I hadn't noticed.
It must be a relief not to be reminded, these last twenty years, of the nature of the employment that made the purchase of this nightclub possible.
You've done extremely well. First, in Bay City, and now, Hollywood.
A friend of celebrities, radio and movie stars.
What do you want, Mr. Baxter? I'm too busy for a trip down memory lane.
One last job.
No!
Regrettably the occasion demands—
Are you hard of hearing?
Have you forgotten who holds the lease on your establishment? And your business has fallen off over the last three years.
Who'd figure a blacklist would put such a damper on night life?
Here is the name of your target.
Lola Burns

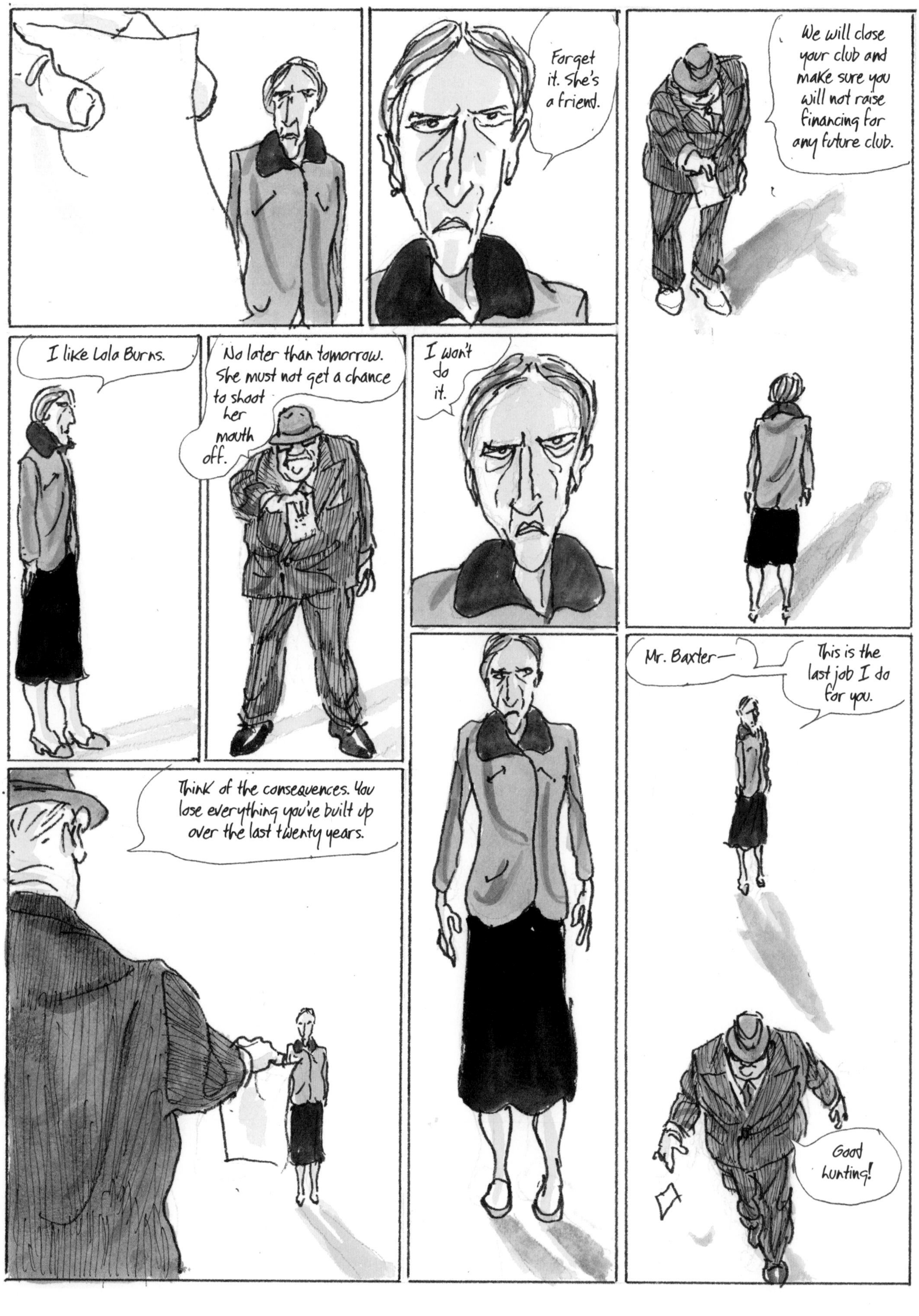

Forget it. She's a friend.
We will close your club and make sure you will not raise financing for any future club.
I like Lola Burns.
No later than tomorrow. She must not get a chance to shoot her mouth off.
I won't do it.
Think of the consequences. You lose everything you've built up over the last twenty years.
Mr. Baxter—
This is the last job I do for you.
Good hunting!

Chapter Forty-Three: Cousin Joseph!

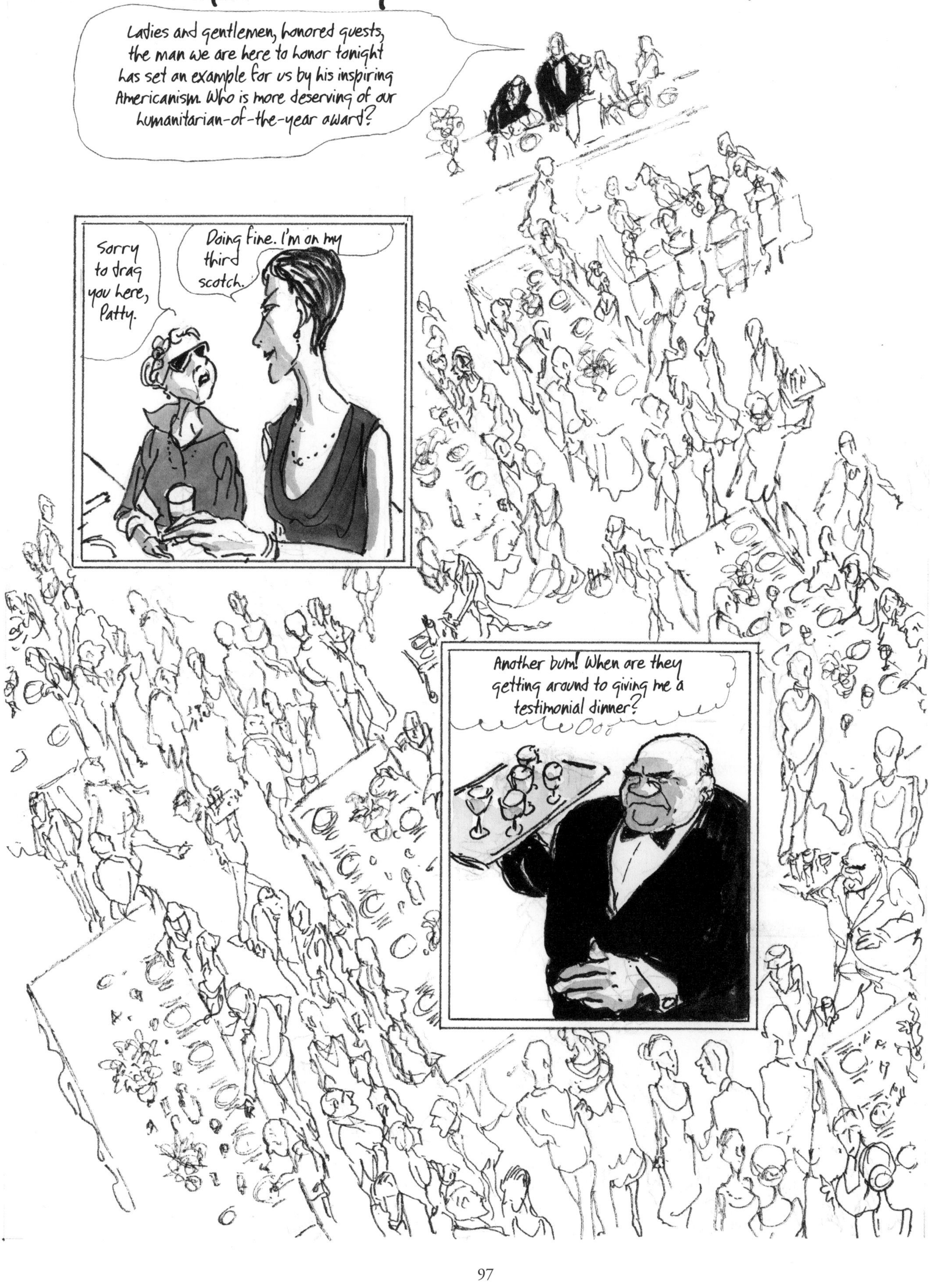

Ladies and gentlemen, honored guests, the man we are here to honor tonight has set an example for us by his inspiring Americanism. Who is more deserving of our humanitarian-of-the-year award?
Sorry to drag you here, Patty.
Doing fine. I'm on my third scotch.
Another bum! When are they getting around to giving me a testimonial dinner?

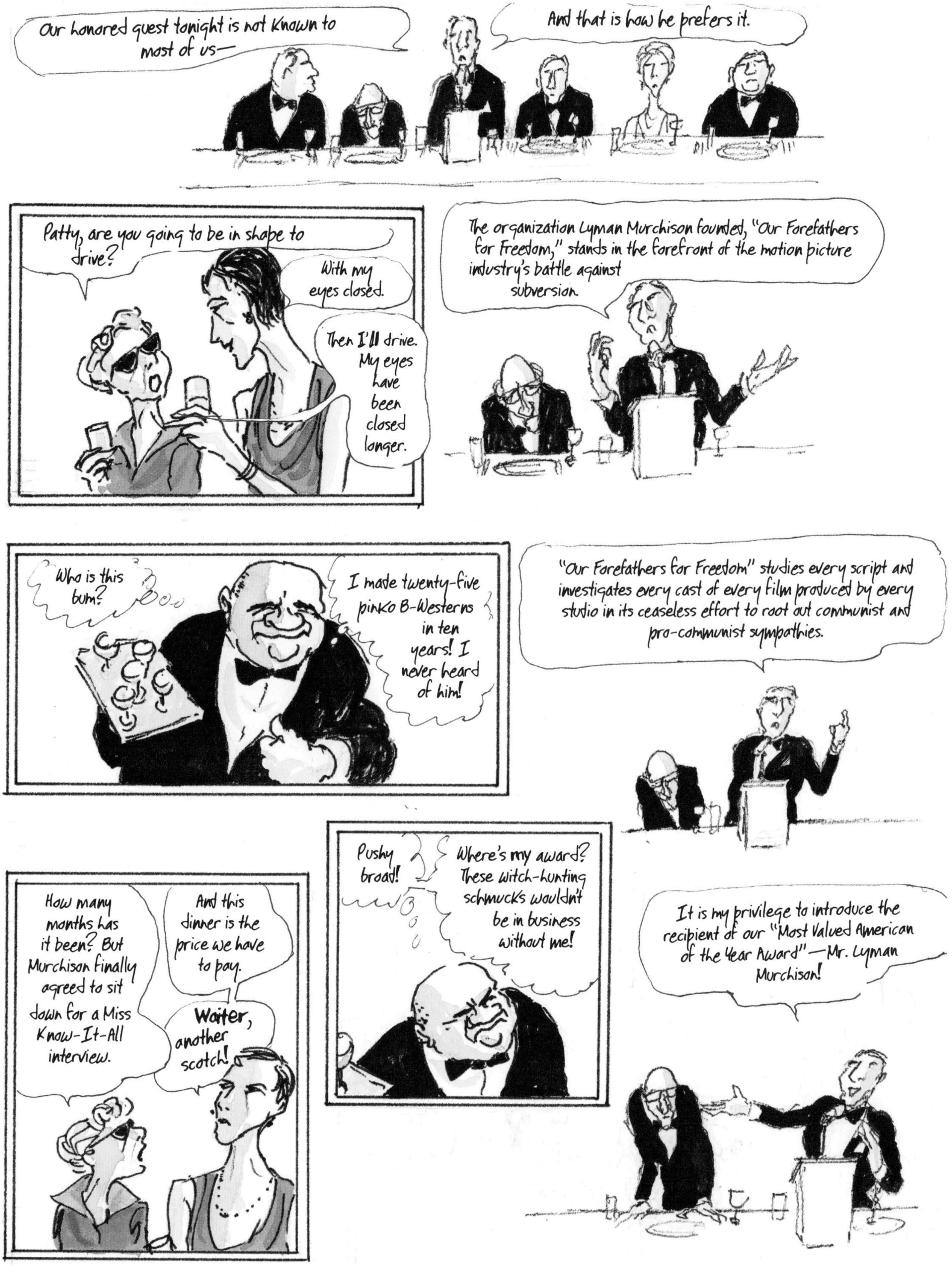
Our honored guest tonight is not known to most of us—
And that is how he prefers it.
Patty, are you going to be in shape to drive?
With my eyes closed.
Then I'll drive. My eyes have been closed longer.
The organization Lyman Murchison founded, "Our Forefathers for Freedom," stands in the forefront of the motion picture industry's battle against subversion.
Who is this bum?
I made twenty-five pinko B-Westerns in ten years! I never heard of him!
"Our Forefathers for Freedom" studies every script and investigates every cast of every film produced by every studio in its ceaseless effort to root out communist and pro-communist sympathies.
How many months has it been? But Murchison finally agreed to sit down for a Miss Know-It-All interview.
And this dinner is the price we have to pay.
Waiter, another scotch!
Pushy broad!
Where's my award? These witch-hunting schmucks wouldn't be in business without me!
It is my privilege to introduce the recipient of our "Most Valued American of the Year Award"—Mr. Lyman Murchison!

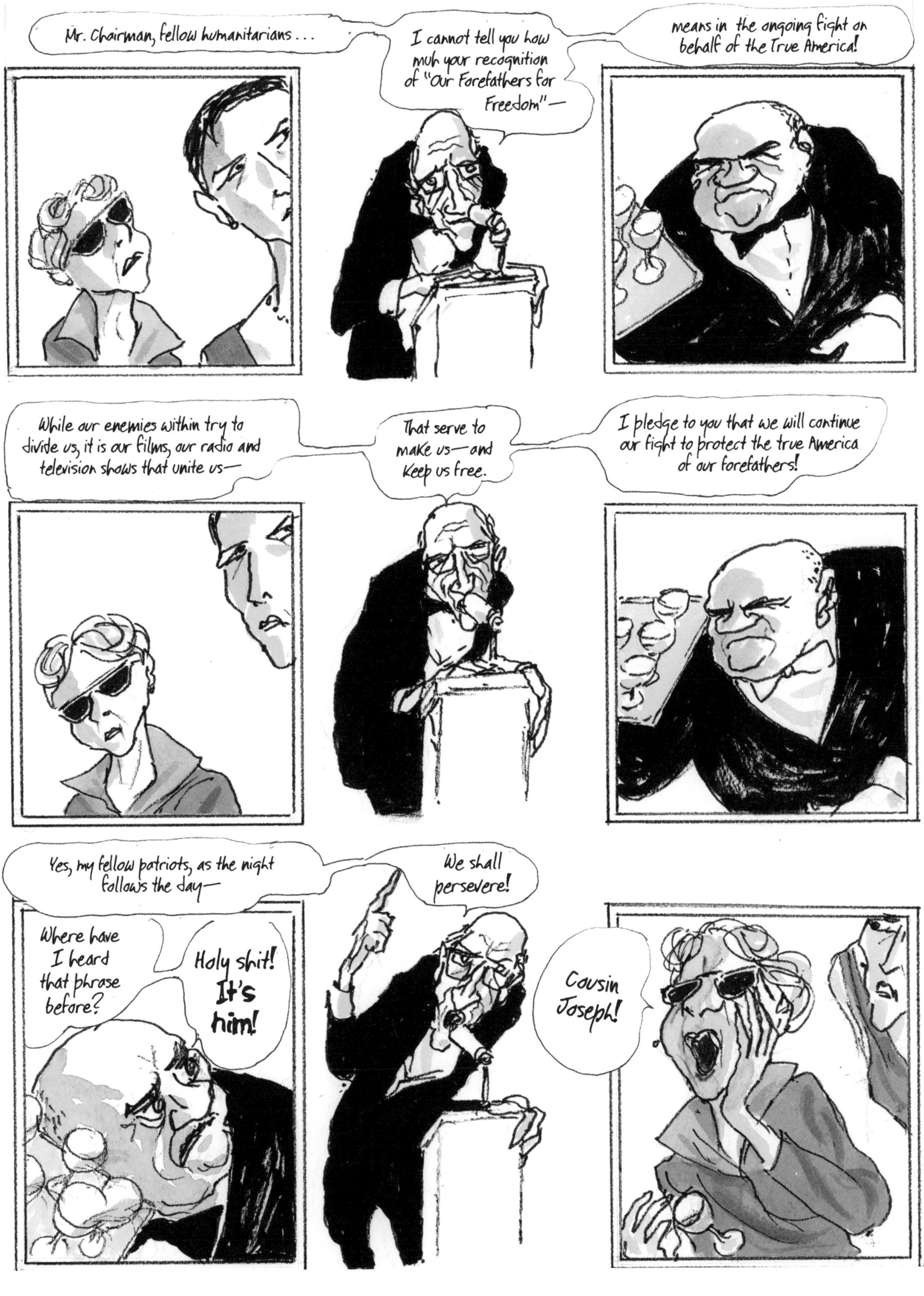

Mr. Chairman, fellow humanitarians . . .
I cannot tell you how muh your recognition of "Our Forefathers for Freedom"—
means in the ongoing fight on behalf of the True America!
While our enemies within try to divide us, it is our films, our radio and television shows that unite us—
That serve to make us—and keep us free.
I pledge to you that we will continue our fight to protect the true America of our forefathers!
Yes, my fellow patriots, as the night follows the day—
We shall persevere!
Where have I heard that phrase before?
Holy shit! It's him!
Cousin Joseph!

Chapter Forty-Four: Ackerman's Farewell

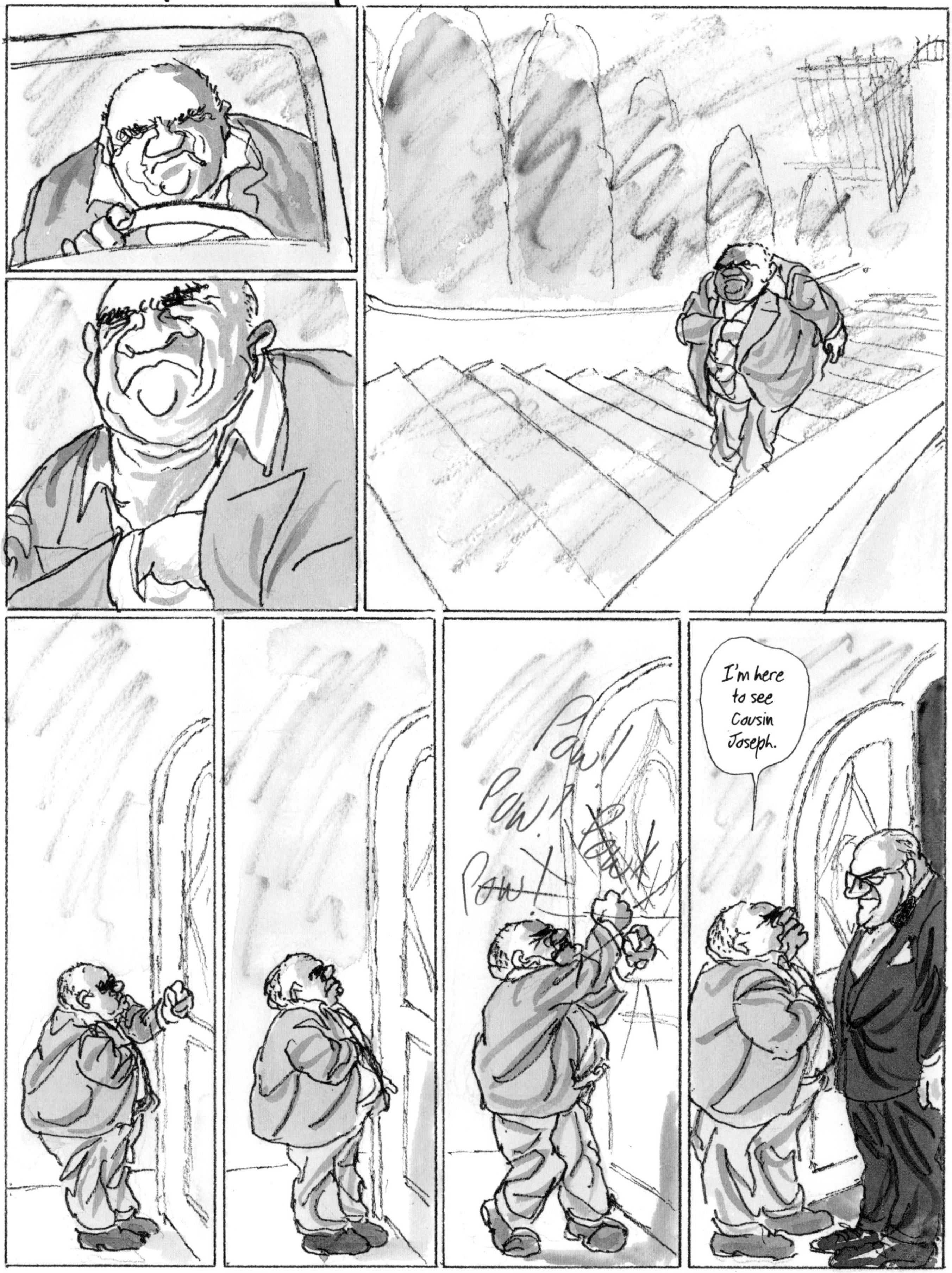

Pow!
Pow!
Pow!
Pow!
I'm here to see Cousin Joseph.

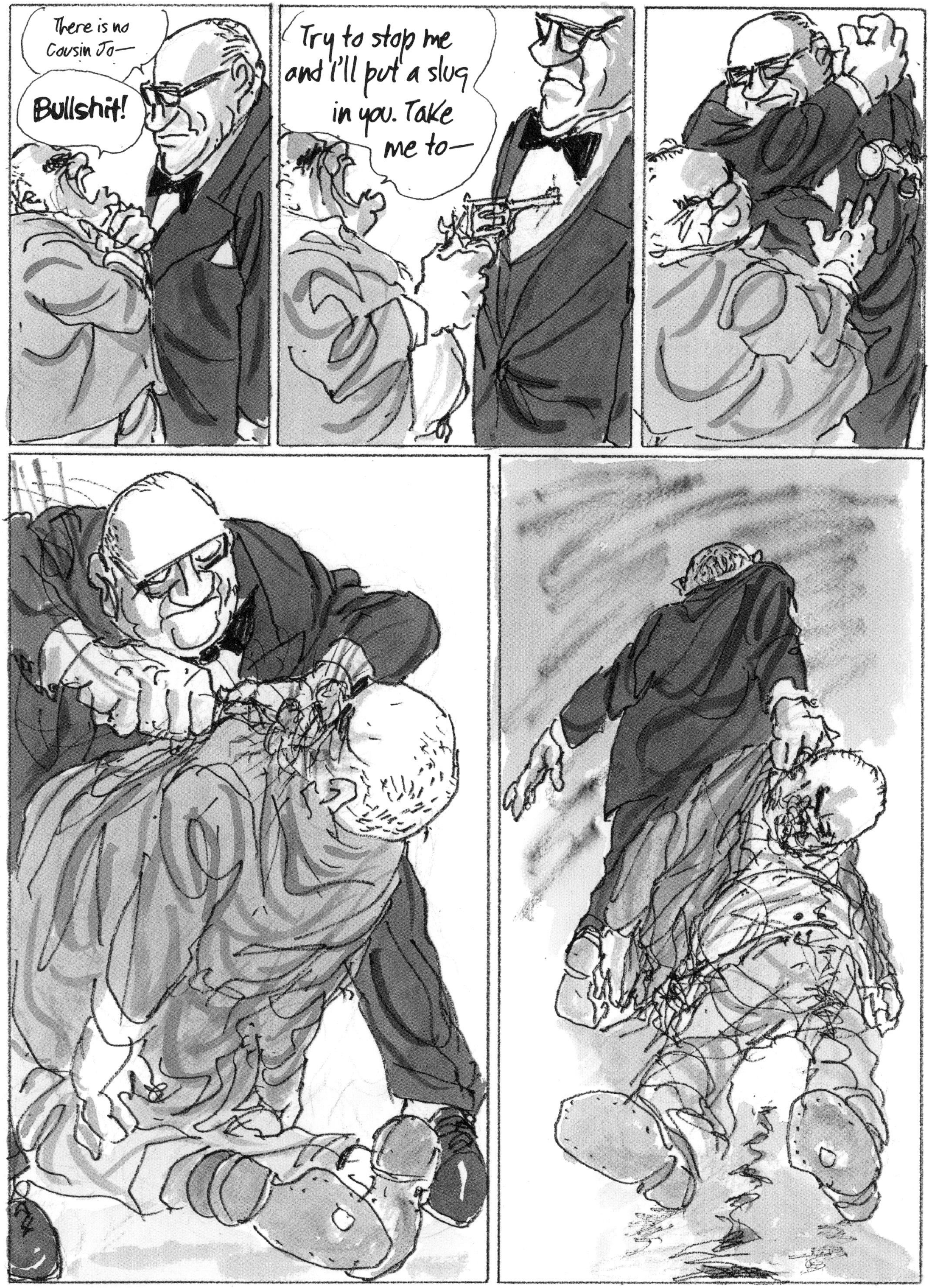
There is no Cousin Jo—
Bullshit!
Try to stop me and I'll put a slug in you. Take me to—

Chapter Forty-Five: Sammy Waves the Flag

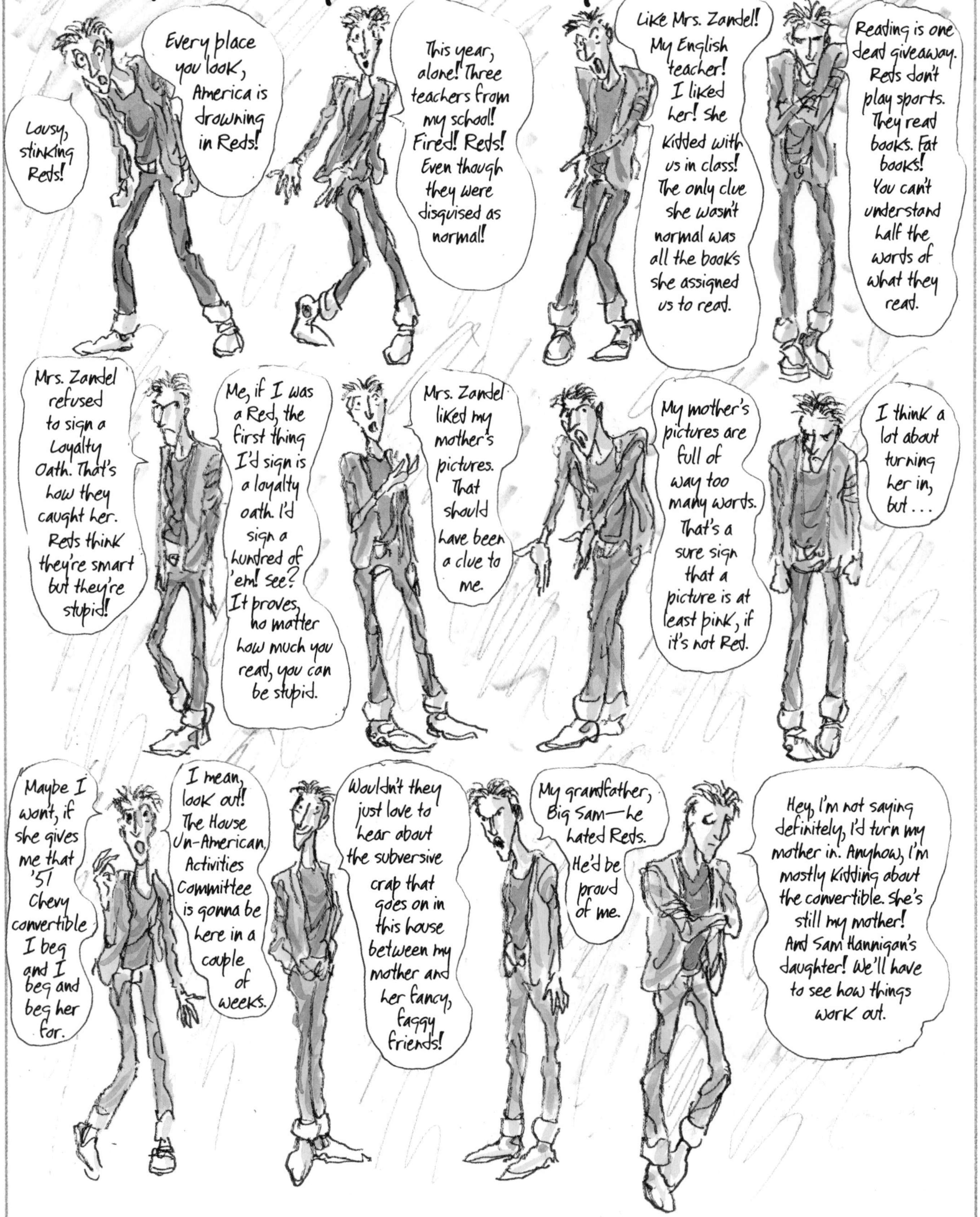
Lousy, stinking Reds!
Every place you look, America is drowning in Reds!
This year, alone! Three teachers from my school! Fired! Reds! Even though they were disguised as normal!
Like Mrs. Zandel! My English teacher! I liked her! She kidded with us in class! The only clue she wasn't normal was all the books she assigned us to read.
Reading is one dead giveaway. Reds don't play sports. They read books. Fat books! You can't understand half the words of what they read.
Mrs. Zandel refused to sign a Loyalty Oath. That's how they caught her. Reds think they're smart but they're stupid!
Me, if I was a Red, the first thing I'd sign is a loyalty oath. I'd sign a hundred of 'em! See? It proves, no matter how much you read, you can be stupid.
Mrs. Zandel liked my mother's pictures. That should have been a clue to me.
My mother's pictures are full of way too many words. That's a sure sign that a picture is at least pink, if it's not Red.
I think a lot about turning her in, but . . .
Maybe I won't, if she gives me that '51 Chevy convertible I beg and I beg and beg her for.
I mean, look out! The House Un-American Activities Committee is gonna be here in a couple of weeks.
Wouldn't they just love to hear about the subversive crap that goes on in this house between my mother and her fancy, faggy friends!
My grandfather, Big Sam—he hated Reds.
He'd be proud of me.
Hey, I'm not saying definitely, I'd turn my mother in. Anyhow, I'm mostly kidding about the convertible. She's still my mother! And Sam Hannigan's daughter! We'll have to see how things work out.

Chapter Forty-Six: Orville and the Wannabe Killers

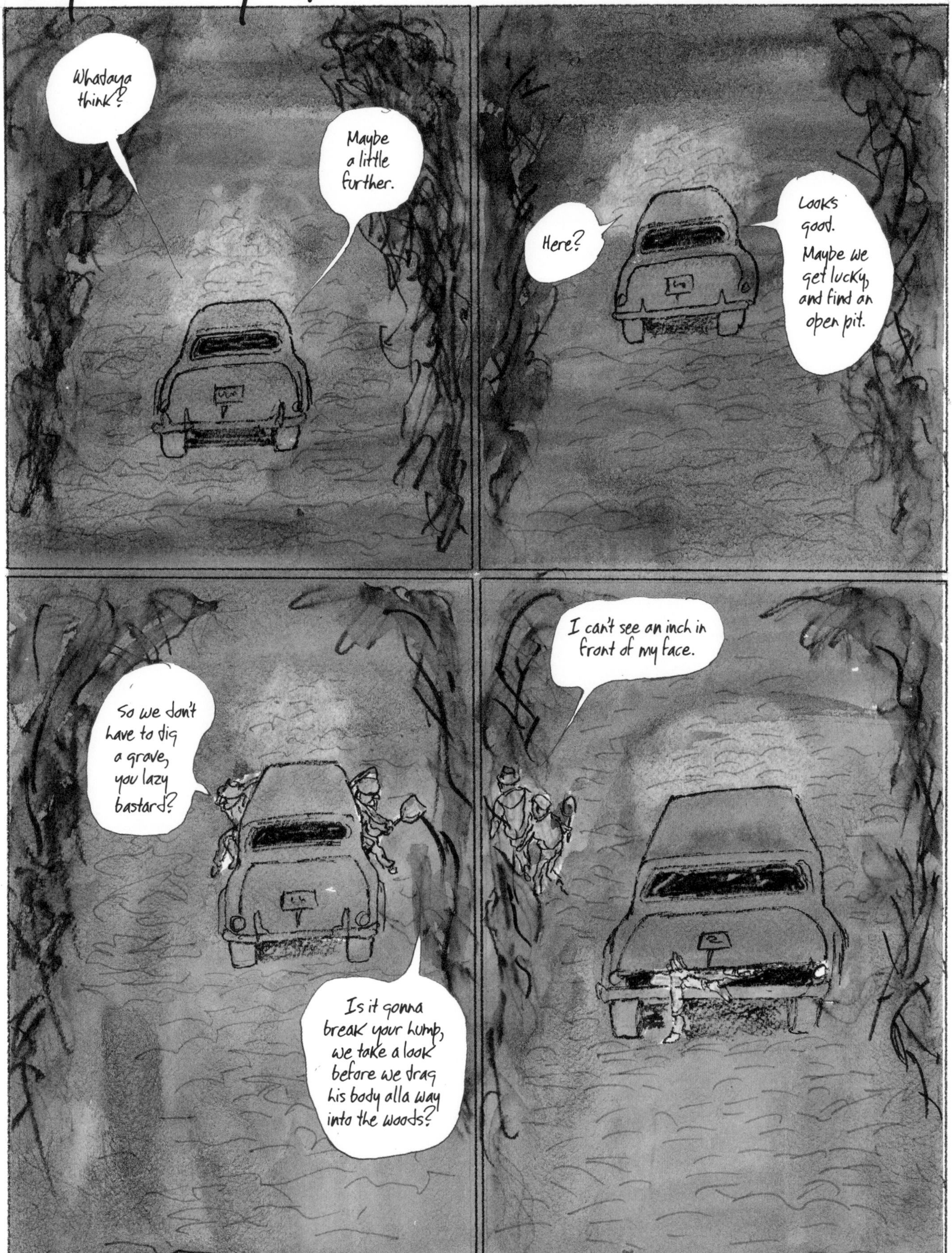

Whadaya think?
Maybe a little further.
Here?
Looks good. Maybe we get lucky, and find an open pit.
So we don't have to dig a grave, you lazy bastard?
Is it gonna break your hump, we take a look before we drag his body alla way into the woods?
I can't see an inch in front of my face.

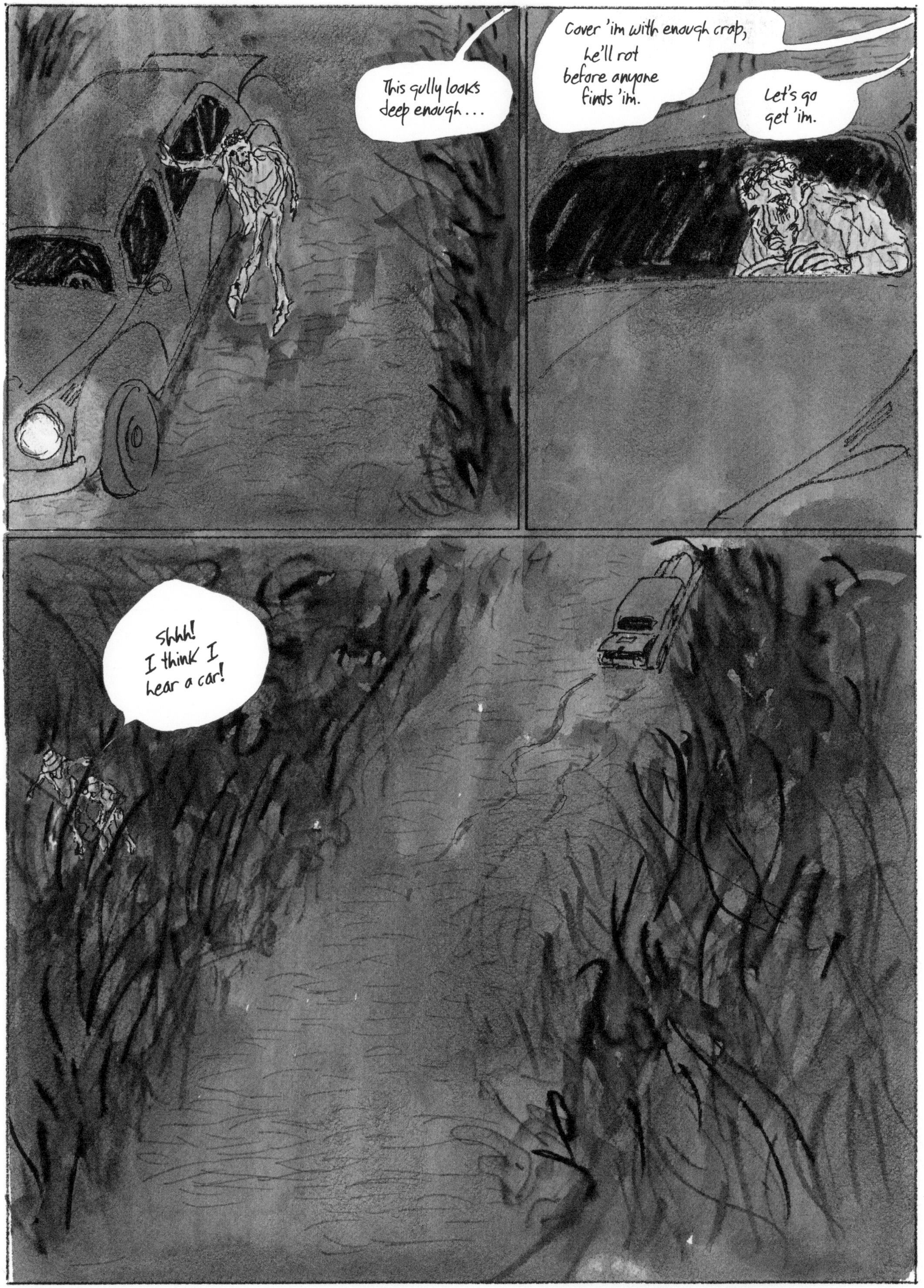
This gully looks deep enough . . .
Cover 'im with enough crap, he'll rot before anyone finds 'im.
Let's go get 'im.
Shhh! I think I hear a car!

Chapter Forty-Seven: Lady Unveiled

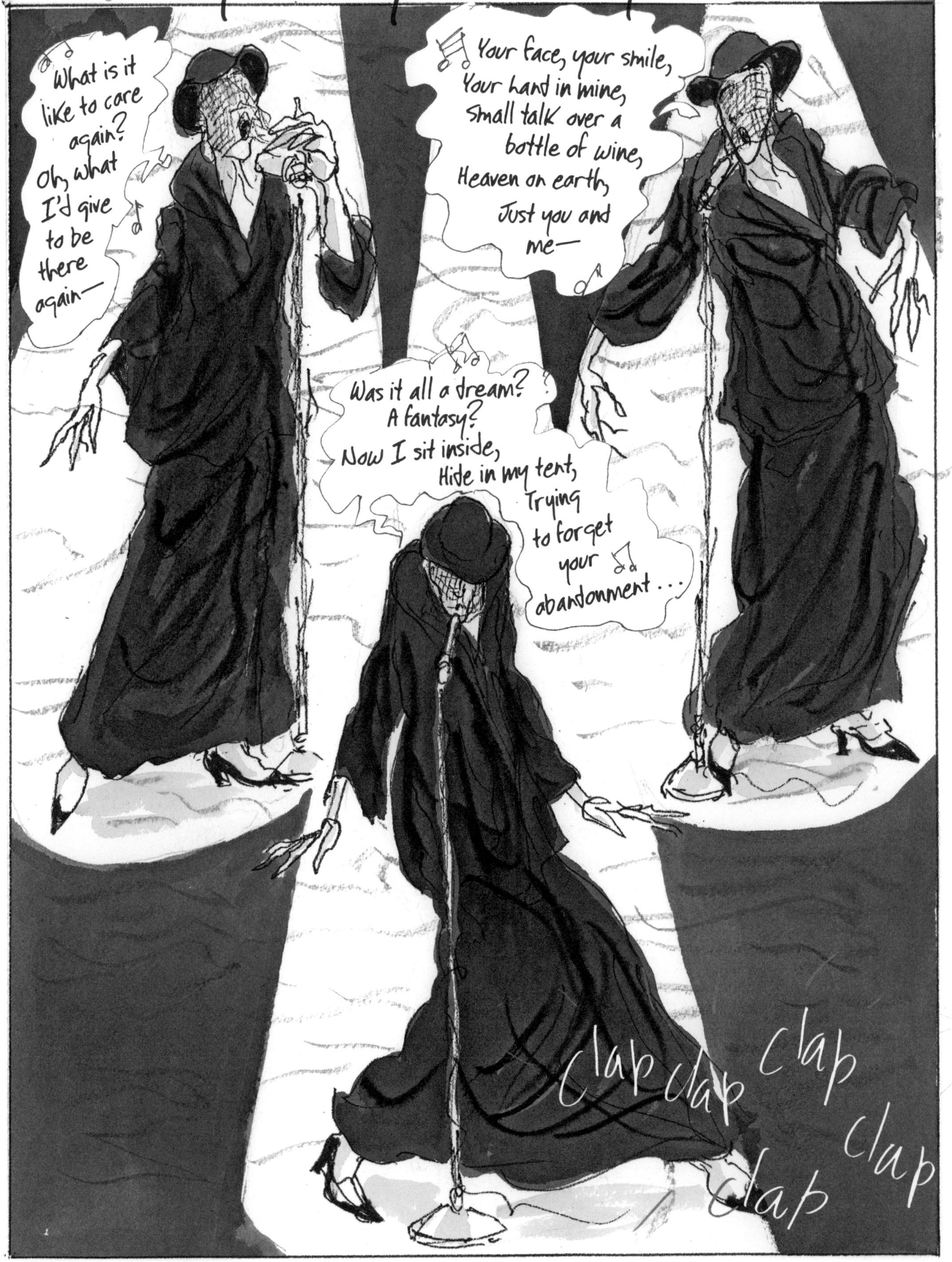

What is it like to care again? Oh, what I'd give to be there again—
Your face, your smile, Your hand in mine, Small talk over a bottle of wine, Heaven on earth, Just you and me—
Was it all a dream? A fantasy? Now I sit inside, Hide in my tent, Trying to forget your abandonment . . .
clap clap clap clap clap

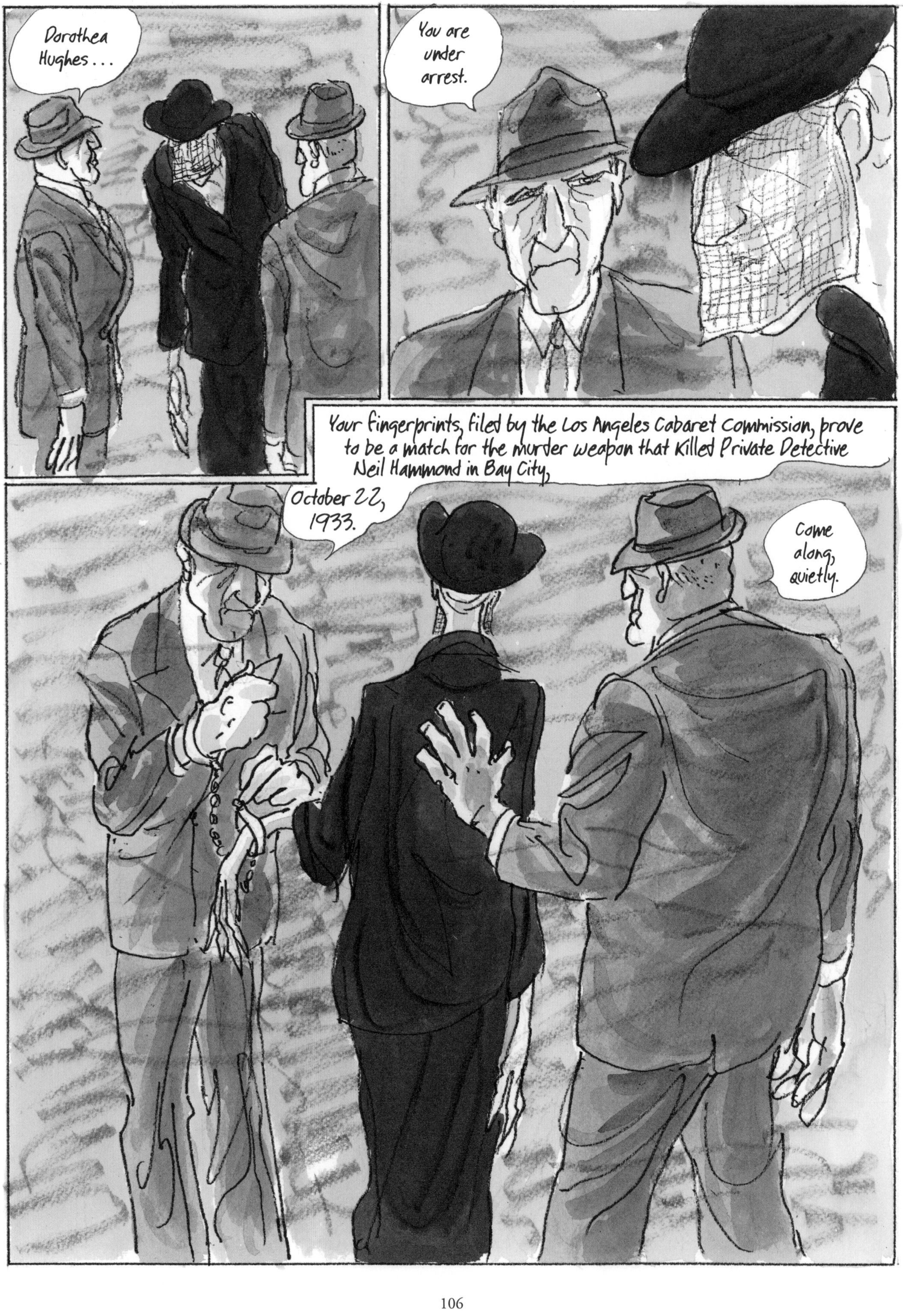
Dorothea Hughes . . .
You are under arrest.
Your fingerprints, filed by the Los Angeles Cabaret Commission, prove to be a match for the murder weapon that Killed Private Detective Neil Hammond in Bay City,
October 22, 1933.
Come along, quietly.

Chapter Forty-Eight: Crisis

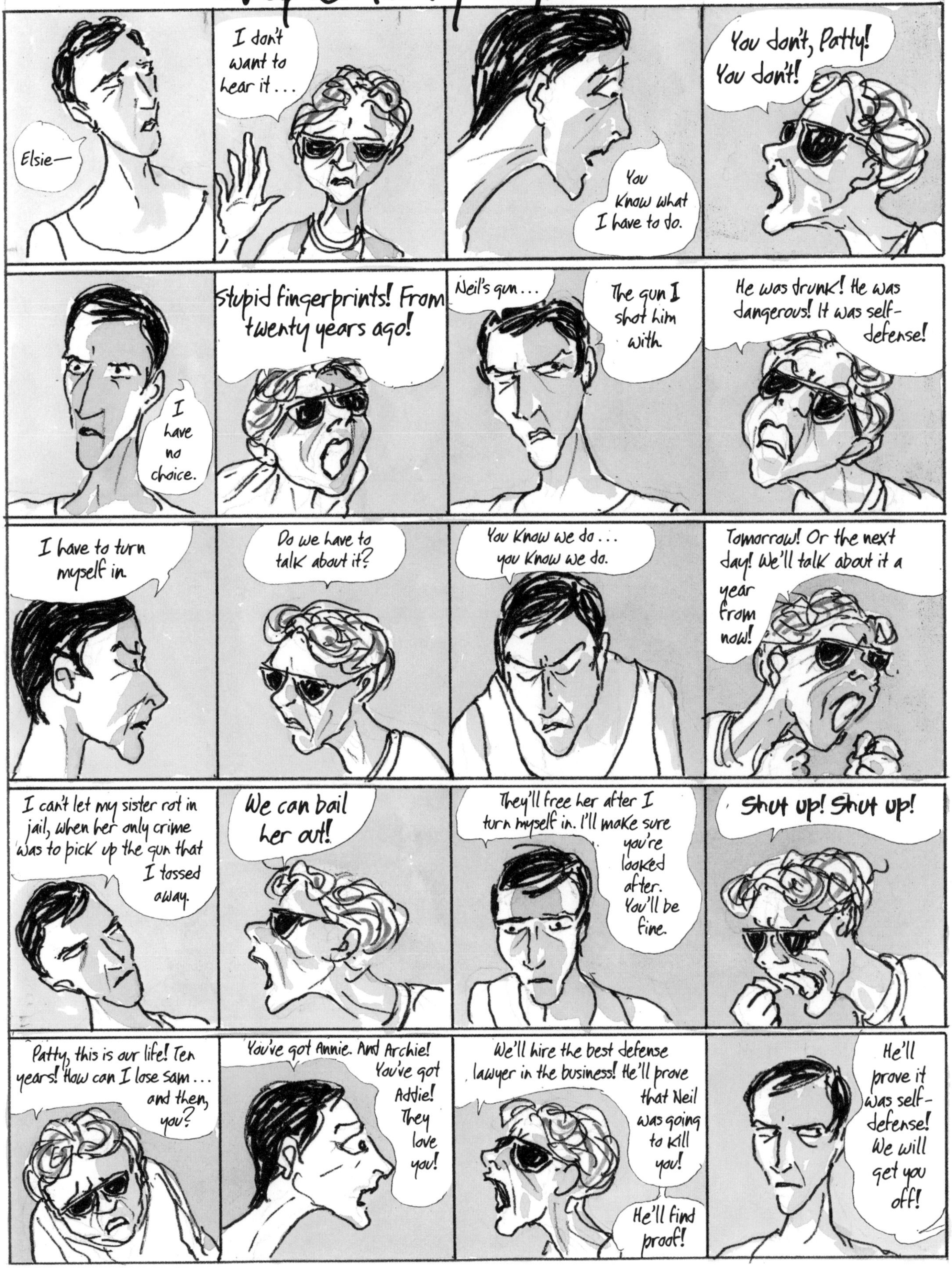
Elsie—
I don't want to hear it . . .
You know what I have to do.
You don't, Patty! You don't!
I have no choice.
Stupid fingerprints! From twenty years ago!
Neil's gun . . .
The gun I shot him with.
He was drunk! He was dangerous! It was self-defense!
I have to turn myself in.
Do we have to talk about it?
You know we do . . . you know we do.
Tomorrow! Or the next day! We'll talk about it a year from now!
I can't let my sister rot in jail, when her only crime was to pick up the gun that I tossed away.
We can bail her out!
They'll free her after I turn myself in. I'll make sure you're looked after. You'll be fine.
Shut up! Shut up!
Patty, this is our life! Ten years! How can I lose Sam . . . and then, you?
You've got Annie. And Archie! You've got Addie! They love you!
We'll hire the best defense lawyer in the business! He'll prove that Neil was going to kill you!
He'll find proof!
He'll prove it was self-defense! We will get you off!

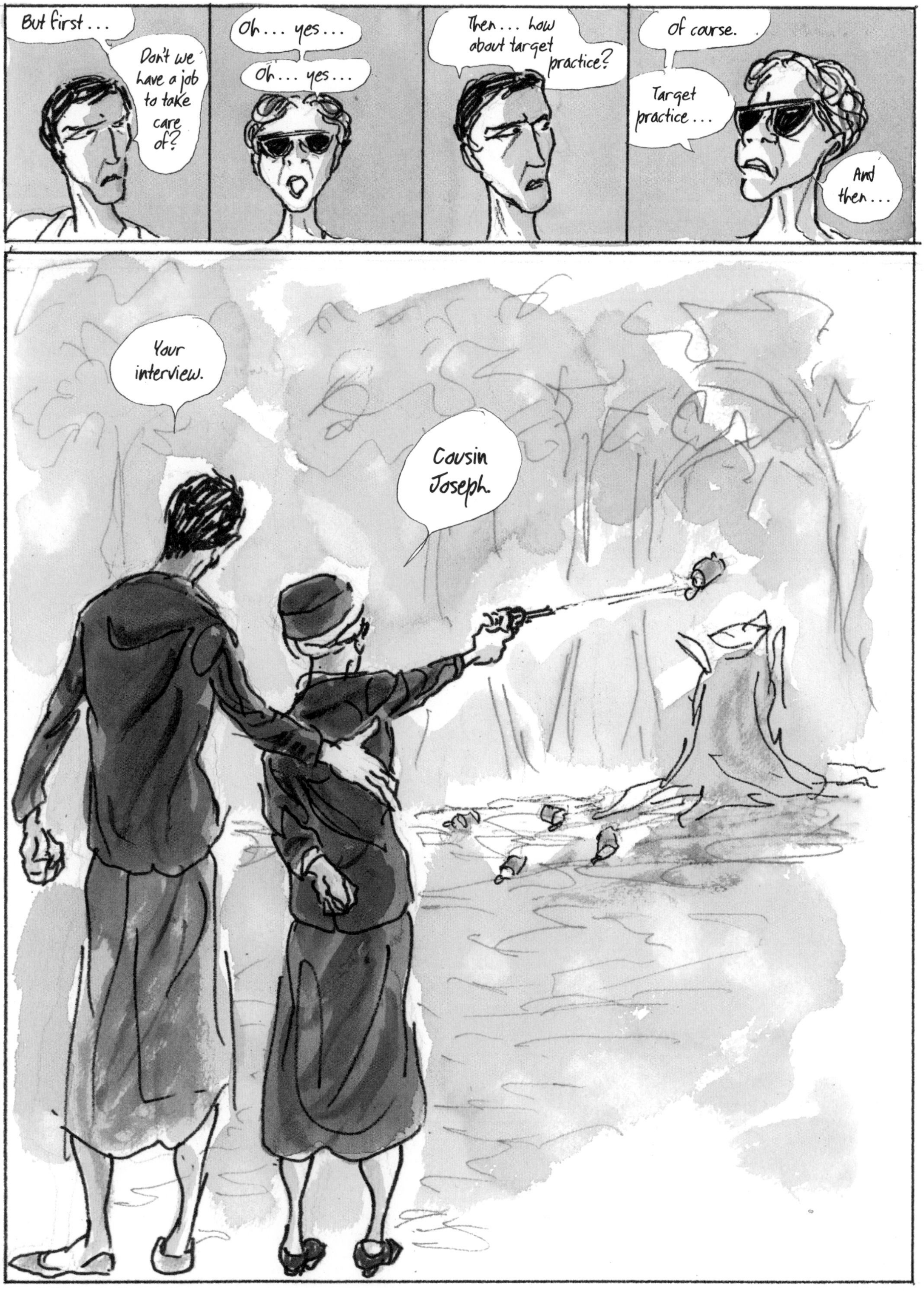
But first . . .
Don't we have a job to take care of?
Oh . . . yes . . .
Oh . . . yes . . .
Then . . . how about target practice?
Of course.
Target practice . . .
And then . . .
Your interview.
Cousin Joseph.

Chapter Forty-Nine: The Getaway

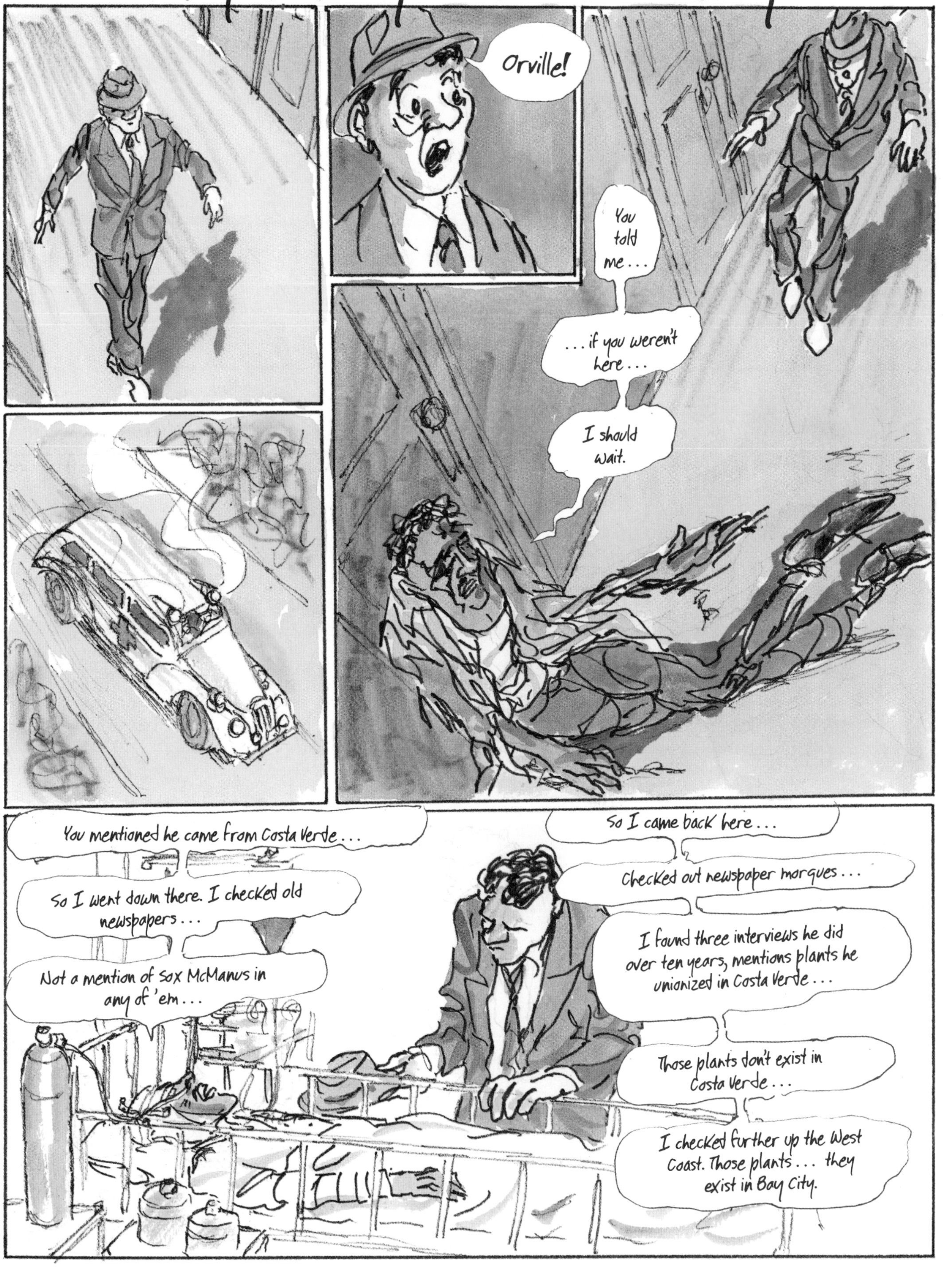

Orville!
You told me . . .
. . . if you weren't here . . .
I should wait.
You mentioned he came from Costa Verde . . .
So I went down there. I checked old newspapers . . .
Not a mention of Sox McManus in any of 'em . . .
So I came back here . . .
Checked out newspaper morgues . . .
I found three interviews he did over ten years, mentions plants he unionized in Costa Verde . . .
Those plants don't exist in Costa Verde . . .
I checked further up the West Coast. Those plants . . . they exist in Bay City.

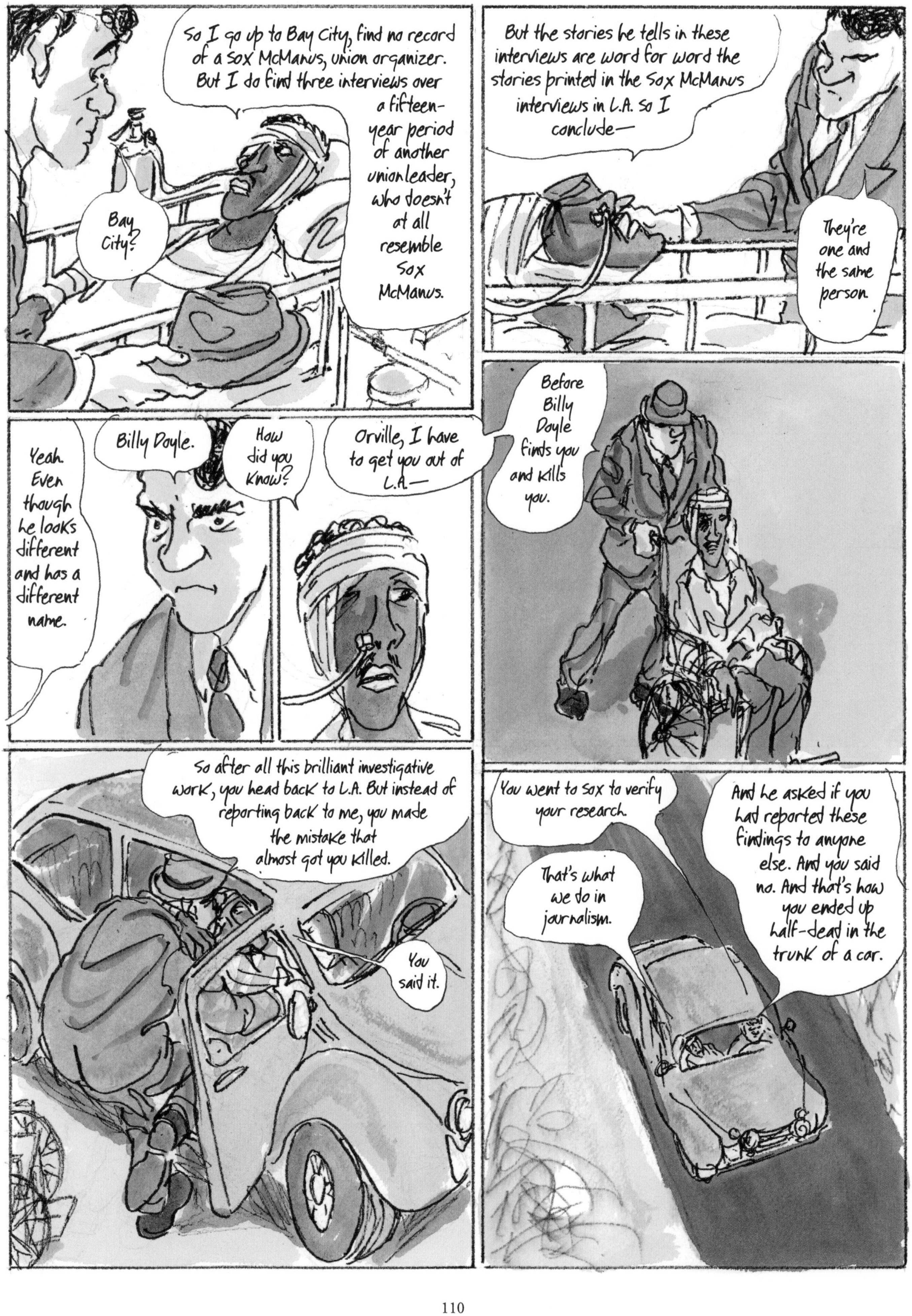
So I go up to Bay City, find no record of a Sox McManus, union organizer. But I do find three interviews over a fifteen-year period of another unionleader, who doesn't at all resemble Sox McManus.
Bay City?
But the stories he tells in these interviews are word for word the stories printed in the Sox McManus interviews in L.A. So I conclude—
They're one and the same person.
Yeah. Even though he looks different and has a different name.
Billy Doyle.
How did you know?
Orville, I have to get you out of L.A.—
Before Billy Doyle finds you and kills you.
So after all this brilliant investigative work, you head back to L.A. But instead of reporting back to me, you made the mistake that almost got you killed.
You said it.
You went to Sox to verify your research.
That's what we do in journalism.
And he asked if you had reported these findings to anyone else. And you said no. And that's how you ended up half-dead in the trunk of a car.

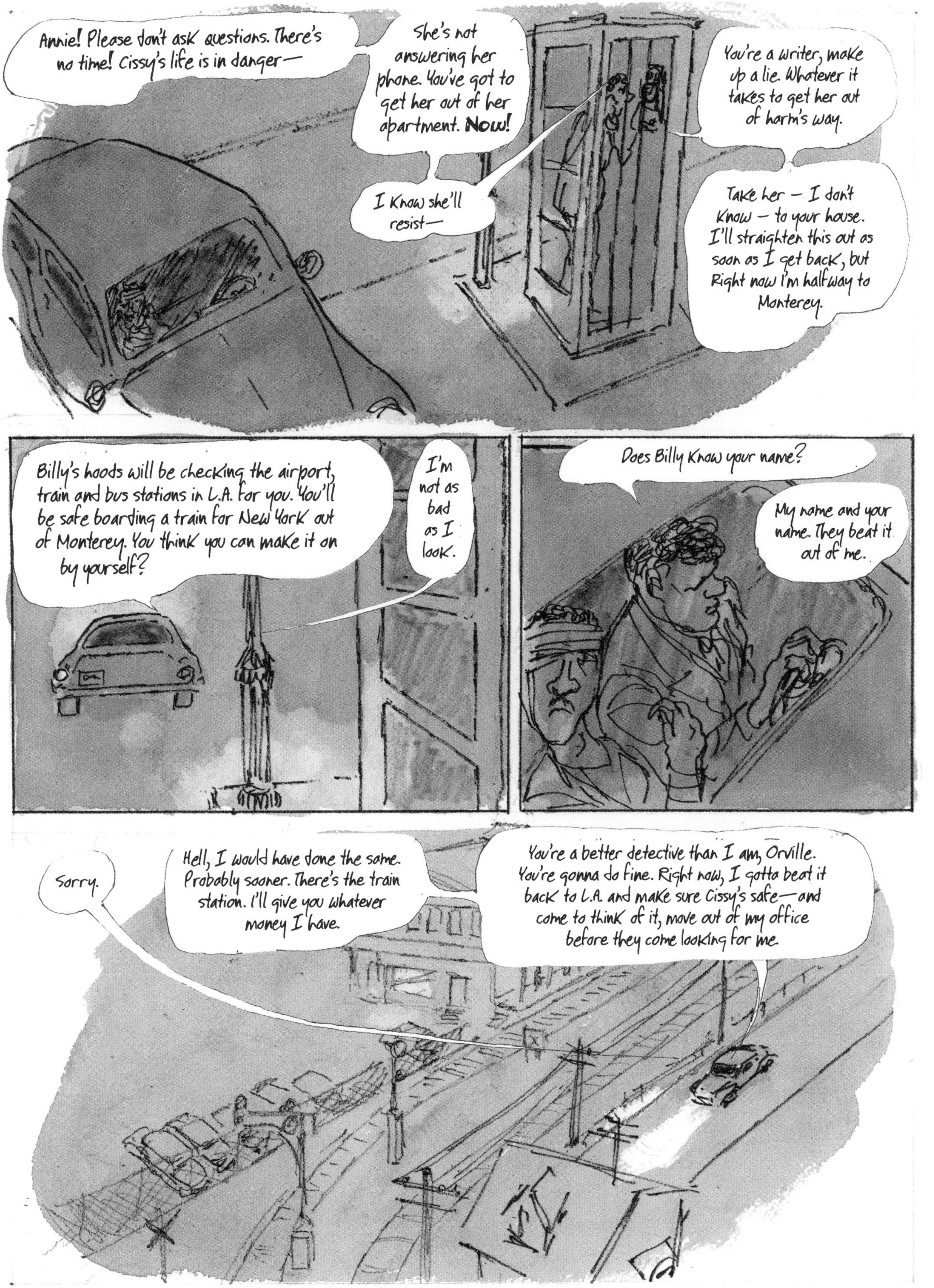
Annie! Please don't ask questions. There's no time! Cissy's life is in danger—
She's not answering her phone. You've got to get her out of her apartment. Now!
I know she'll resist—
You're a writer, make up a lie. Whatever it takes to get her out of harm's way.
Take her — I don't know — to your house. I'll straighten this out as soon as I get back, but right now I'm halfway to Monterey.
Billy's hoods will be checking the airport, train and bus stations in L.A. for you. You'll be safe boarding a train for New York out of Monterey. You think you can make it on by yourself?
I'm not as bad as I look.
Does Billy know your name?
My name and your name. They beat it out of me.
Sorry.
Hell, I would have done the same. Probably sooner. There's the train station. I'll give you whatever money I have.
You're a better detective than I am, Orville. You're gonna do fine. Right now, I gotta beat it back to L.A. and make sure Cissy's safe—and come to think of it, move out of my office before they come looking for me.

Chapter Fifty: Annie at the Door

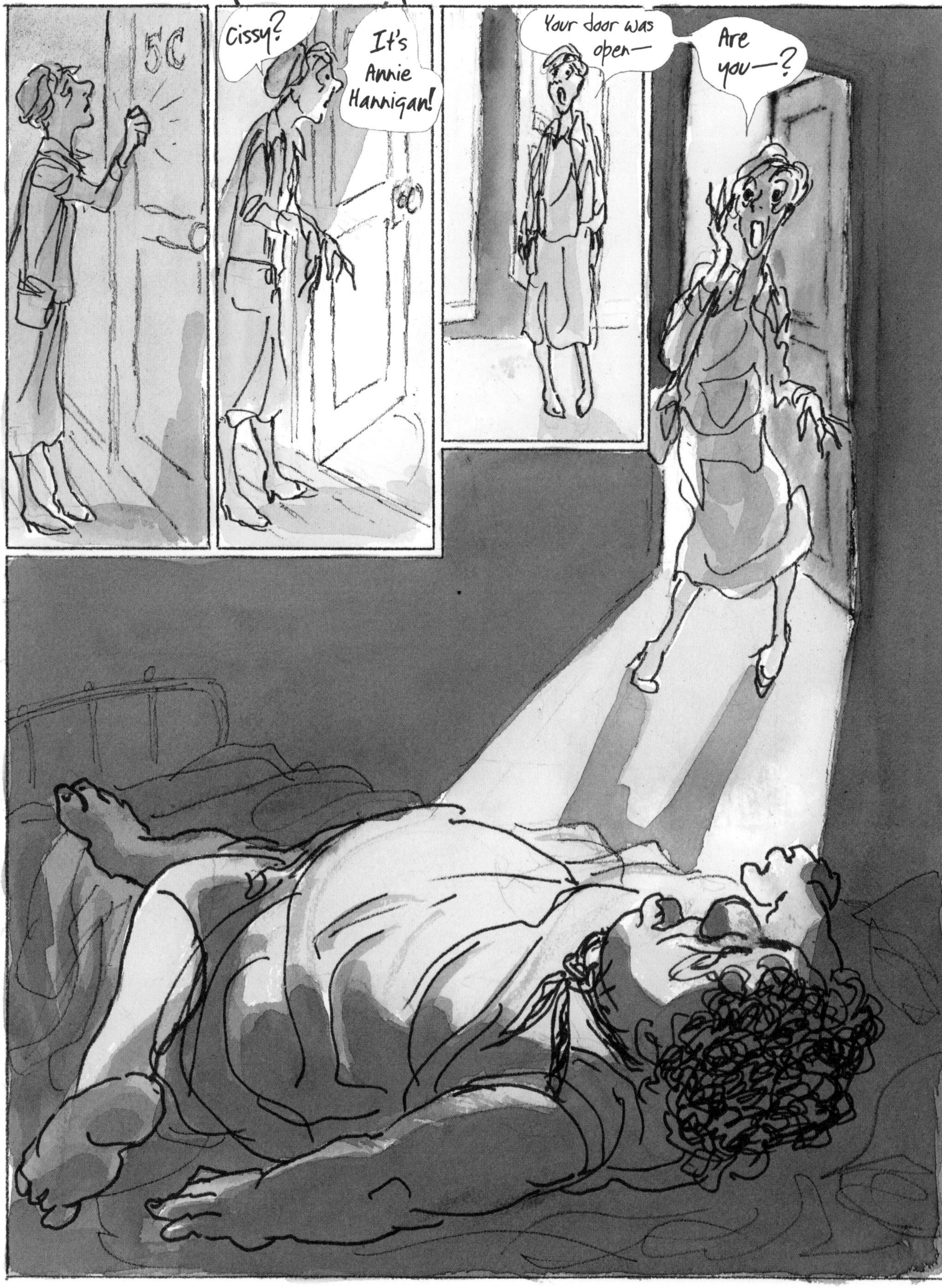

Cissy?
It's Annie Hannigan!
Your door was open—
Are you—?

Chapter Fifty-One: Insanity

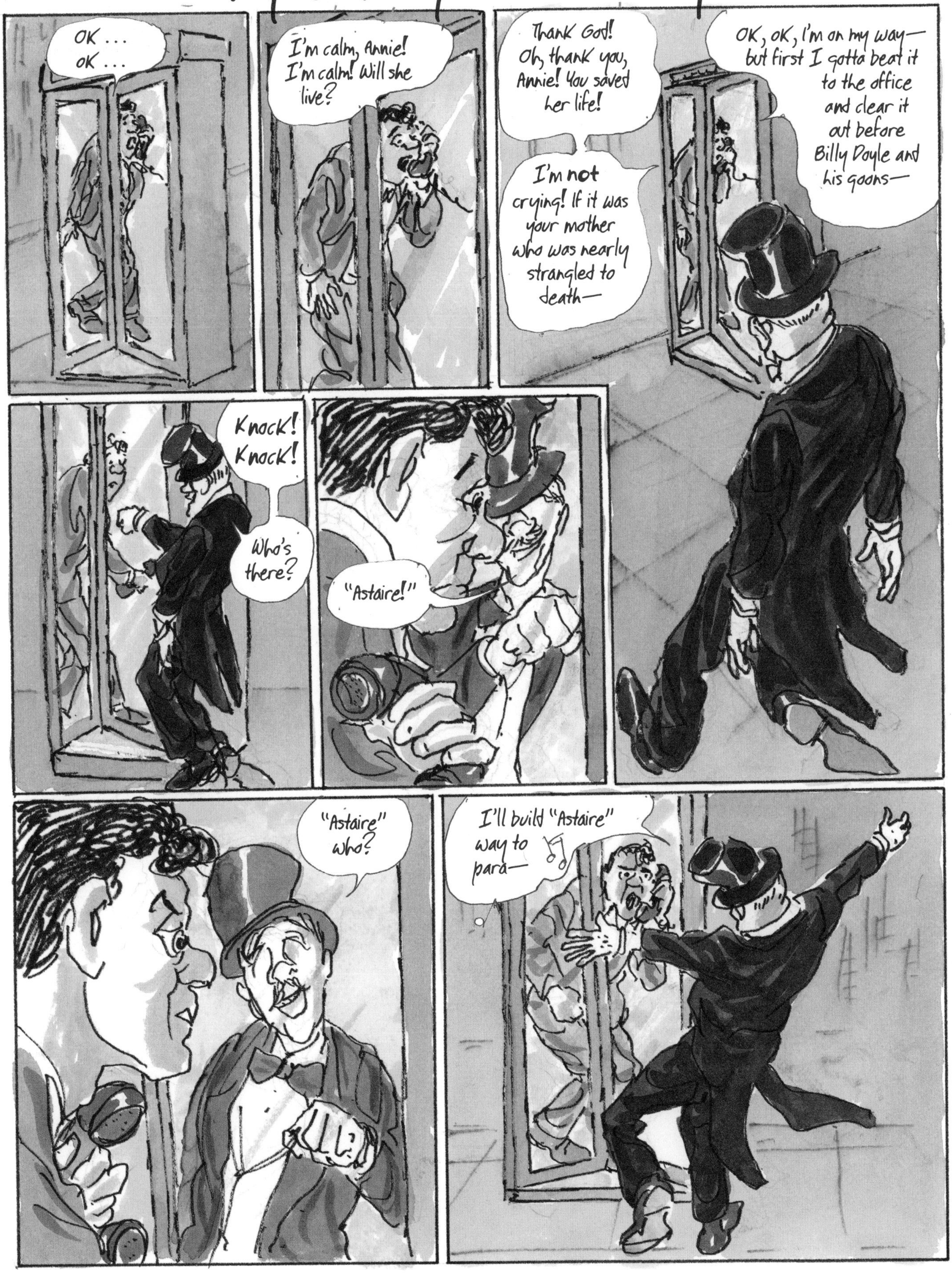

OK . . .
OK . . .
I'm calm, Annie! I'm calm! Will she live?
Thank God! Oh, thank you, Annie! You saved her life!
I'm not crying! If it was your mother who was nearly strangled to death—
OK, ok, I'm on my way—but first I gotta beat it to the office and clear it out before Billy Doyle and his goons—
Knock! Knock!
Who's there?
"Astaire!"
"Astaire" who?
I'll build "Astaire" way to para—

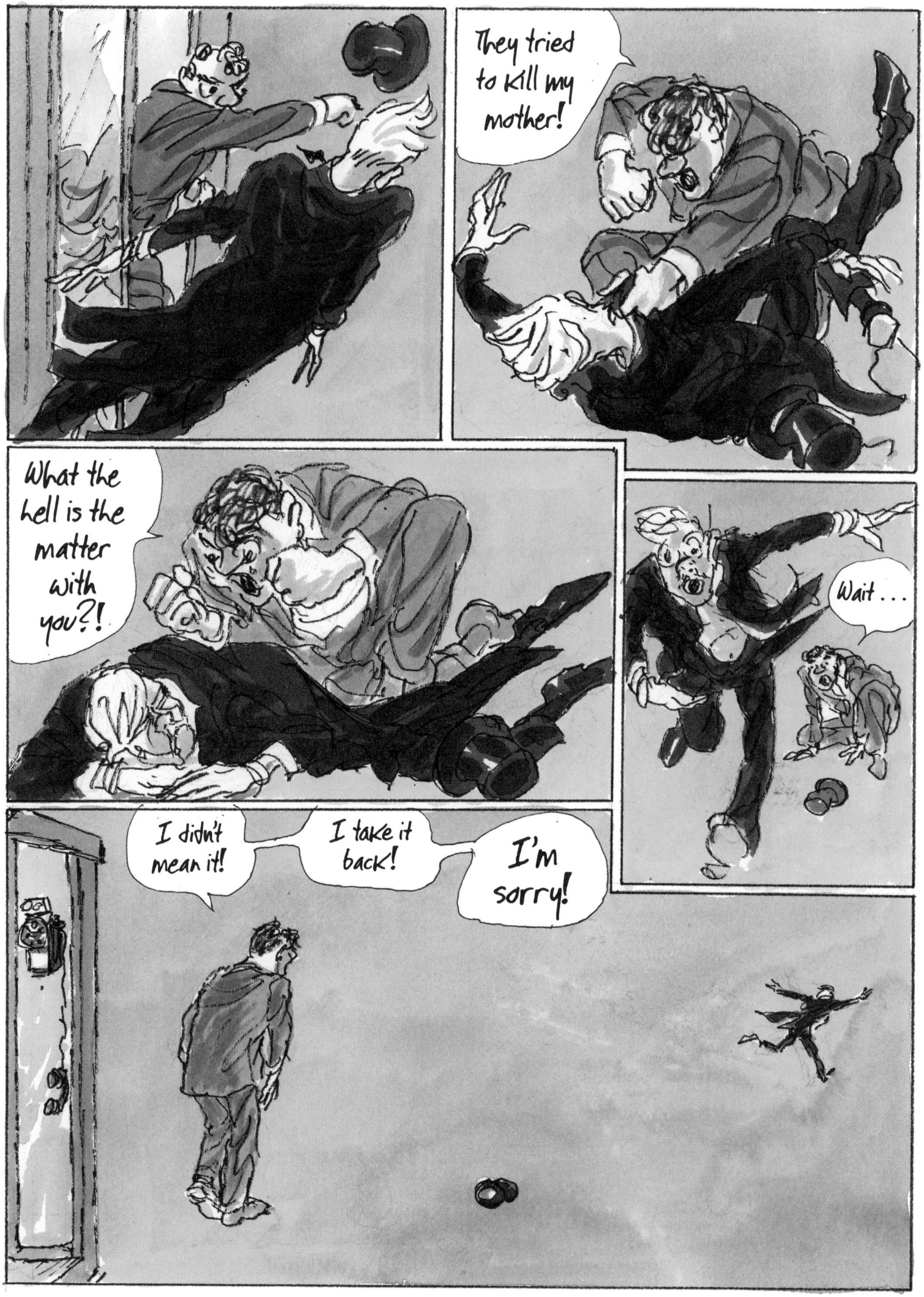
They tried to kill my mother!
What the hell is the matter with you?!
Wait . . .
I didn't mean it!
I take it back!
I'm sorry!

Chapter Fifty-Two: Flashback—Bay City, 1931

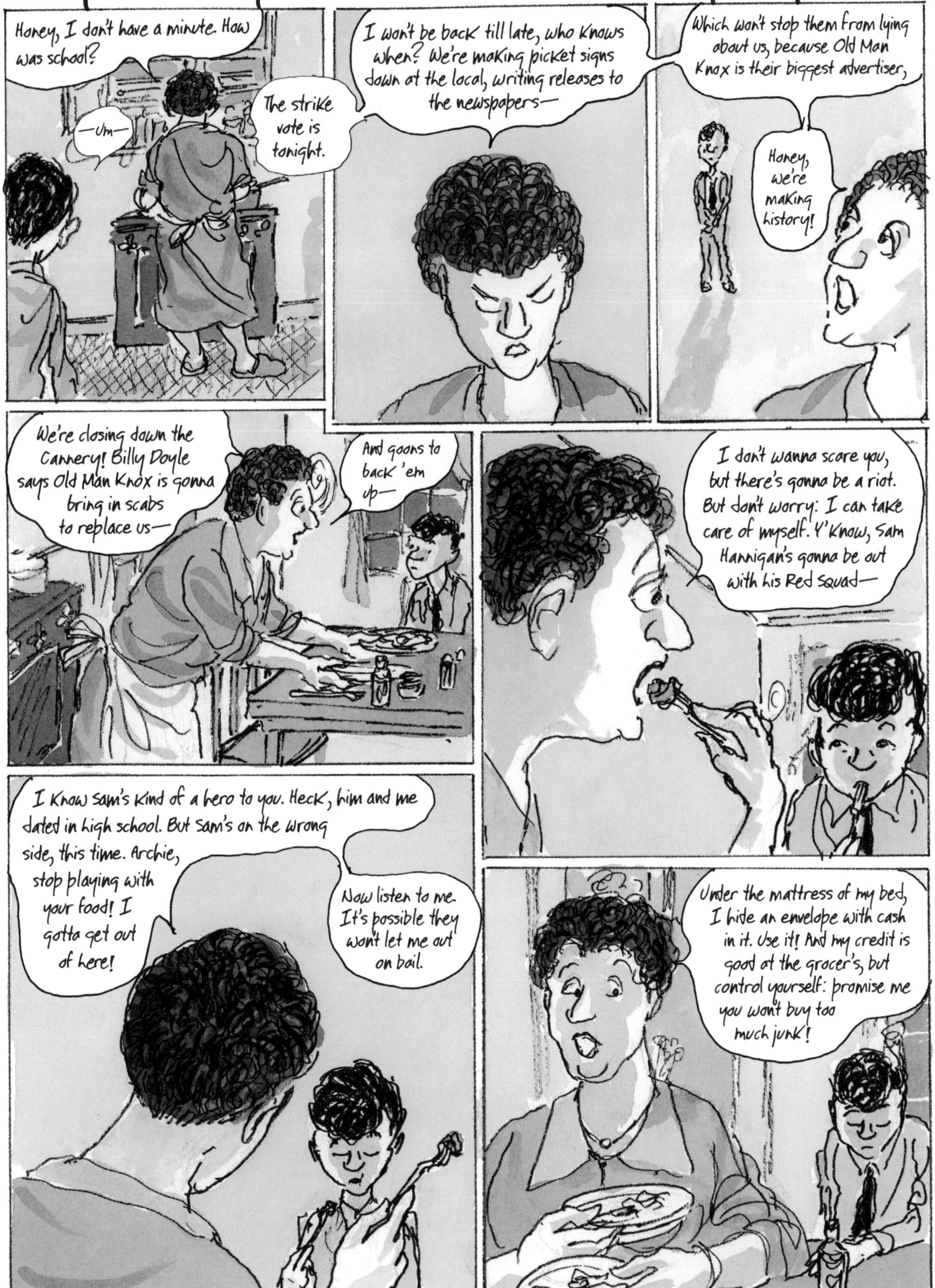
Honey, I don't have a minute. How was school?
—Um—
The strike vote is tonight.
I won't be back till late, who knows when? We're making picket signs down at the local, writing releases to the newspapers—
Which won't stop them from lying about us, because Old Man Knox is their biggest advertiser,
Honey, we're making history!
We're closing down the cannery! Billy Doyle says Old Man Knox is gonna bring in scabs to replace us—
And goons to back 'em up—
I don't wanna scare you, but there's gonna be a riot. But don't worry: I can take care of myself. Y'know, Sam Hannigan's gonna be out with his Red Squad—
I know Sam's kind of a hero to you. Heck, him and me dated in high school. But Sam's on the wrong side, this time. Archie, stop playing with your food! I gotta get out of here!
Now listen to me. It's possible they won't let me out on bail.
Under the mattress of my bed, I hide an envelope with cash in it. Use it! And my credit is good at the grocer's, but control yourself: promise me you won't buy too much junk!

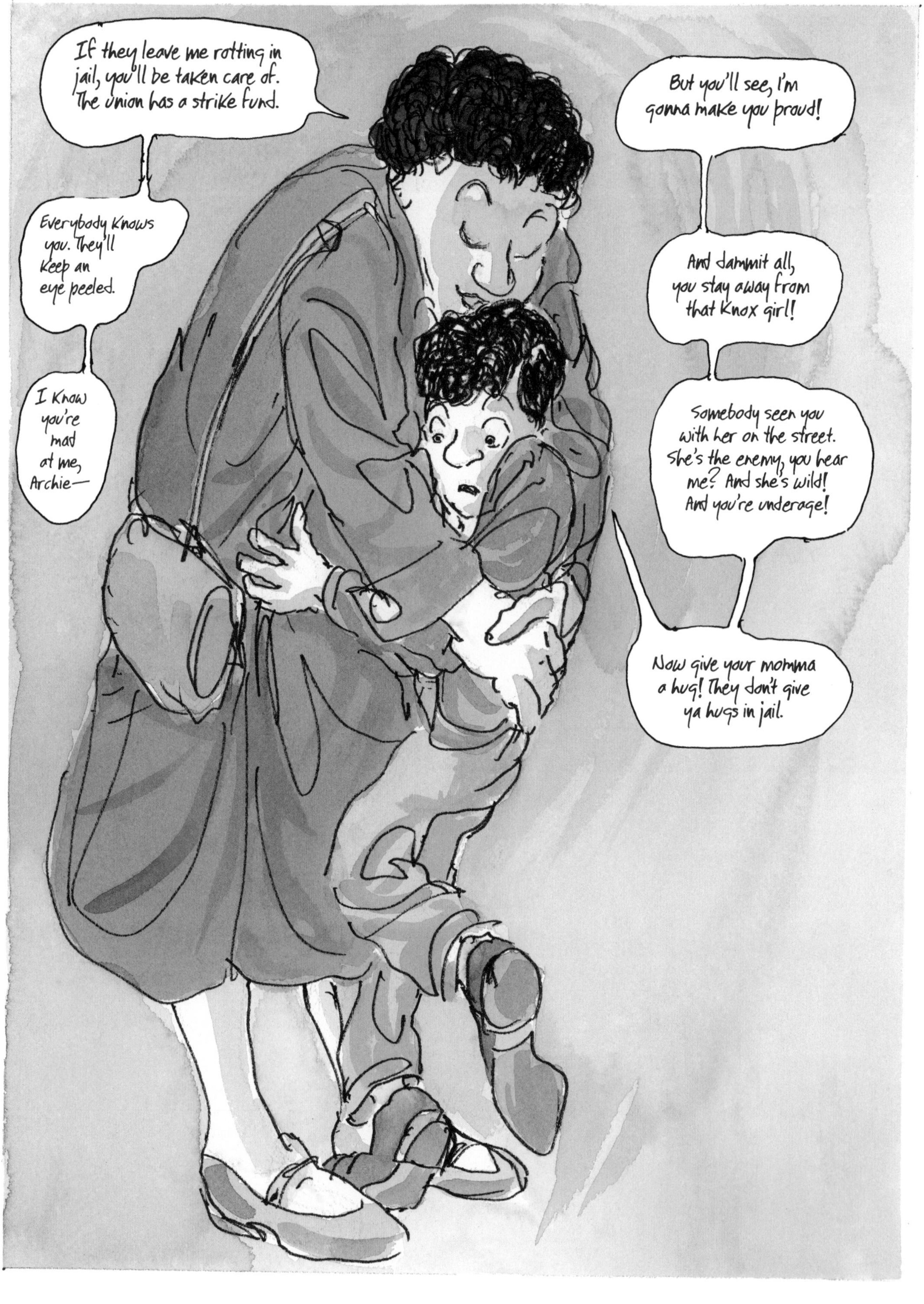
If they leave me rotting in jail, you'll be taken care of. The union has a strike fund.
Everybody knows you. They'll keep an eye peeled.
I know you're mad at me, Archie—
But you'll see, I'm gonna make you proud!
And dammit all, you stay away from that Knox girl!
Somebody seen you with her on the street. She's the enemy, you hear me? And she's wild! And you're underage!
Now give your momma a hug! They don't give ya hugs in jail.

Chapter Fifty-Three: Lights Out

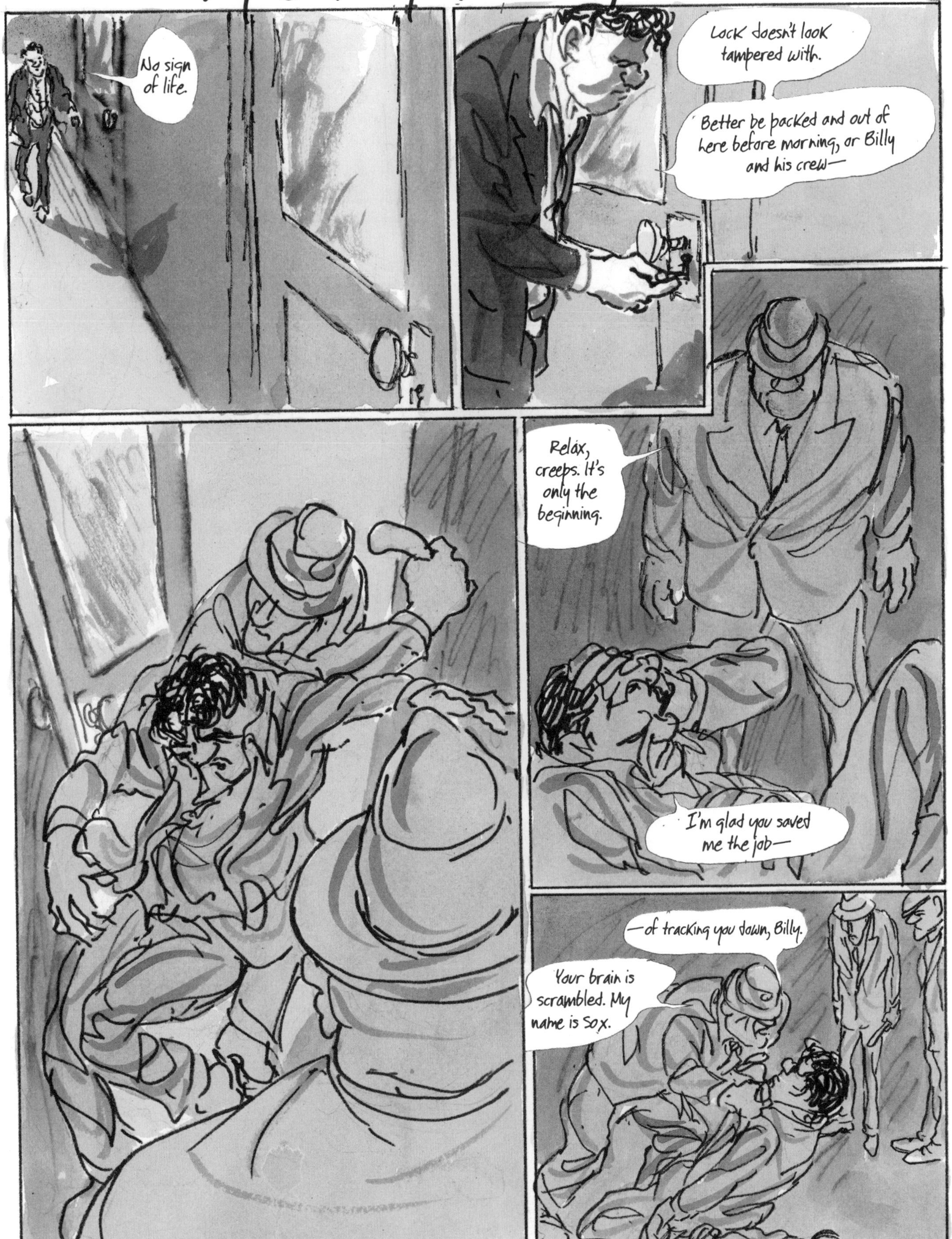
No sign of life.
Lock doesn't look tampered with.
Better be packed and out of here before morning, or Billy and his crew—
Relax, creeps. It's only the beginning.
I'm glad you saved me the job—
—of tracking you down, Billy.
Your brain is scrambled. My name is Sox.

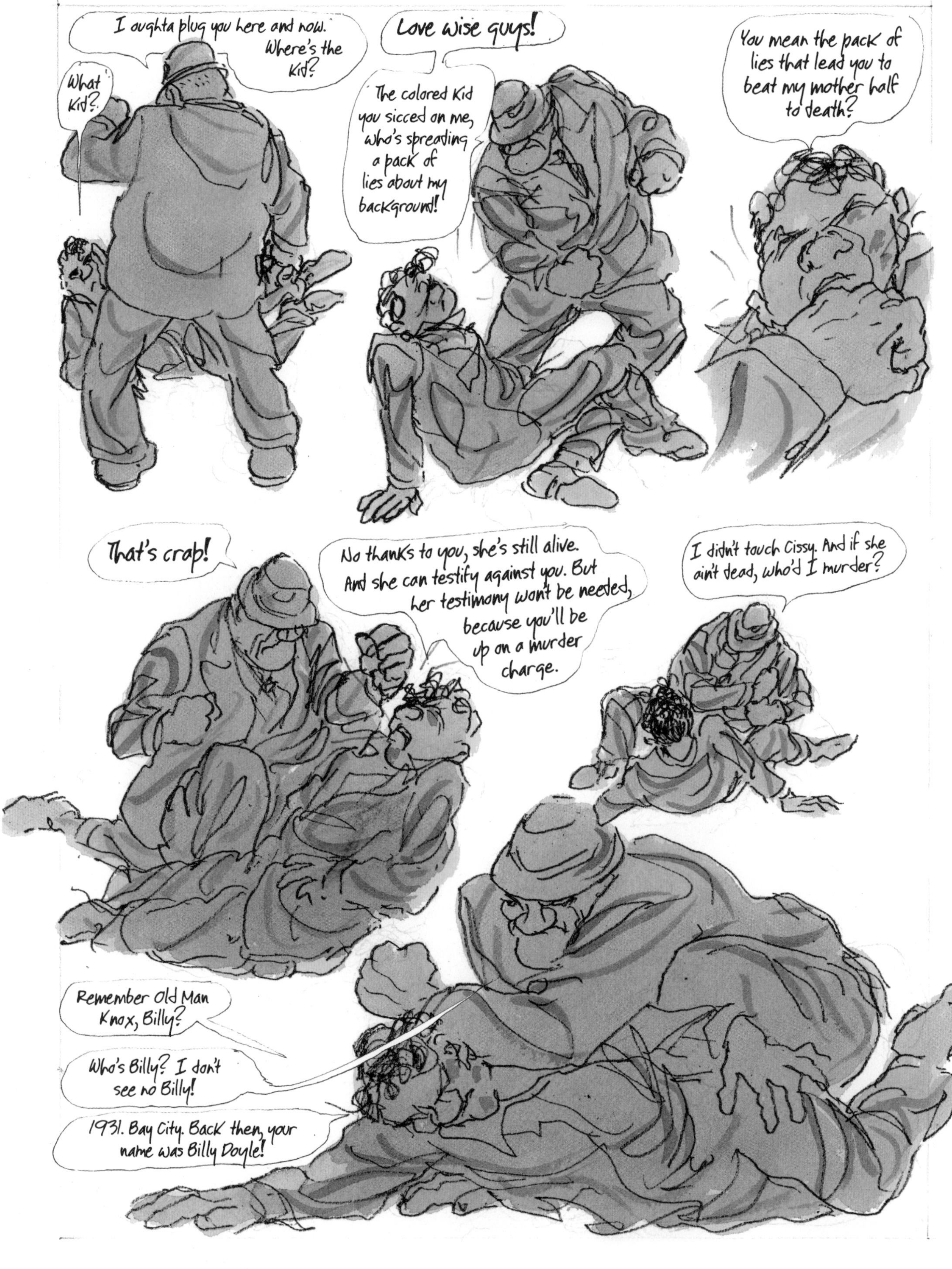

I oughta plug you here and now. Where's the kid?
What kid?
Love wise guys!
The colored kid you sicced on me, who's spreading a pack of lies about my background!
You mean the pack of lies that lead you to beat my mother half to death?
That's crap!
No thanks to you, she's still alive. And she can testify against you. But her testimony won't be needed, because you'll be up on a murder charge.
I didn't touch Cissy. And if she ain't dead, who'd I murder?
Remember Old Man Knox, Billy?
Who's Billy? I don't see no Billy!
1931. Bay City. Back then, your name was Billy Doyle!

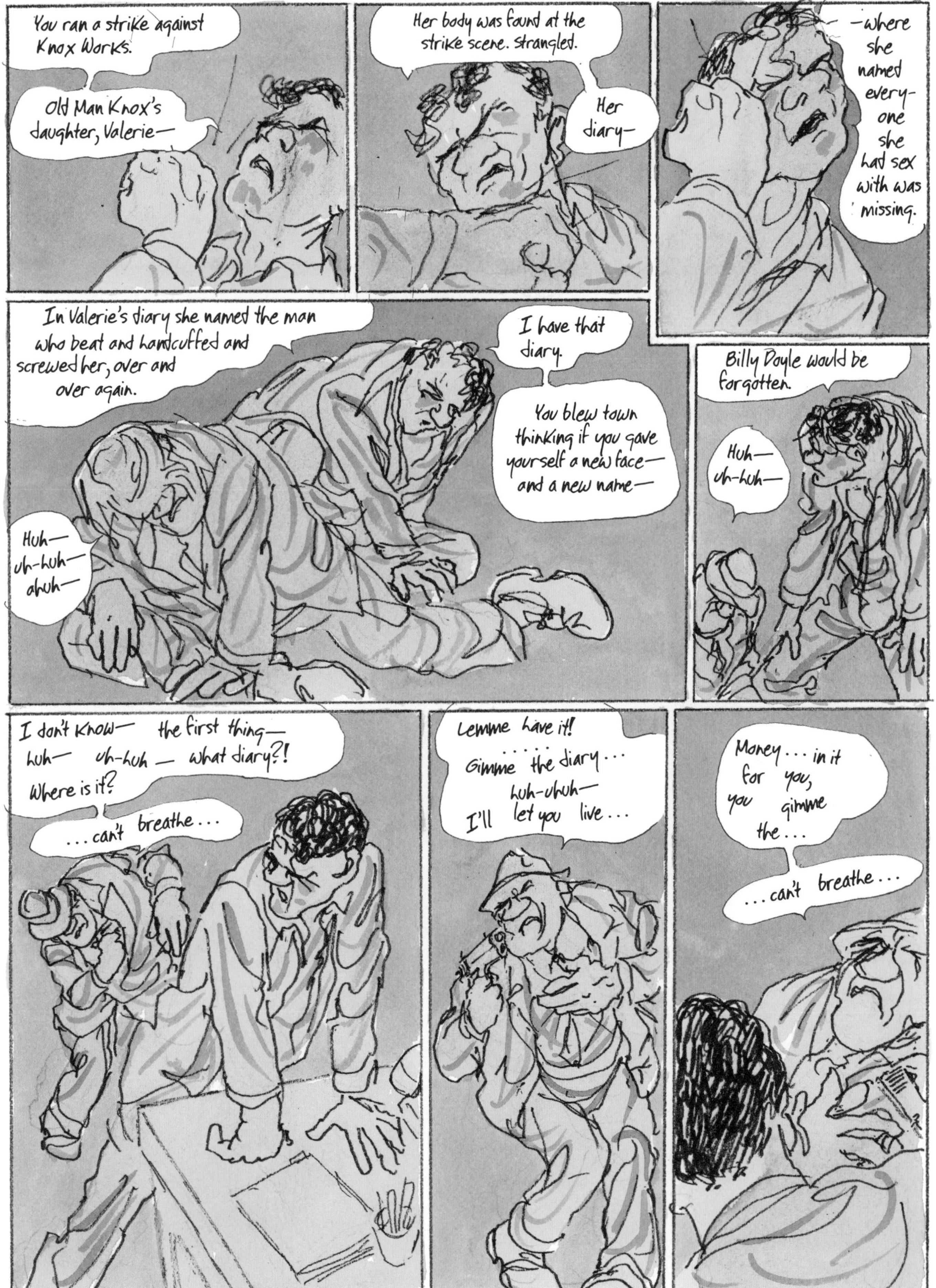
You ran a strike against Knox Works.
Old Man Knox's daughter, Valerie—
Her body was found at the strike scene. Strangled.
Her diary—
—where she named every-one she had sex with was missing.
In Valerie's diary she named the man who beat and handcuffed and screwed her, over and over again.
I have that diary.
You blew town thinking if you gave yourself a new face— and a new name—
Huh— uh-huh— ahuh—
Billy Doyle would be forgotten.
Huh— uh-huh—
I don't know— the first thing— huh— uh-huh — what diary?! Where is it?
...can't breathe...
Lemme have it!
Gimme the diary... huh-uhuh— I'll let you live...
Money... in it for you, you gimme the...
...can't breathe...

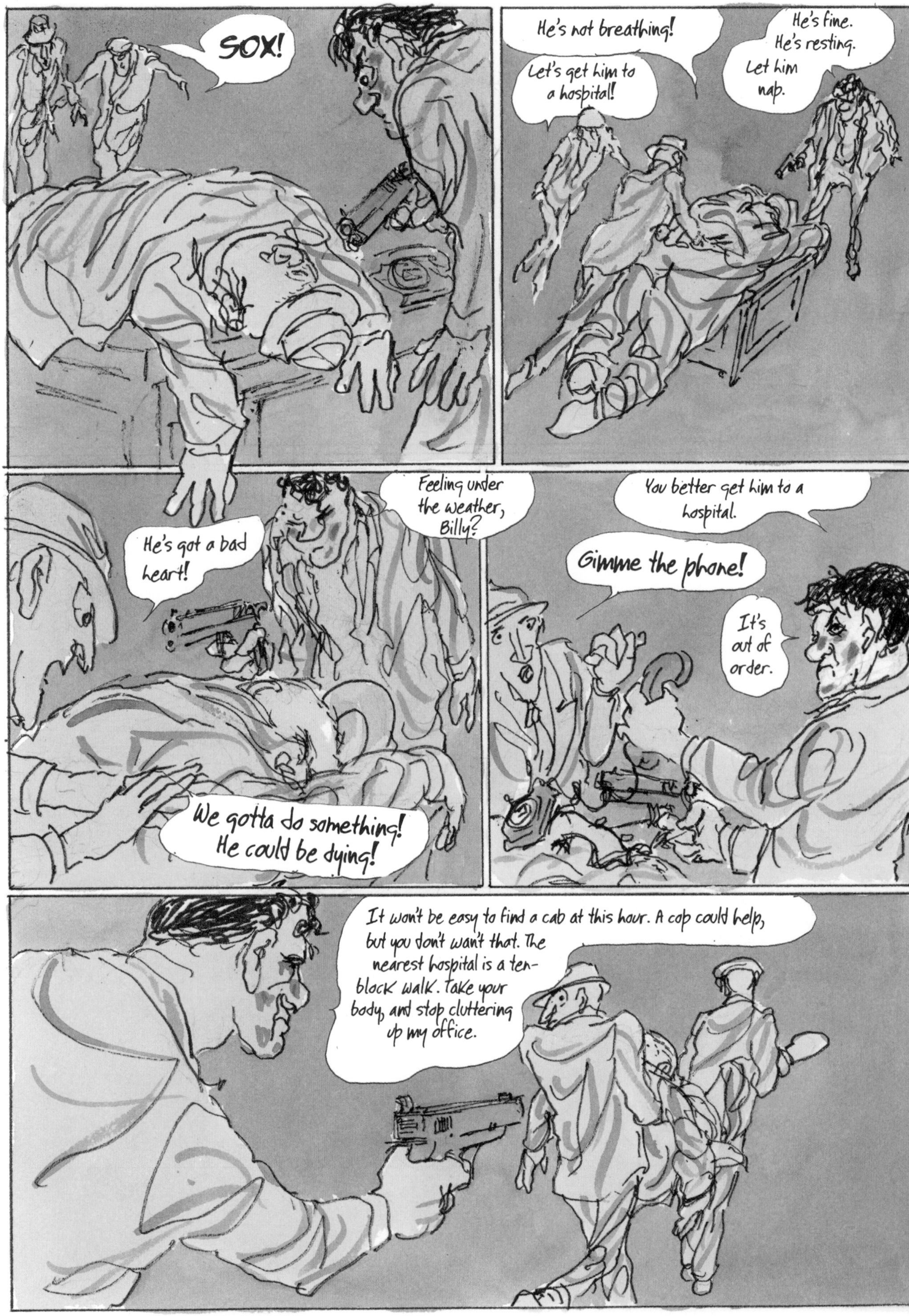
SOX!
He's not breathing!
Let's get him to a hospital!
He's fine. He's resting.
Let him nap.
He's got a bad heart!
Feeling under the weather, Billy?
We gotta do something! He could be dying!
You better get him to a hospital.
Gimme the phone!
It's out of order.
It won't be easy to find a cab at this hour. A cop could help, but you don't want that. The nearest hospital is a ten-block walk. Take your body, and stop cluttering up my office.

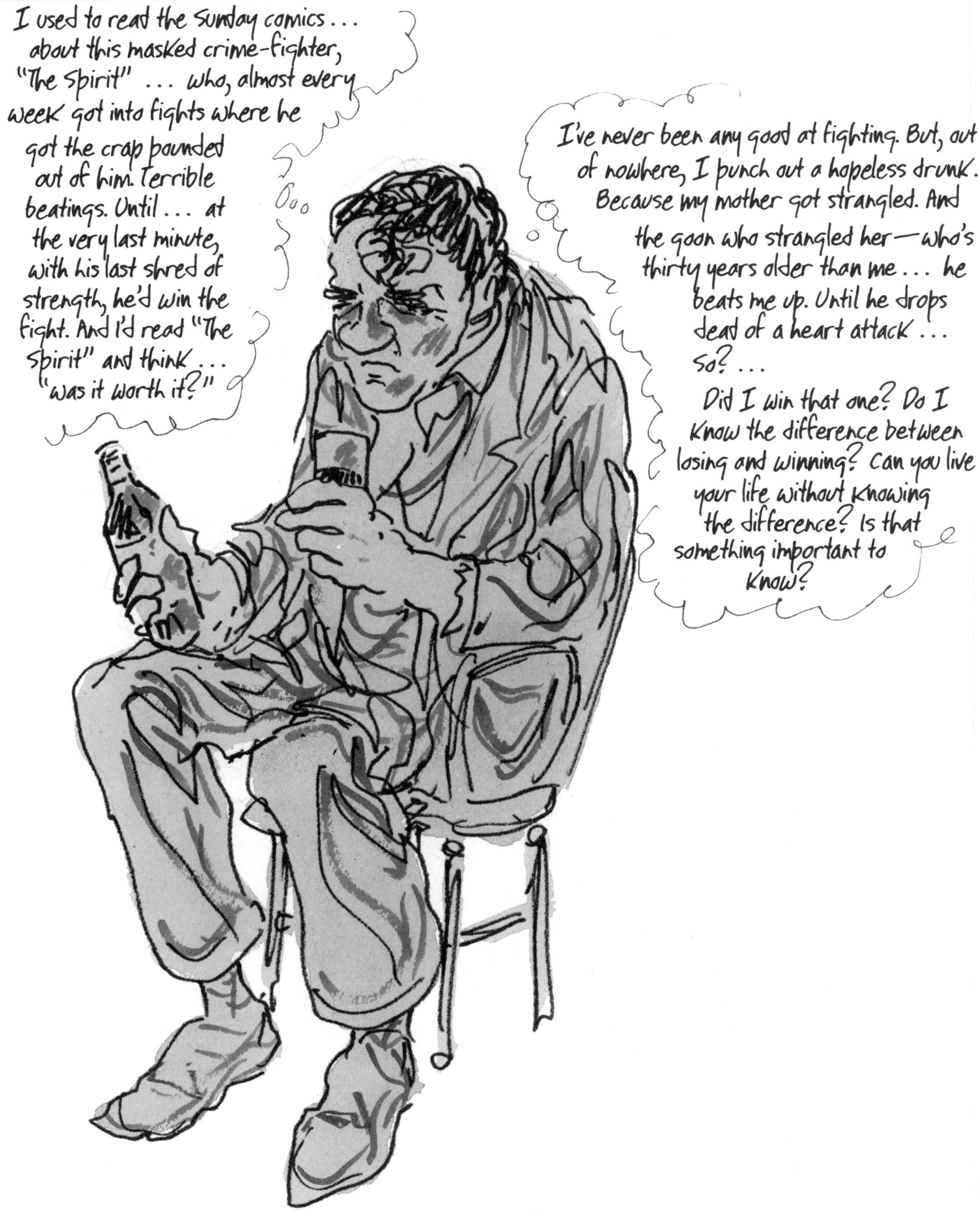
I used to read the Sunday comics . . . about this masked crime-fighter, "The Spirit" . . . who, almost every week got into fights where he got the crap pounded out of him. Terrible beatings. Until . . . at the very last minute, with his last shred of strength, he'd win the fight. And I'd read "The Spirit" and think . . . "was it worth it?"
I've never been any good at fighting. But, out of nowhere, I punch out a hopeless drunk. Because my mother got strangled. And the goon who strangled her—who's thirty years older than me . . . he beats me up. Until he drops dead of a heart attack . . . so? . . .
Did I win that one? Do I know the difference between losing and winning? Can you live your life without knowing the difference? Is that something important to know?

Chapter Fifty-Four: Conspirators

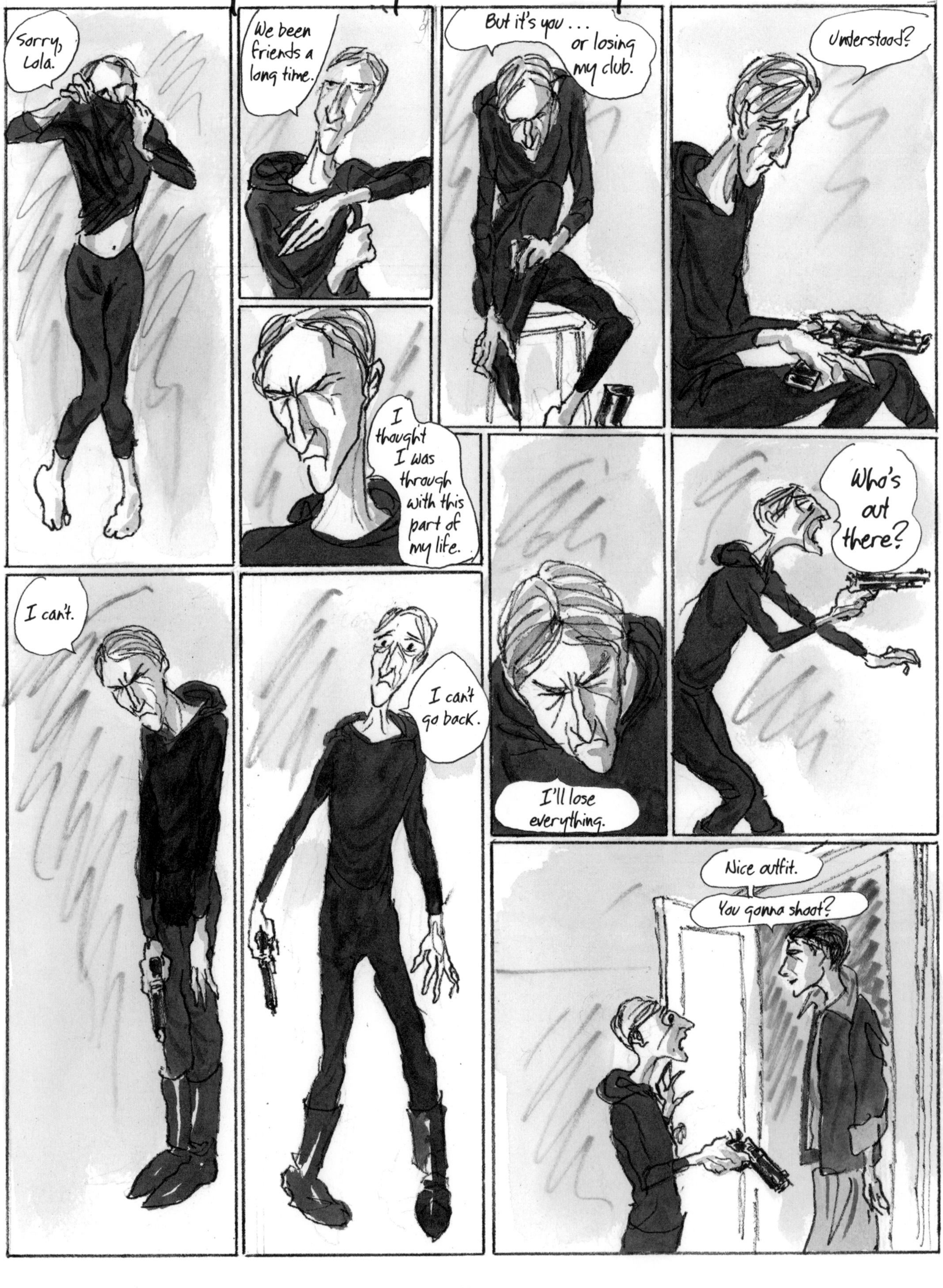
Sorry, Lola.
We been friends a long time.
I thought I was through with this part of my life.
But it's you . . . or losing my club.
Understood?
I can't.
I can't go back.
I'll lose everything.
Who's out there?
Nice outfit.
You gonna shoot?

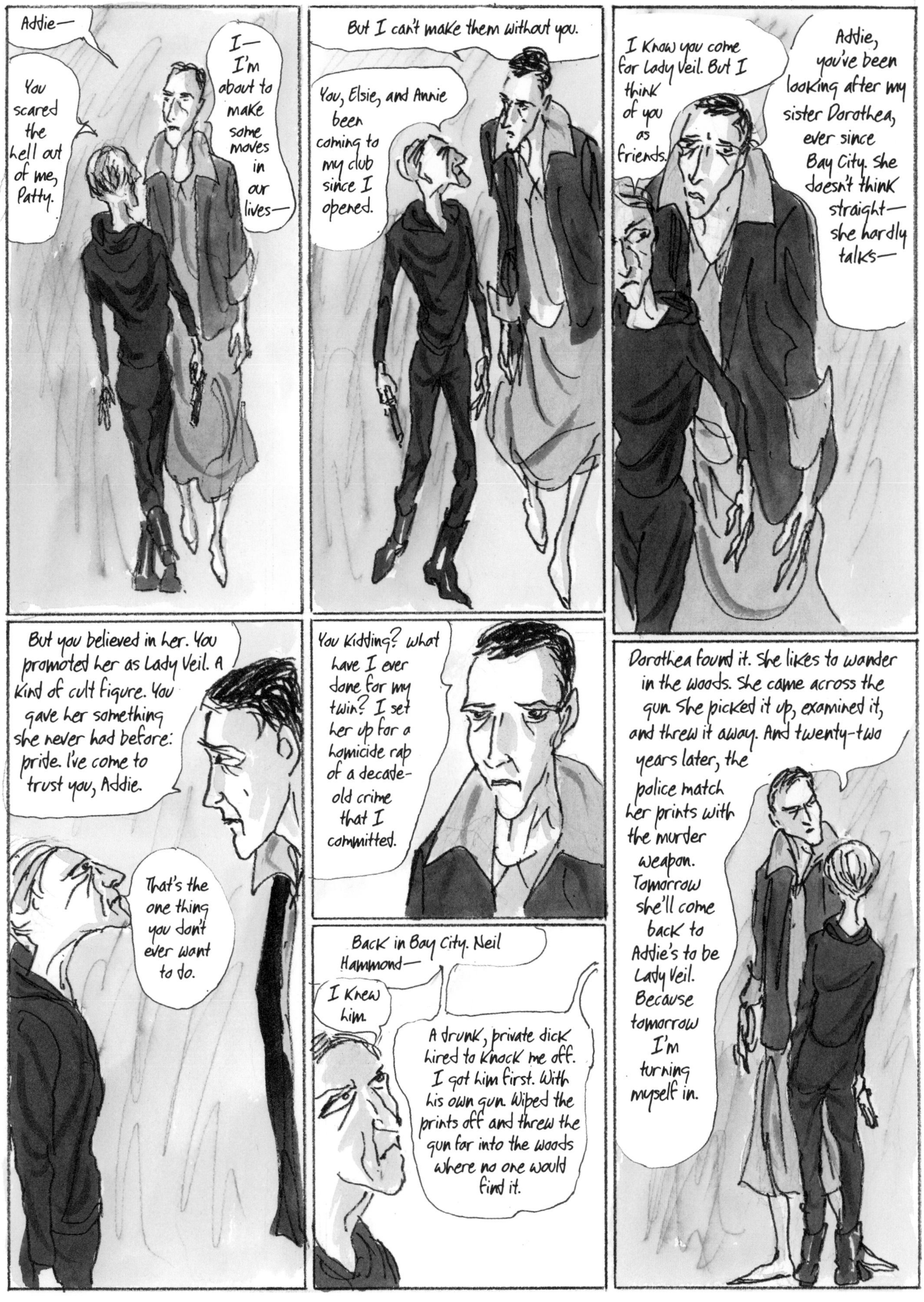

Addie—
I— I'm about to make some moves in our lives—
You scared the hell out of me, Patty.
But I can't make them without you.
You, Elsie, and Annie been coming to my club since I opened.
I know you come for Lady Veil. But I think of you as friends.
Addie, you've been looking after my sister Dorothea, ever since Bay City. She doesn't think straight— she hardly talks—
But you believed in her. You promoted her as Lady Veil. A kind of cult figure. You gave her something she never had before: pride. I've come to trust you, Addie.
That's the one thing you don't ever want to do.
You kidding? what have I ever done for my twin? I set her up for a homicide rap of a decade-old crime that I committed.
Back in Bay City. Neil Hammond—
I knew him.
A drunk, private dick hired to knock me off. I got him first. With his own gun. Wiped the prints off and threw the gun far into the woods where no one would find it.
Dorothea found it. She likes to wander in the woods. She came across the gun. She picked it up, examined it, and threw it away. And twenty-two years later, the police match her prints with the murder weapon. Tomorrow she'll come back to Addie's to be Lady Veil. Because tomorrow I'm turning myself in.

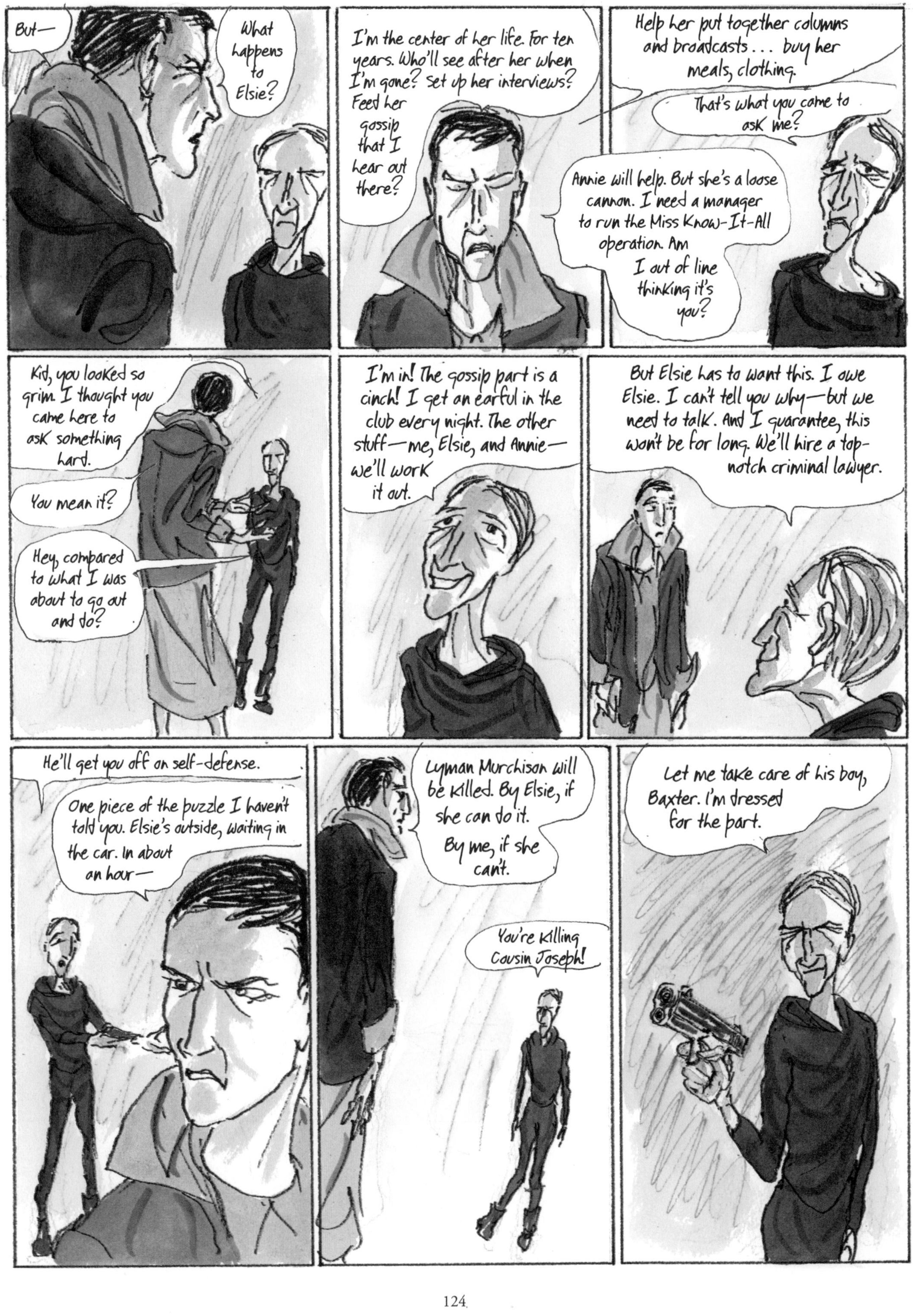
But—
What happens to Elsie?
I'm the center of her life. For ten years. Who'll see after her when I'm gone? Set up her interviews? Feed her gossip that I hear out there?
Help her put together columns and broadcasts . . . buy her meals, clothing.
That's what you came to ask me?
Annie will help. But she's a loose cannon. I need a manager to run the Miss Know-It-All operation. Am I out of line thinking it's you?
Kid, you looked so grim. I thought you came here to ask something hard.
You mean it?
Hey, compared to what I was about to go out and do?
I'm in! The gossip part is a cinch! I get an earful in the club every night. The other stuff—me, Elsie, and Annie—we'll work it out.
But Elsie has to want this. I owe Elsie. I can't tell you why—but we need to talk. And I guarantee, this won't be for long. We'll hire a top-notch criminal lawyer.
He'll get you off on self-defense.
One piece of the puzzle I haven't told you. Elsie's outside, waiting in the car. In about an hour—
Lyman Murchison will be killed. By Elsie, if she can do it.
By me, if she can't.
You're killing Cousin Joseph!
Let me take care of his boy, Baxter. I'm dressed for the part.

Chapter Fifty-Five: Naming Names

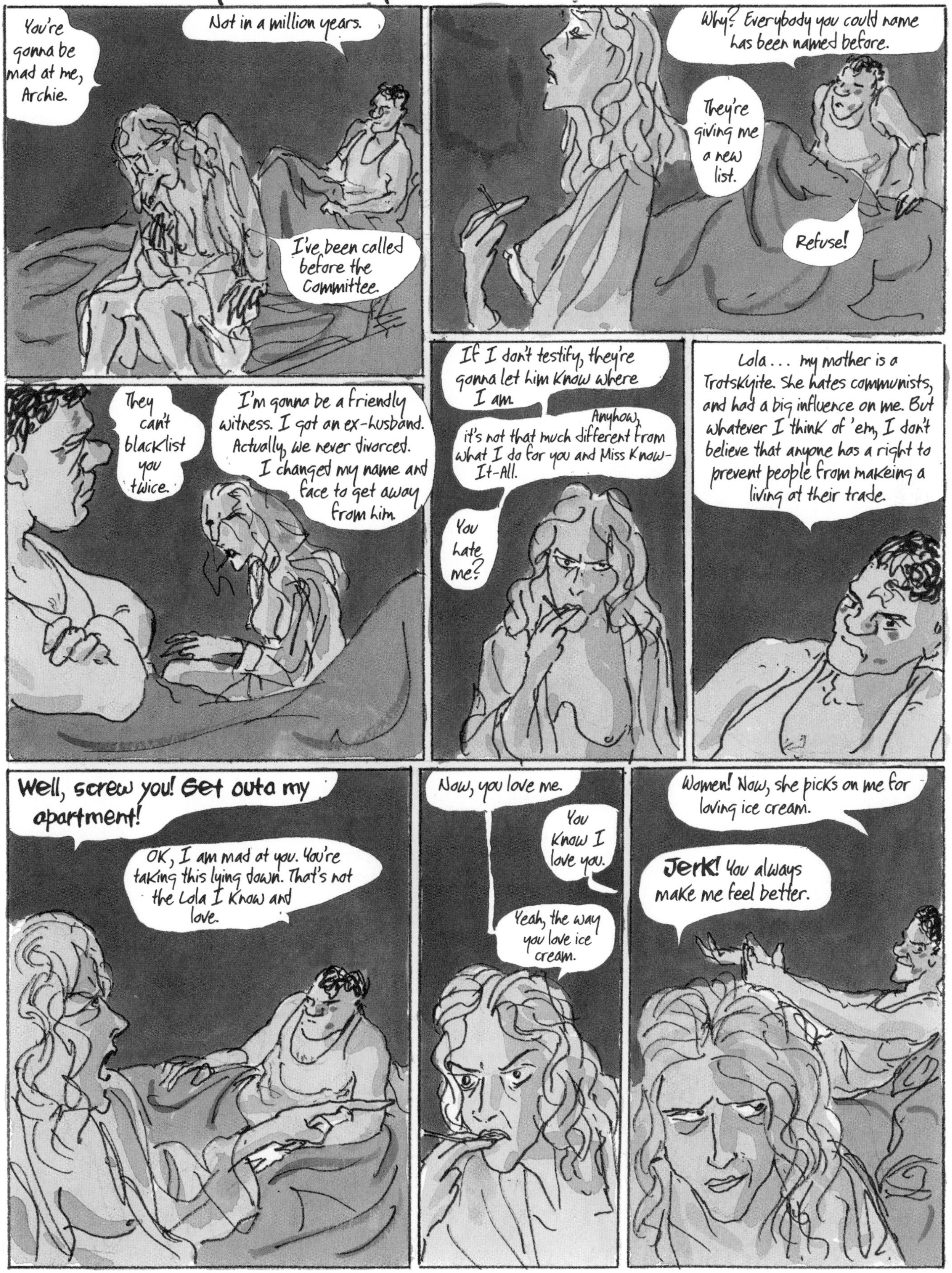
You're gonna be mad at me, Archie.
Not in a million years.
I've been called before the Committee.
Why? Everybody you could name has been named before.
They're giving me a new list.
Refuse!
They can't blacklist you twice.
I'm gonna be a friendly witness. I got an ex-husband. Actually, we never divorced. I changed my name and face to get away from him.
If I don't testify, they're gonna let him know where I am.
Anyhow, it's not that much different from what I do for you and Miss Know-It-All.
You hate me?
Lola... my mother is a Trotskyite. She hates communists, and had a big influence on me. But whatever I think of 'em, I don't believe that anyone has a right to prevent people from makeing a living at their trade.
Well, screw you! Get outa my apartment!
OK, I am mad at you. You're taking this lying down. That's not the Lola I know and love.
Now, you love me.
You know I love you.
Yeah, the way you love ice cream.
Women! Now, she picks on me for loving ice cream.
Jerk! You always make me feel better.

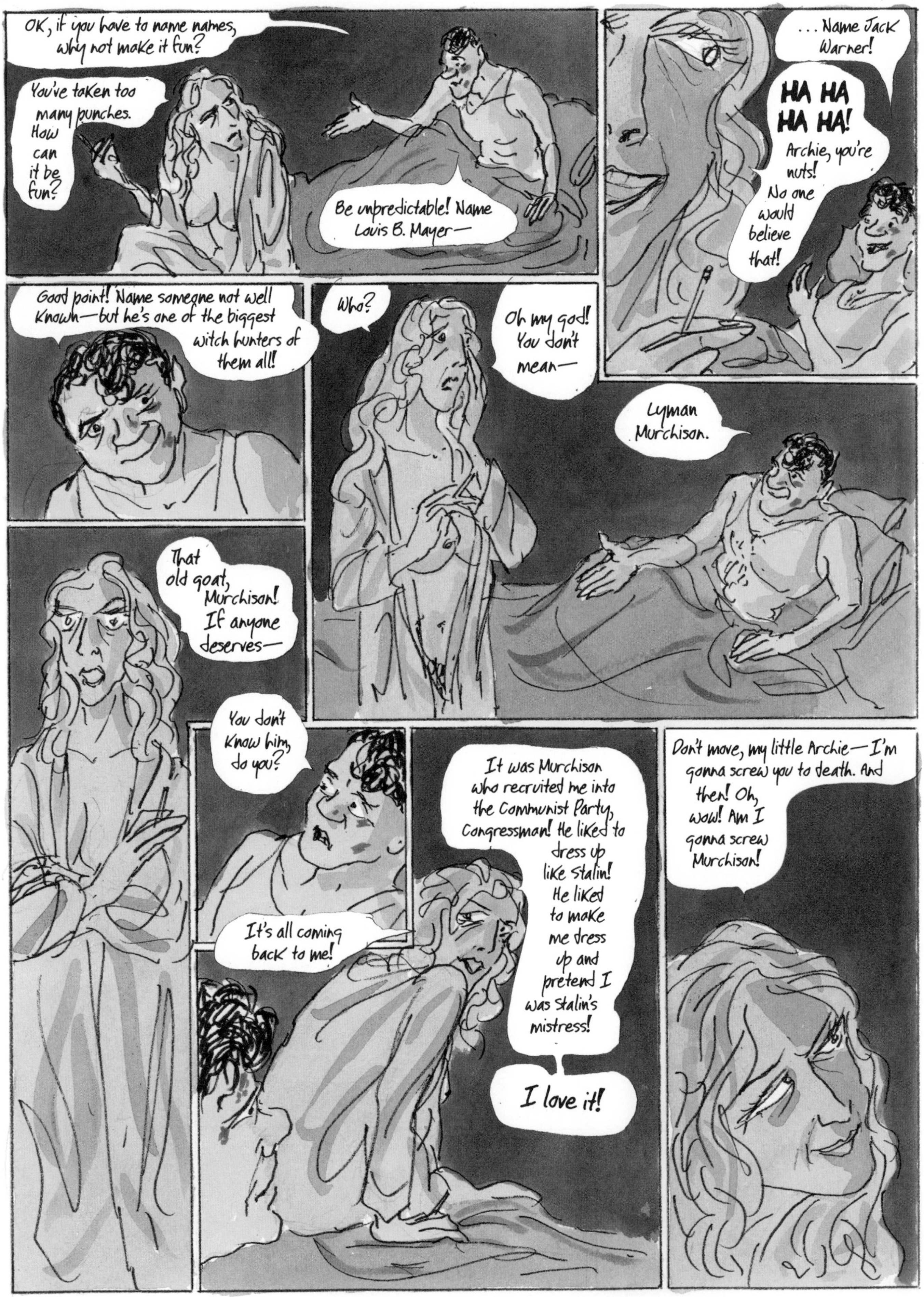
OK, if you have to name names, why not make it fun?
You've taken too many punches. How can it be fun?
Be unpredictable! Name Louis B. Mayer—
. . . Name Jack Warner!
HA HA HA HA!
Archie, you're nuts! No one would believe that!
Good point! Name someone not well known—but he's one of the biggest witch hunters of them all!
Who?
Oh my god! You don't mean—
Lyman Murchison.
That old goat, Murchison! If anyone deserves—
You don't know him, do you?
It's all coming back to me!
It was Murchison who recruited me into the Communist Party, Congressman! He liked to dress up like Stalin! He liked to make me dress up and pretend I was Stalin's mistress!
I love it!
Don't move, my little Archie—I'm gonna screw you to death. And then! Oh, wow! Am I gonna screw Murchison!

Chapter Fifty-Six: Good Riddance

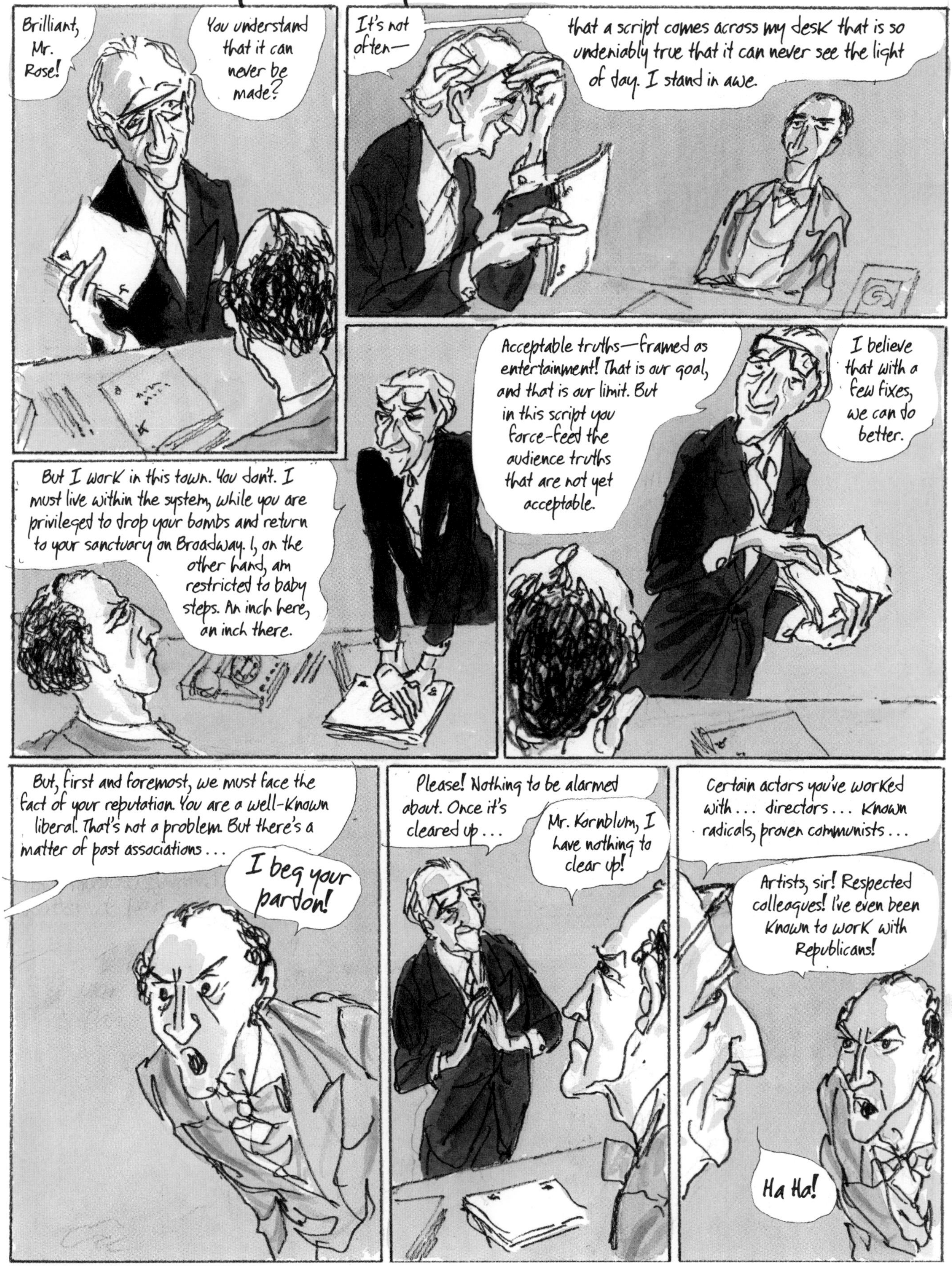

Brilliant, Mr. Rose!
You understand that it can never be made?
It's not often—
that a script comes across my desk that is so undeniably true that it can never see the light of day. I stand in awe.
Acceptable truths—framed as entertainment! That is our goal, and that is our limit. But in this script you force-feed the audience truths that are not yet acceptable.
I believe that with a few fixes, we can do better.
But I work in this town. You don't. I must live within the system, while you are privileged to drop your bombs and return to your sanctuary on Broadway. I, on the other hand, am restricted to baby steps. An inch here, an inch there.
But, first and foremost, we must face the fact of your reputation. You are a well-known liberal. That's not a problem. But there's a matter of past associations . . .
I beg your pardon!
Please! Nothing to be alarmed about. Once it's cleared up . . .
Mr. Kornblum, I have nothing to clear up!
Certain actors you've worked with . . . directors . . . known radicals, proven communists . . .
Artists, sir! Respected colleagues! I've even been known to work with Republicans!
Ha Ha!

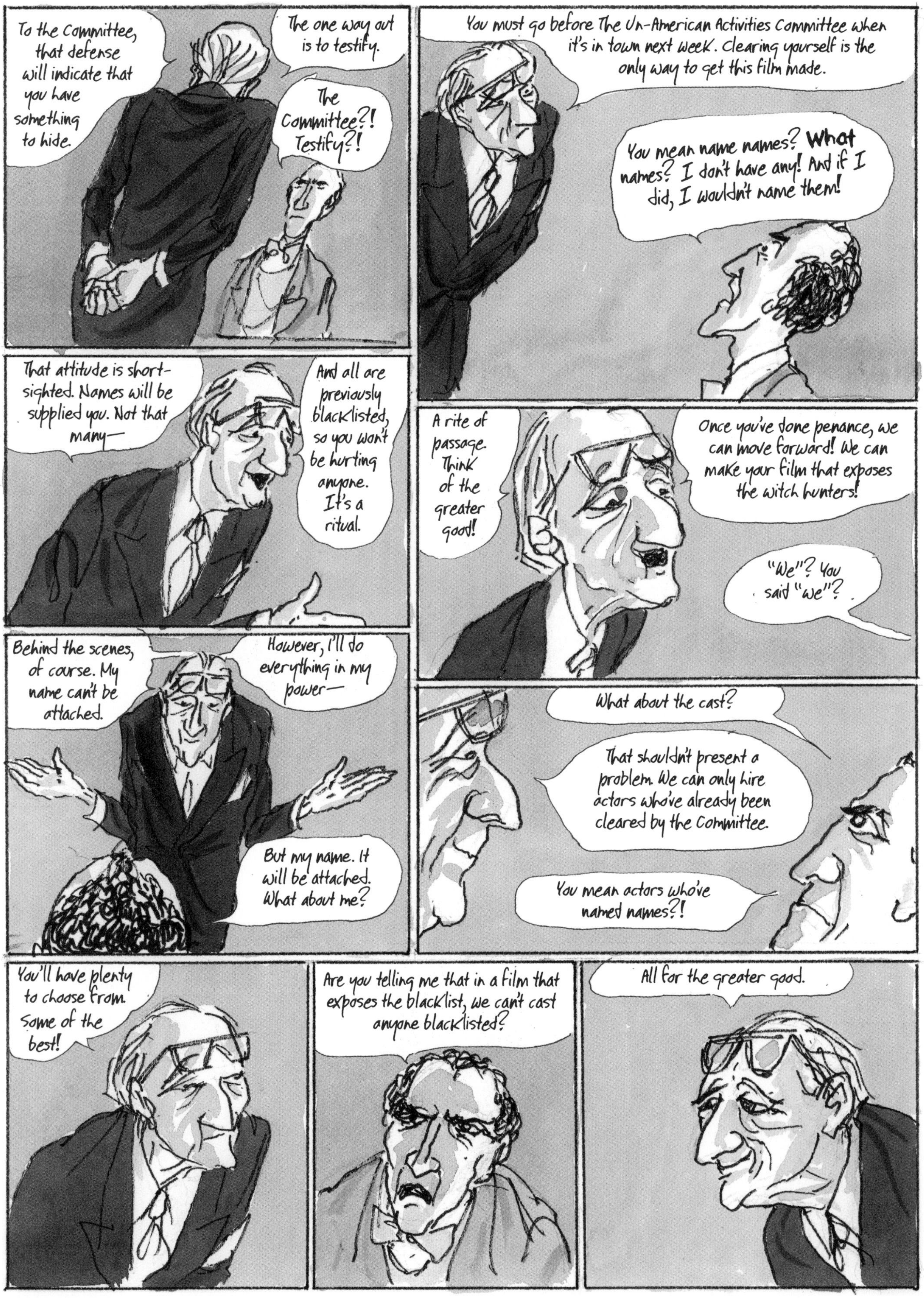
To the Committee, that defense will indicate that you have something to hide.
The one way out is to testify.
The Committee?! Testify?!
You must go before The Un-American Activities Committee when it's in town next week. Clearing yourself is the only way to get this film made.
You mean name names? What names? I don't have any! And if I did, I wouldn't name them!
That attitude is short-sighted. Names will be supplied you. Not that many—
And all are previously blacklisted, so you won't be hurting anyone. It's a ritual.
A rite of passage. Think of the greater good!
Once you've done penance, we can move forward! We can make your film that exposes the witch hunters!
"We"? You said "we"?
Behind the scenes, of course. My name can't be attached.
However, I'll do everything in my power—
But my name. It will be attached. What about me?
What about the cast?
That shouldn't present a problem. We can only hire actors who've already been cleared by the Committee.
You mean actors who've named names?!
You'll have plenty to choose from. Some of the best!
Are you telling me that in a film that exposes the blacklist, we can't cast anyone blacklisted?
All for the greater good.

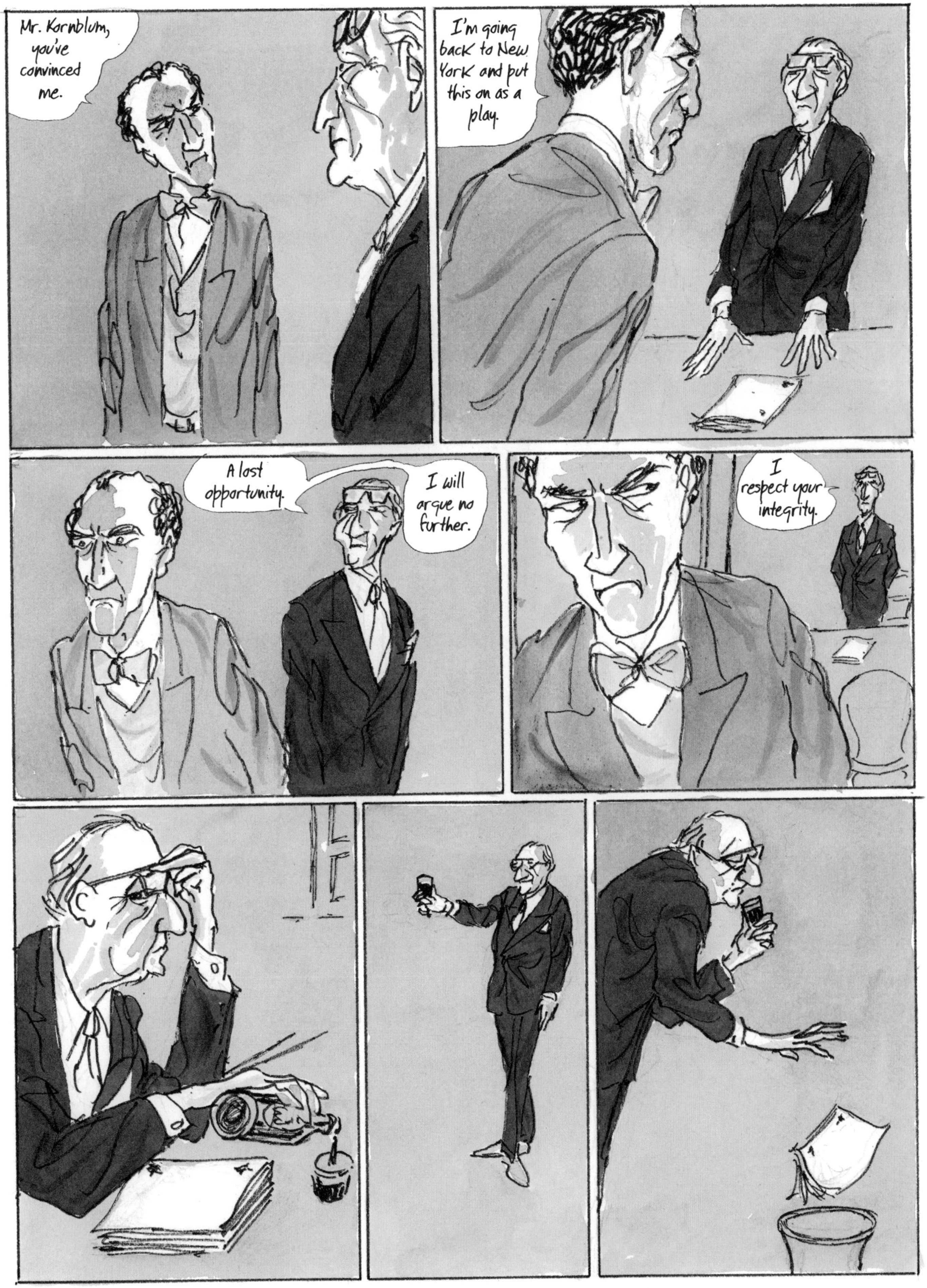
Mr. Kornblum, you've convinced me.
I'm going back to New York and put this on as a play.
A lost opportunity.
I will argue no further.
I respect your integrity.

Chapter Fifty-Seven: For Sam

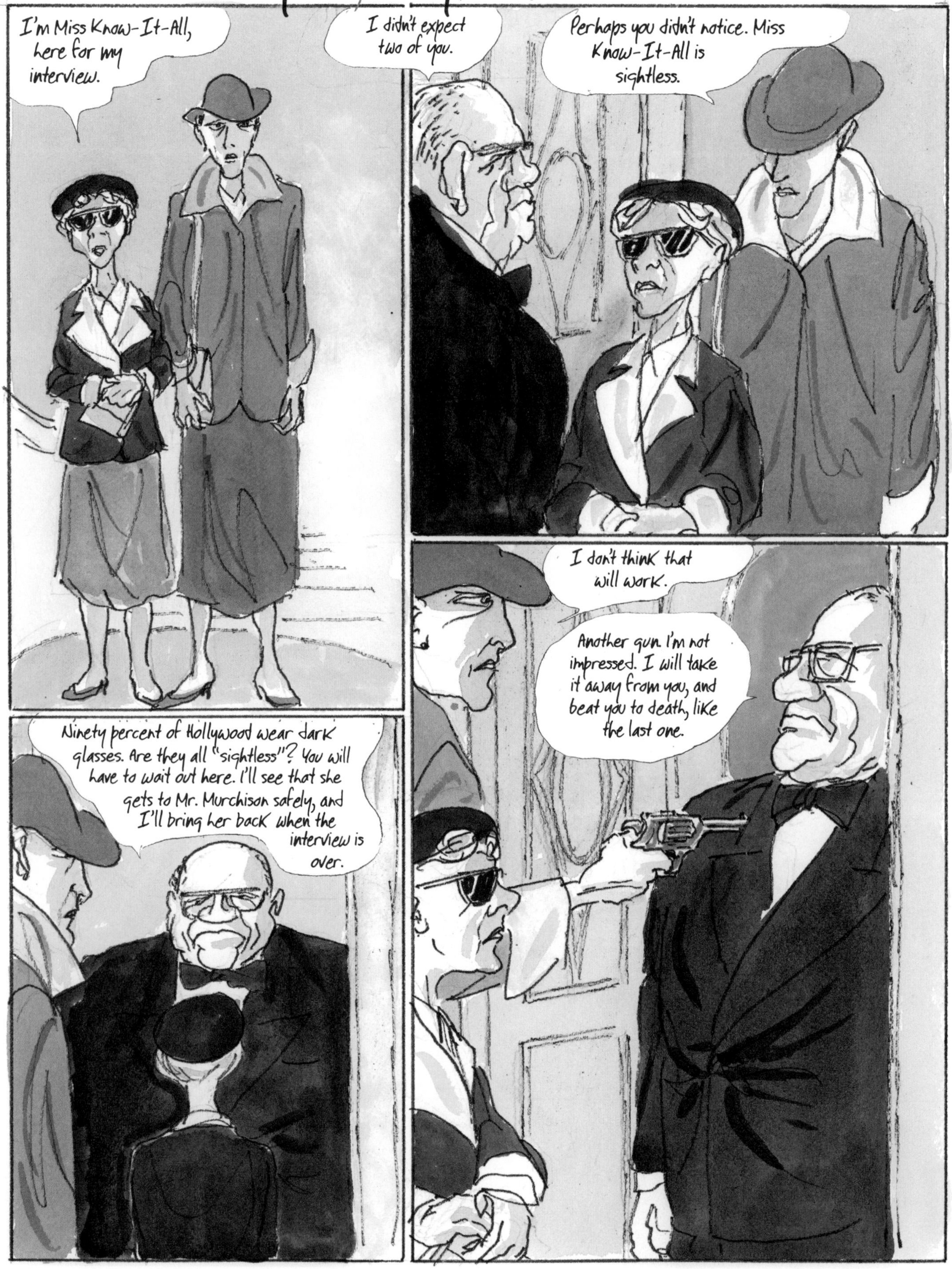
I'm Miss Know-It-All, here for my interview.
I didn't expect two of you.
Perhaps you didn't notice. Miss Know-It-All is sightless.
Ninety percent of Hollywood wear dark glasses. Are they all "sightless"? You will have to wait out here. I'll see that she gets to Mr. Murchison safely, and I'll bring her back when the interview is over.
I don't think that will work.
Another gun I'm not impressed. I will take it away from you, and beat you to death, like the last one.

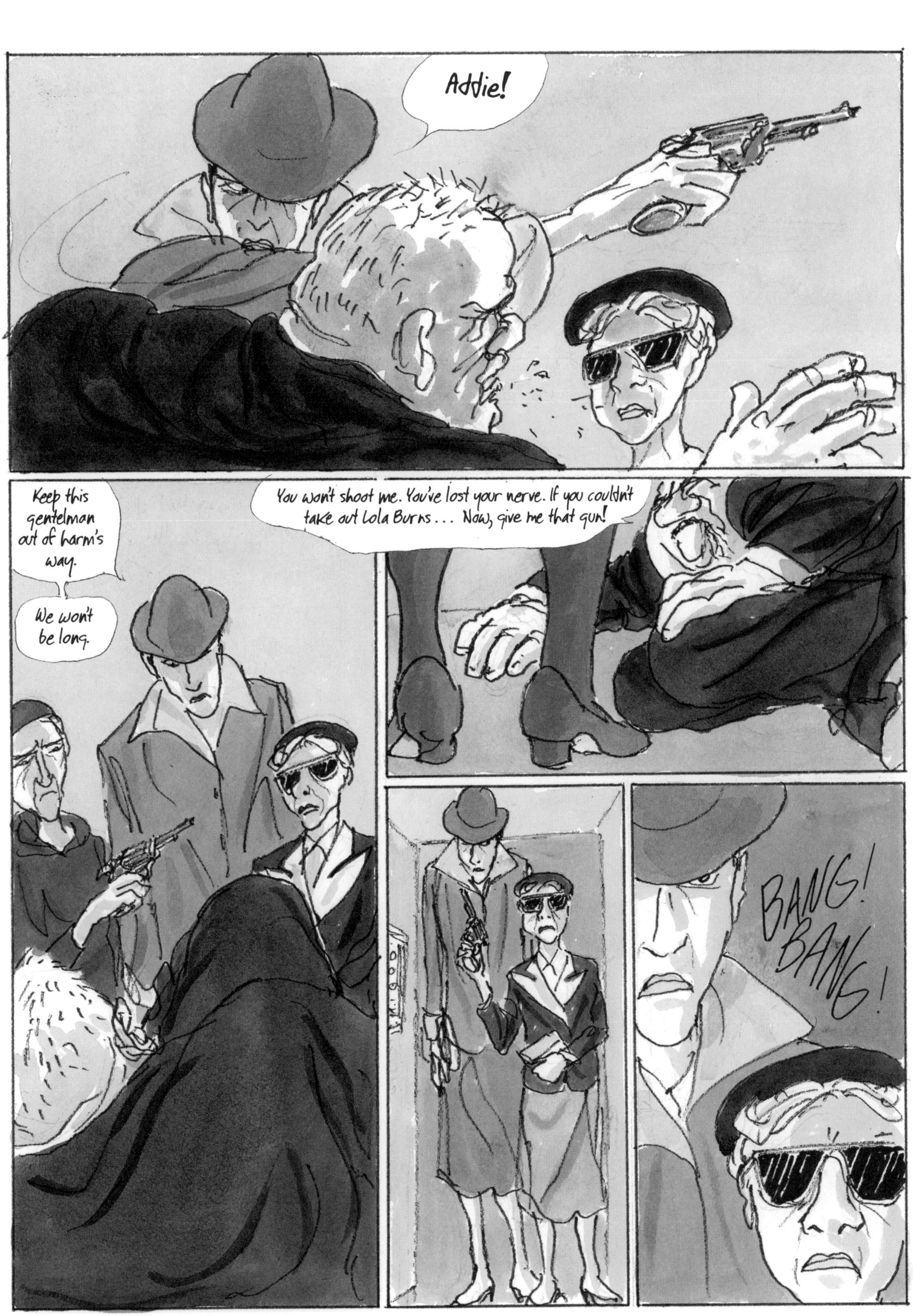
Addie!
Keep this gentelman out of harm's way.
We won't be long.
You won't shoot me. You've lost your nerve. If you couldn't take out Lola Burns . . . Now, give me that gun!
BANG! BANG!

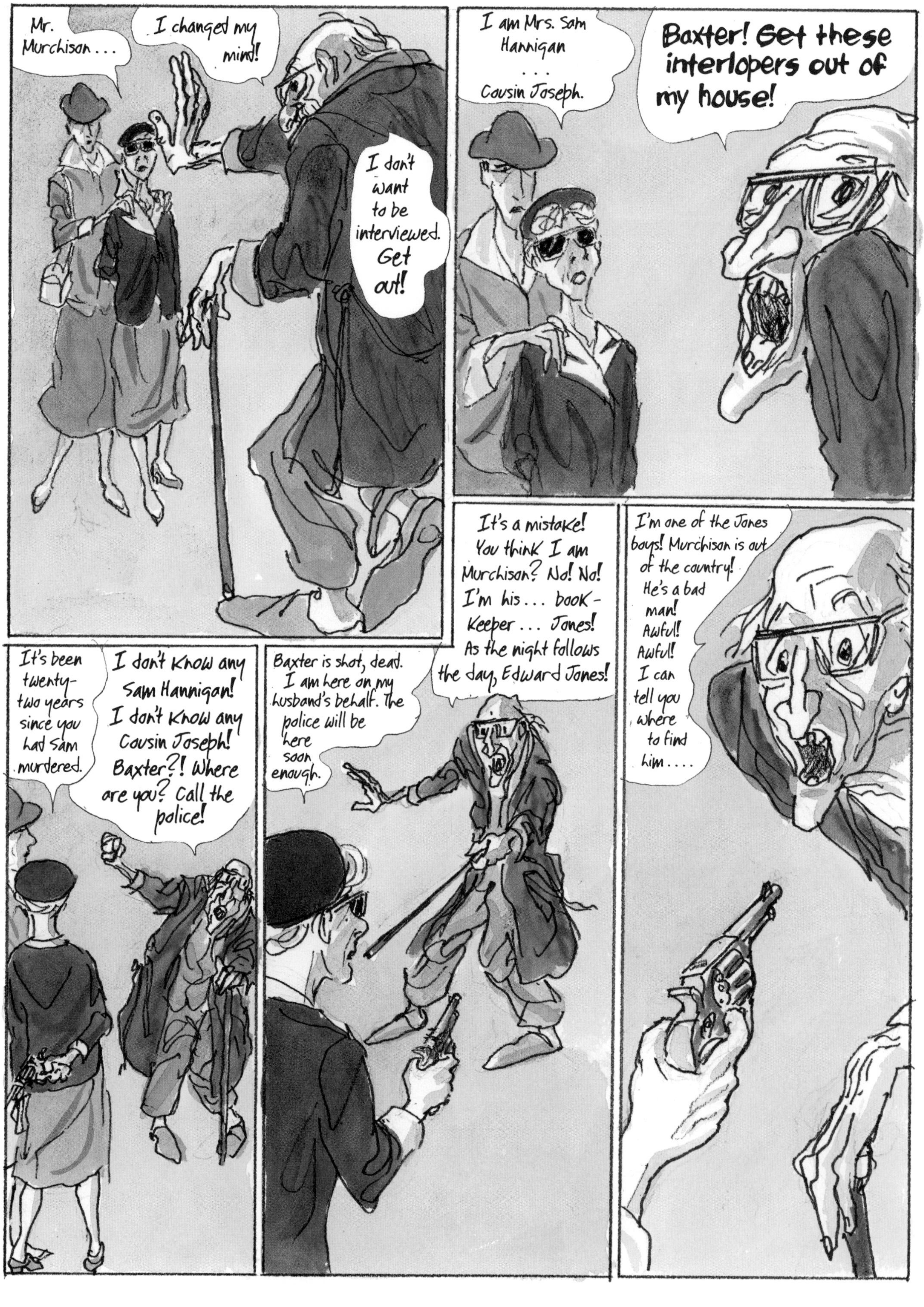
Mr. Murchison . . .
I changed my mind!
I don't want to be interviewed. Get out!
I am Mrs. Sam Hannigan . . . Cousin Joseph.
Baxter! Get these interlopers out of my house!
It's a mistake! You think I am Murchison? No! No! I'm his . . . book-keeper . . . Jones!
As the night follows the day, Edward Jones!
I'm one of the Jones boys! Murchison is out of the country! He's a bad man! Awful! Awful! I can tell you where to find him . . . .
It's been twenty-two years since you had Sam murdered.
I don't know any Sam Hannigan! I don't know any Cousin Joseph! Baxter?! Where are you? Call the police!
Baxter is shot, dead. I am here on my husband's behalf. The police will be here soon enough.

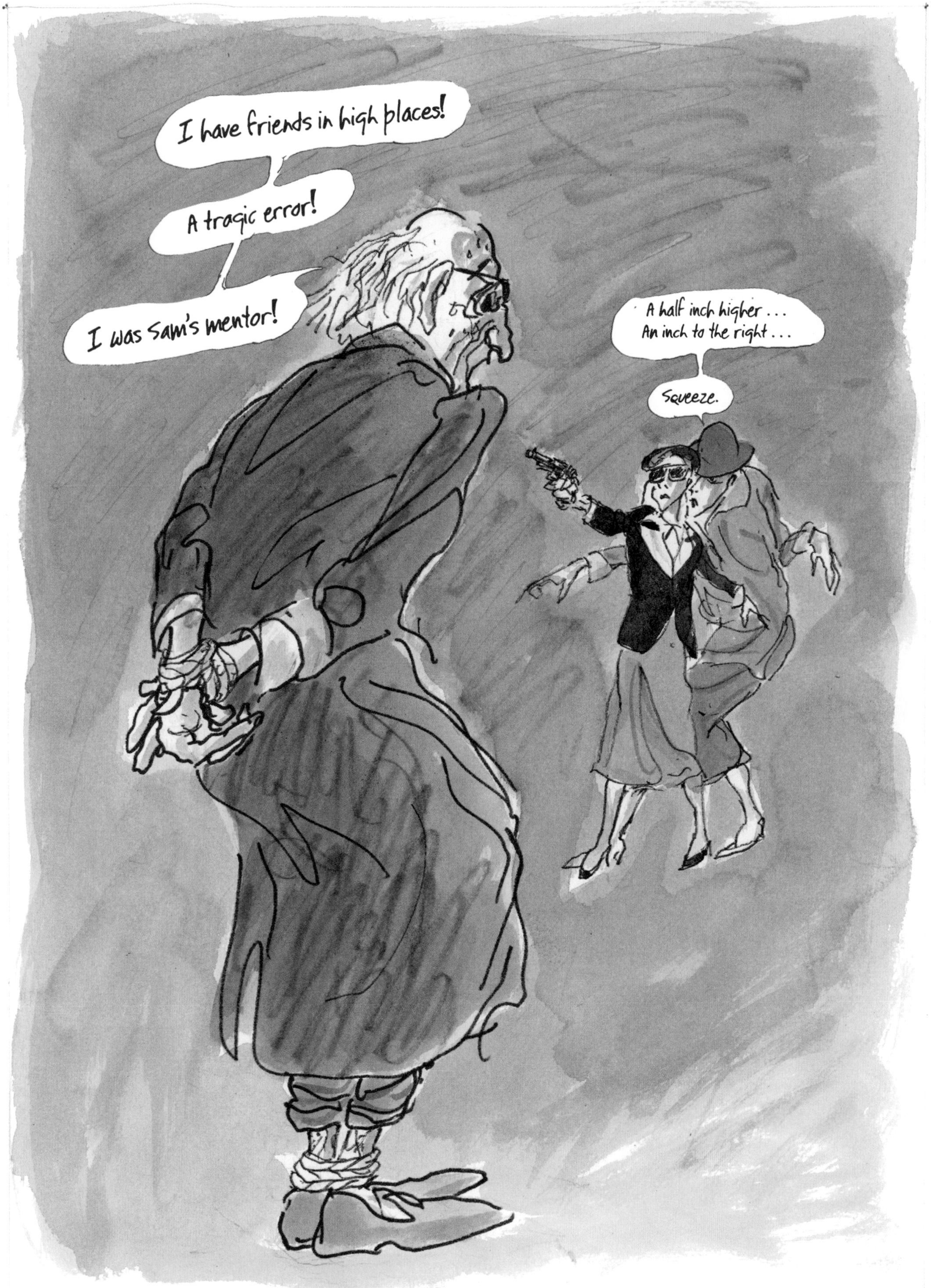
I have friends in high places!
A tragic error!
I was Sam's mentor!
A half inch higher . . .
An inch to the right . . .
Squeeze.

Chapter Fifty-Eight: The Cover-Up

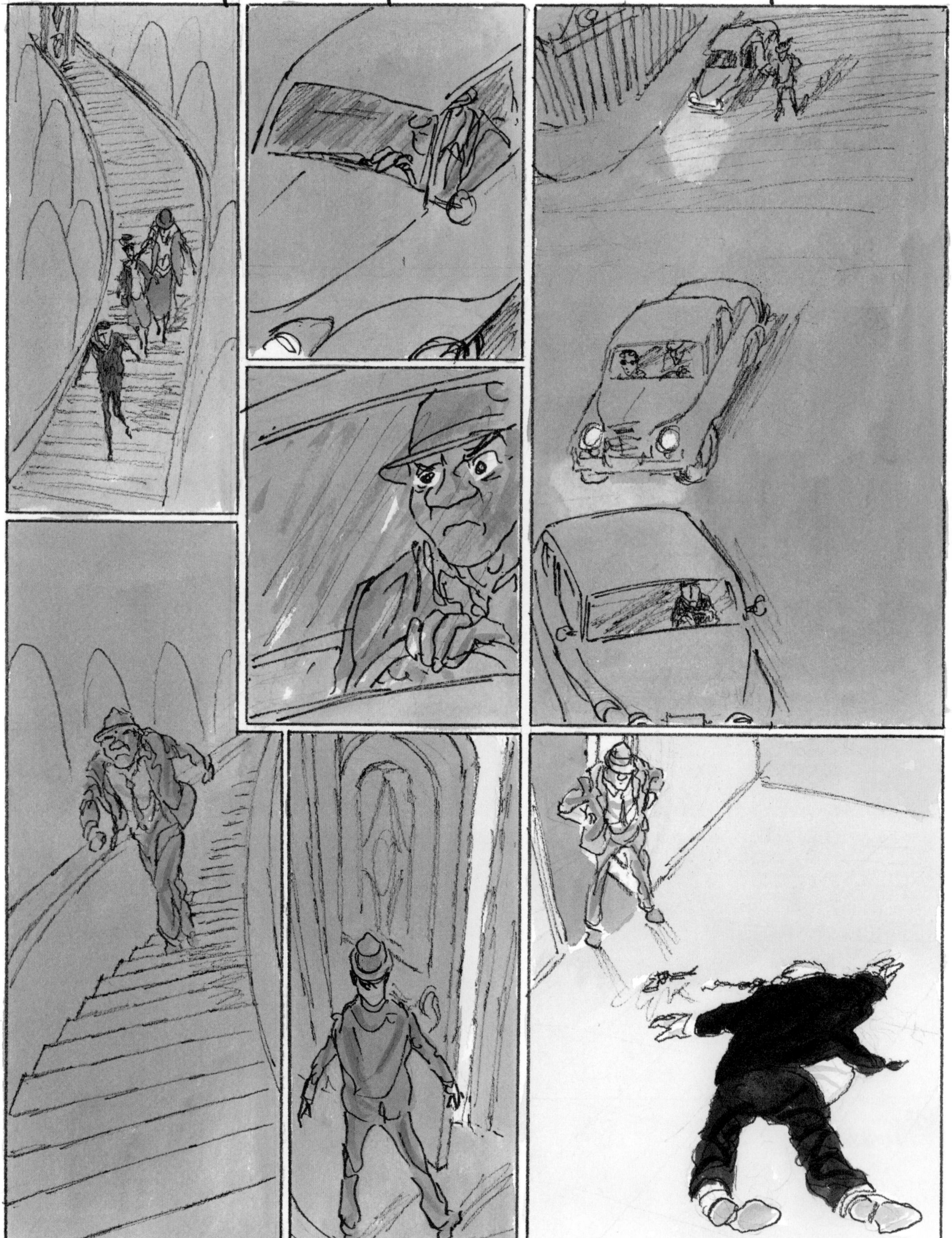

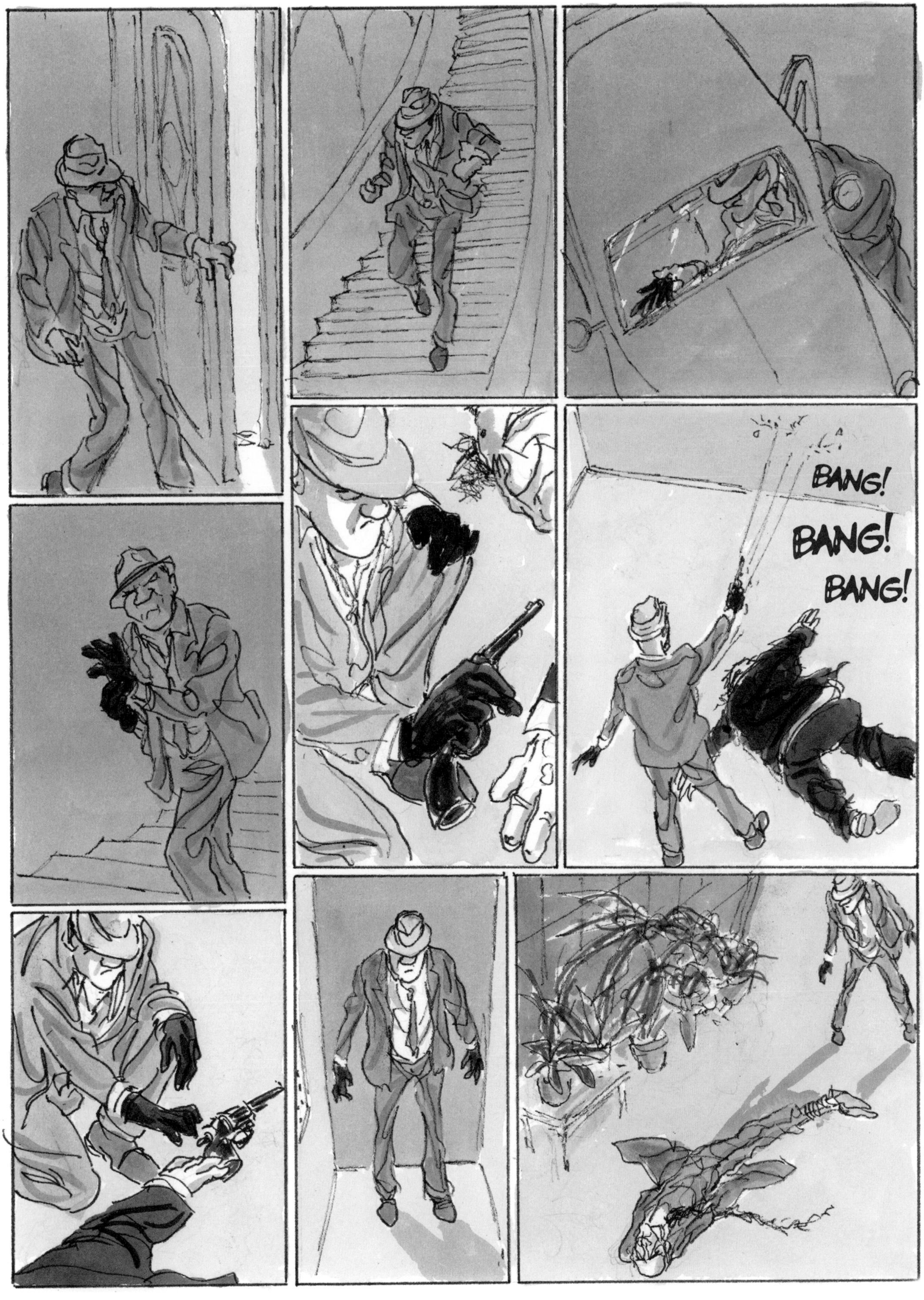
BANG!
BANG!
BANG!

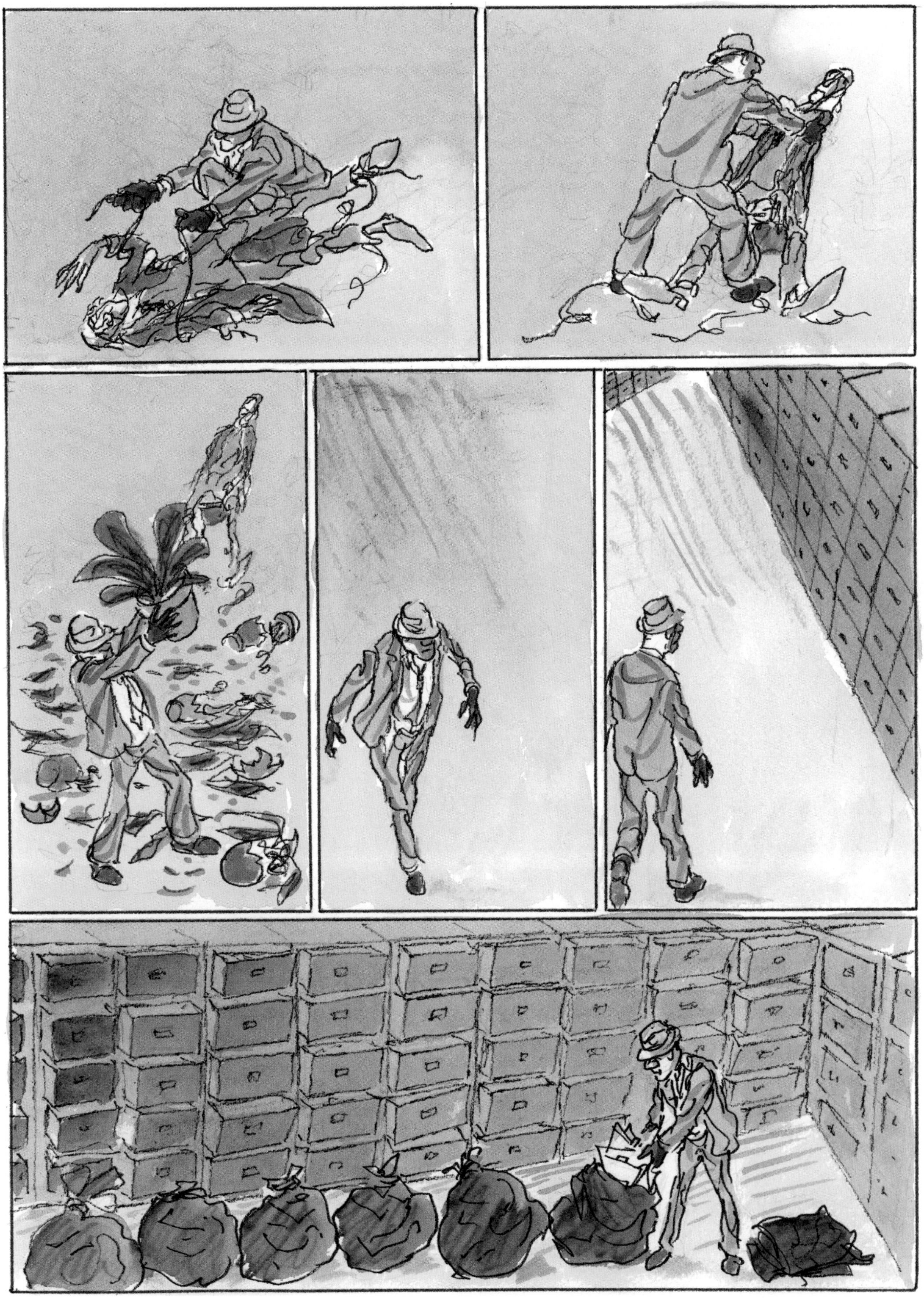

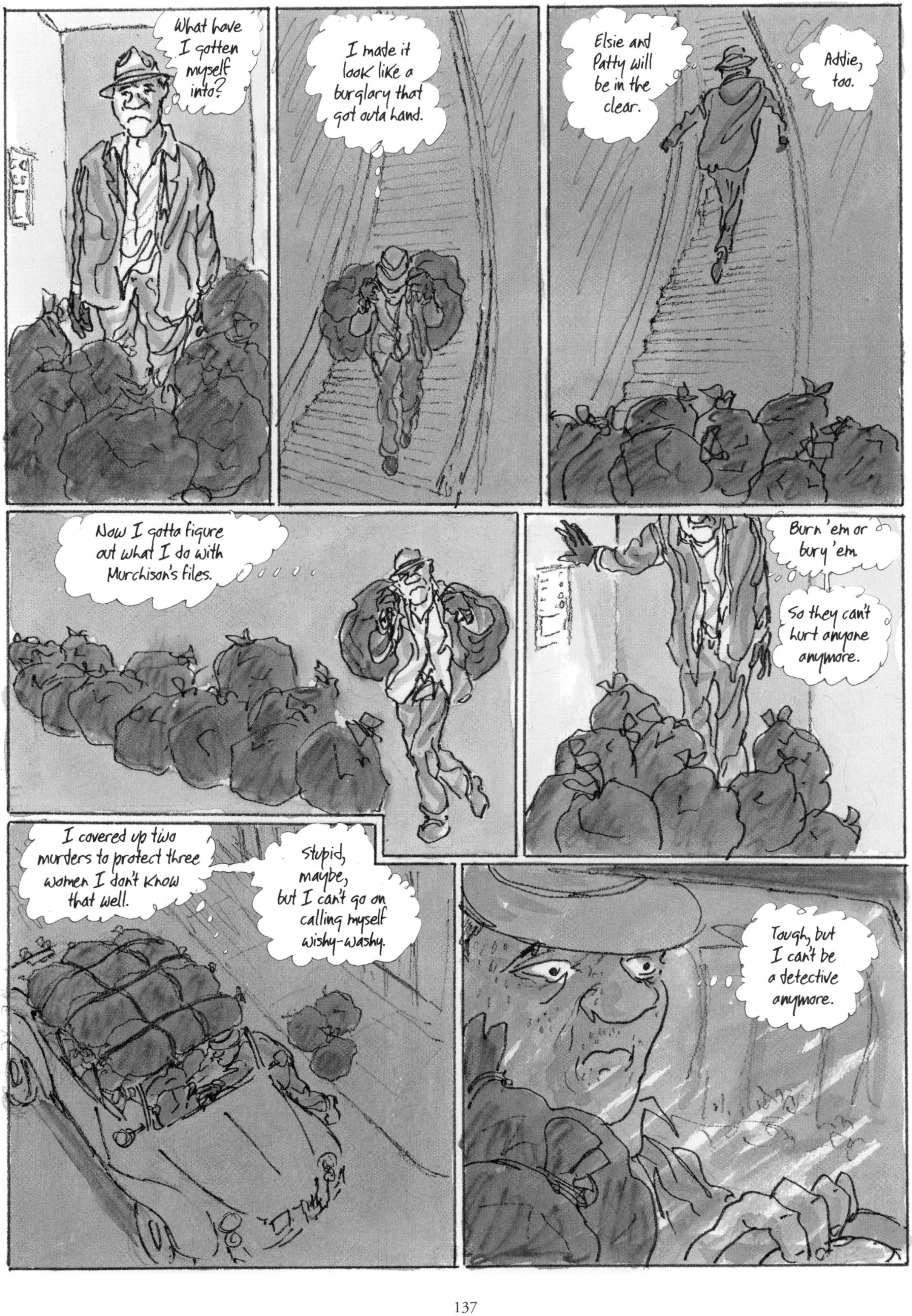
What have I gotten myself into?
I made it look like a burglary that got outa hand.
Elsie and Patty will be in the clear.
Addie, too.
Now I gotta figure out what I do with Murchison's files.
Burn 'em or bury 'em.
So they can't hurt anyone anymore.
I covered up two murders to protect three women I don't know that well.
Stupid, maybe, but I can't go on calling myself wishy-washy.
Tough, but I can't be a detective anymore.

Chapter Fifty-Nine: In Session

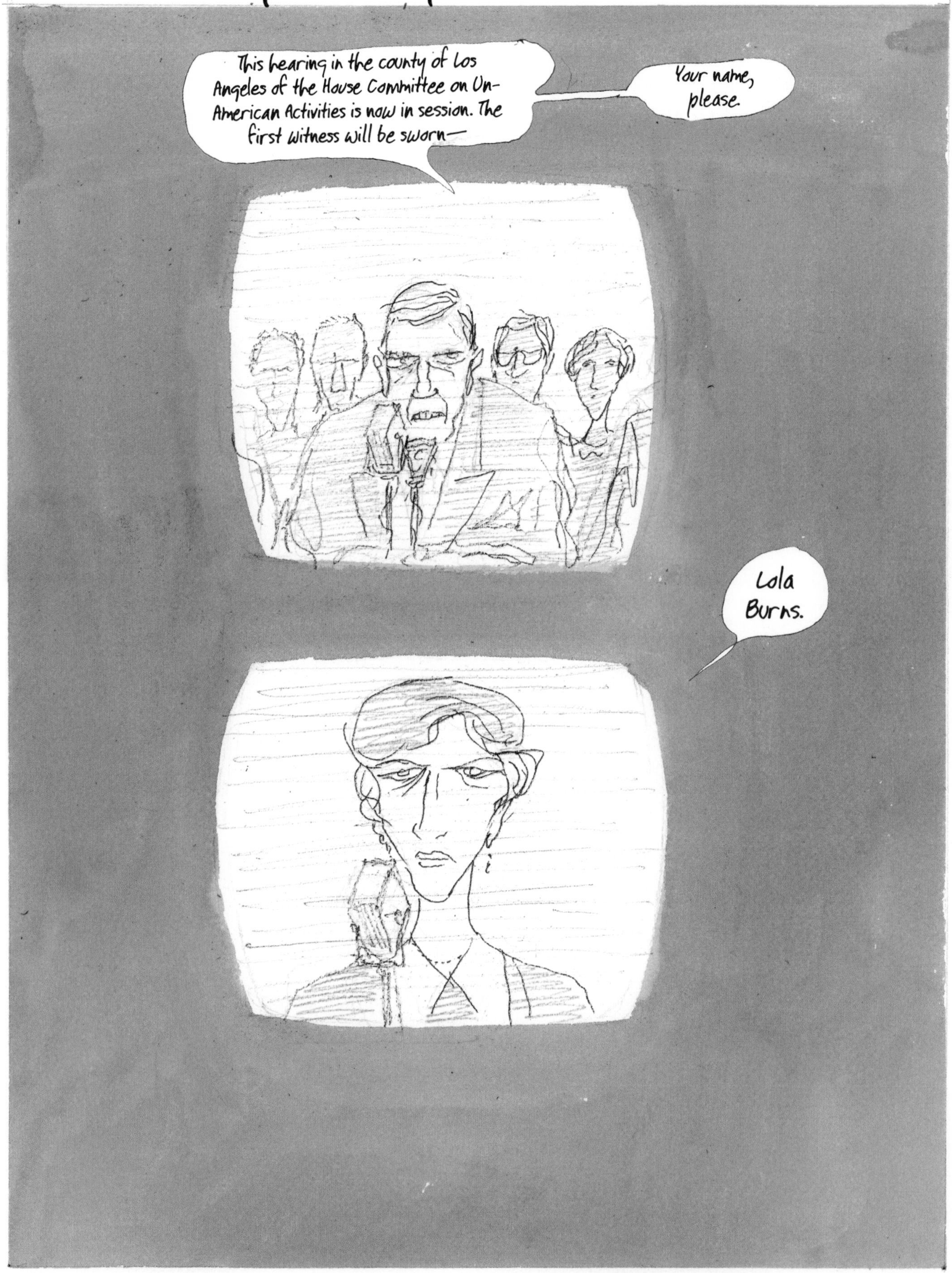
This hearing in the county of Los Angeles of the House Committee on Un-American Activities is now in session. The first witness will be sworn—
Your name, please.
Lola Burns.

Chapter Sixty: Swan Song

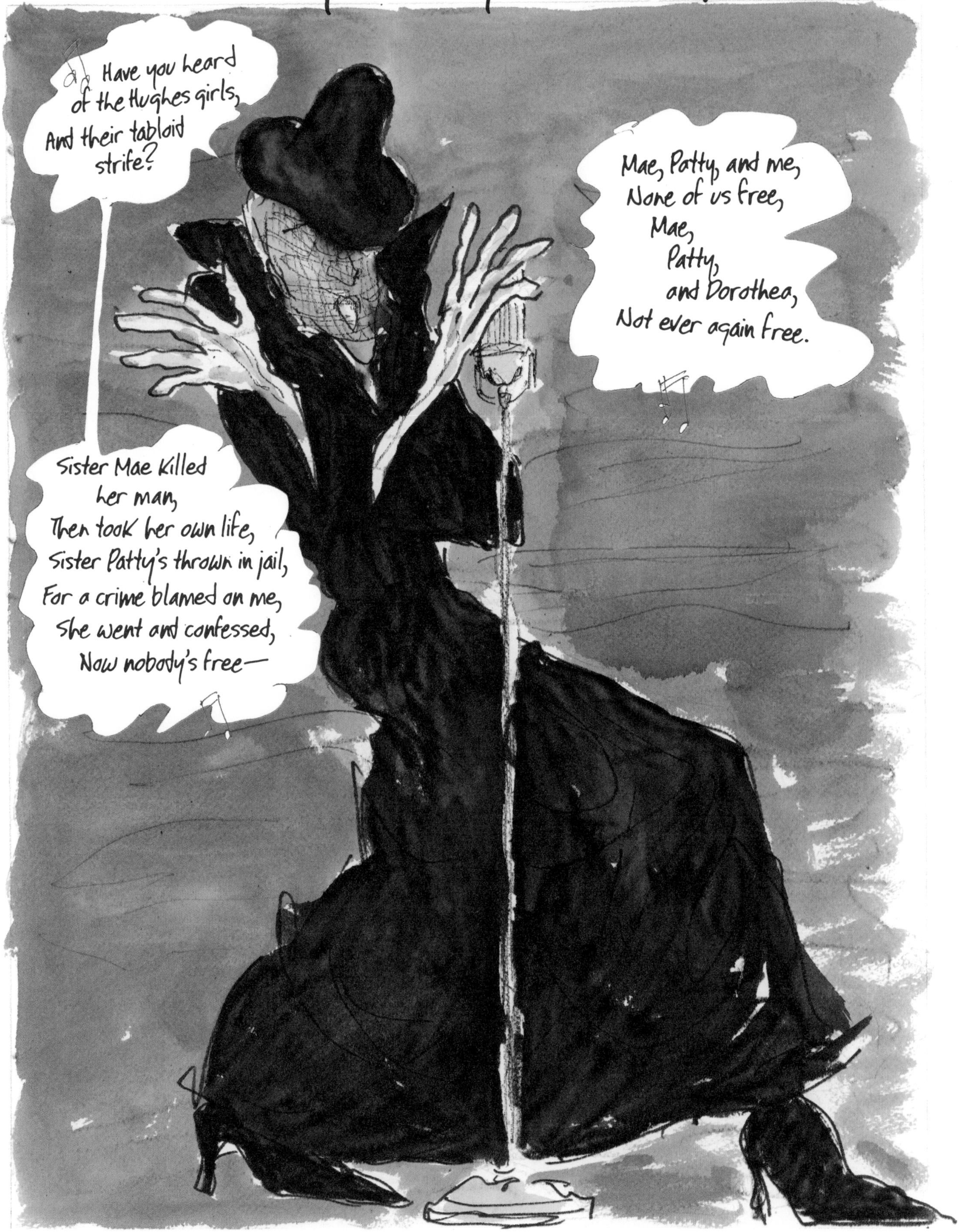

Chapter Sixty-One: The Big Broadcast of 1953

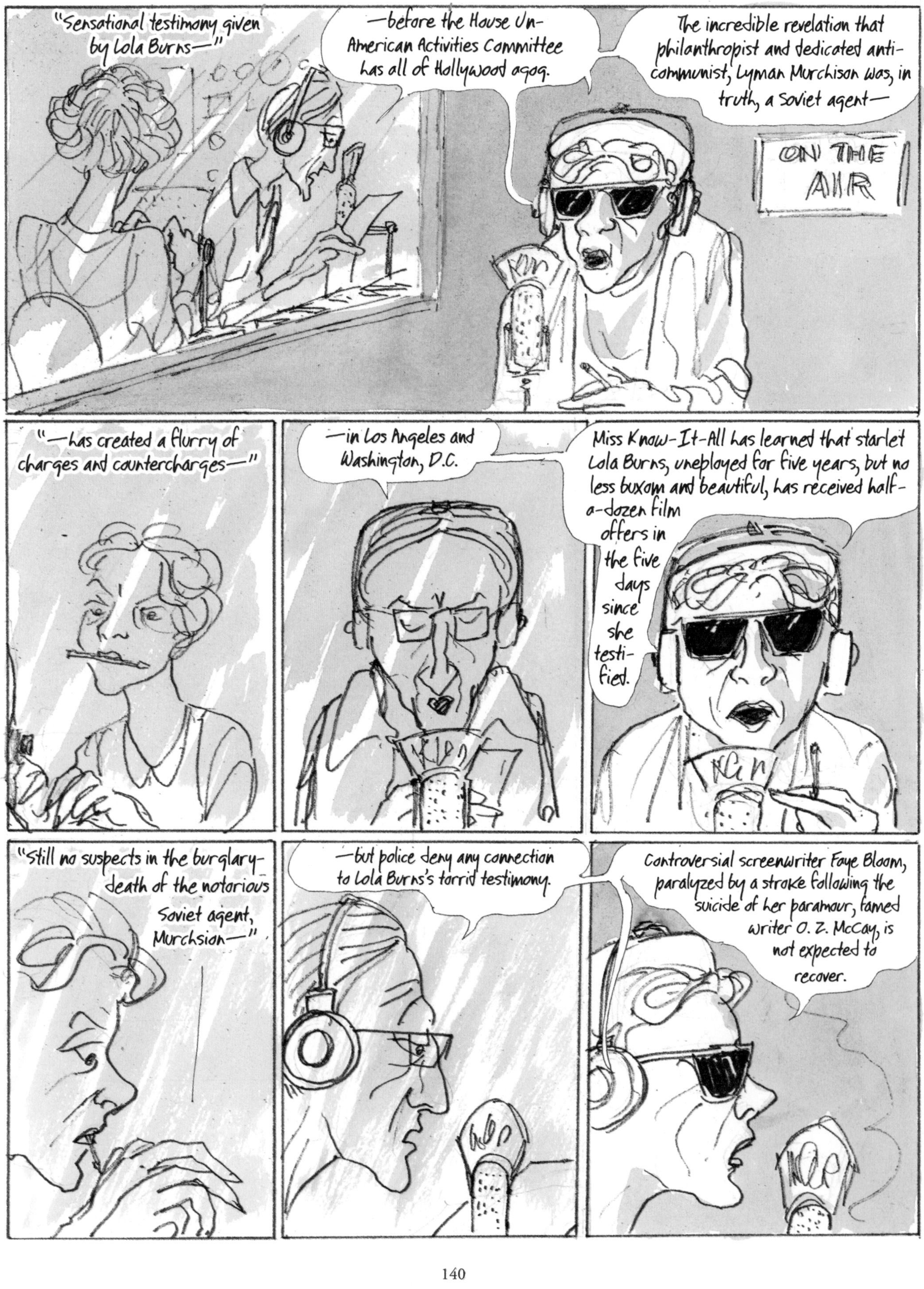
"Sensational testimony given by Lola Burns—"
—before the House Un-American Activities Committee has all of Hollywood agog.
The incredible revelation that philanthropist and dedicated anti-communist, Lyman Murchison was, in truth, a Soviet agent—
ON THE AIR
"—has created a flurry of charges and countercharges—"
—in Los Angeles and Washington, D.C.
Miss Know-It-All has learned that starlet Lola Burns, unebloyed for five years, but no less buxom and beautiful, has received half-a-dozen film offers in the five days since she testi-fied.
"Still no suspects in the burglary-death of the notorious Soviet agent, Murchsion—"
—but police deny any connection to Lola Burns's torrid testimony.
Controversial screenwriter Faye Bloom, paralyzed by a stroke following the suicide of her paramour, famed writer O. Z. McCay, is not expected to recover.

Chapter Sixty-Two: Summing Upward

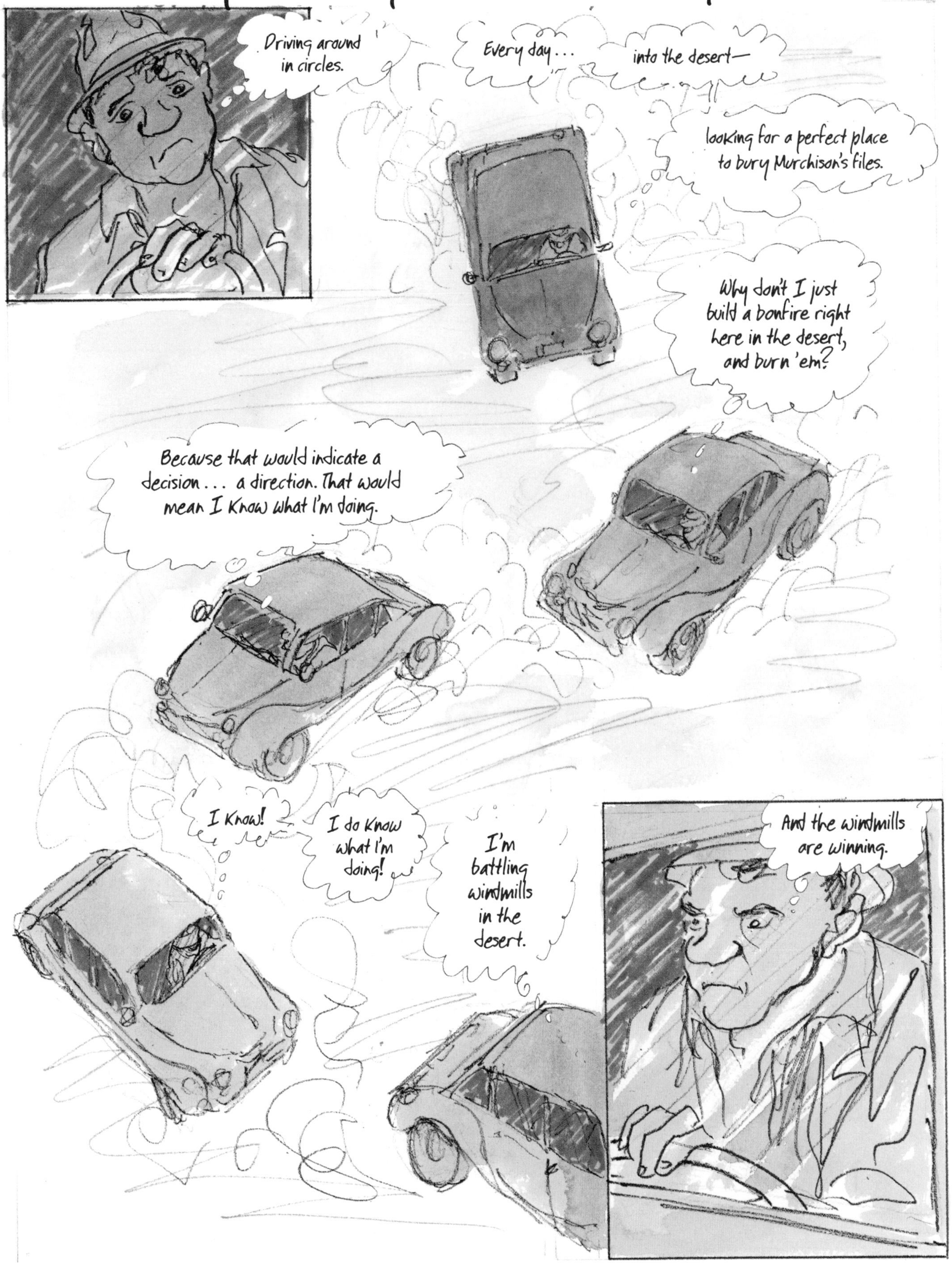

Driving around in circles.
Every day . . .
into the desert—
looking for a perfect place to bury Murchison's files.
Why don't I just build a bonfire right here in the desert, and burn 'em?
Because that would indicate a decision . . . a direction. That would mean I know what I'm doing.
I know!
I do know what I'm doing!
I'm battling windmills in the desert.
And the windmills are winning.

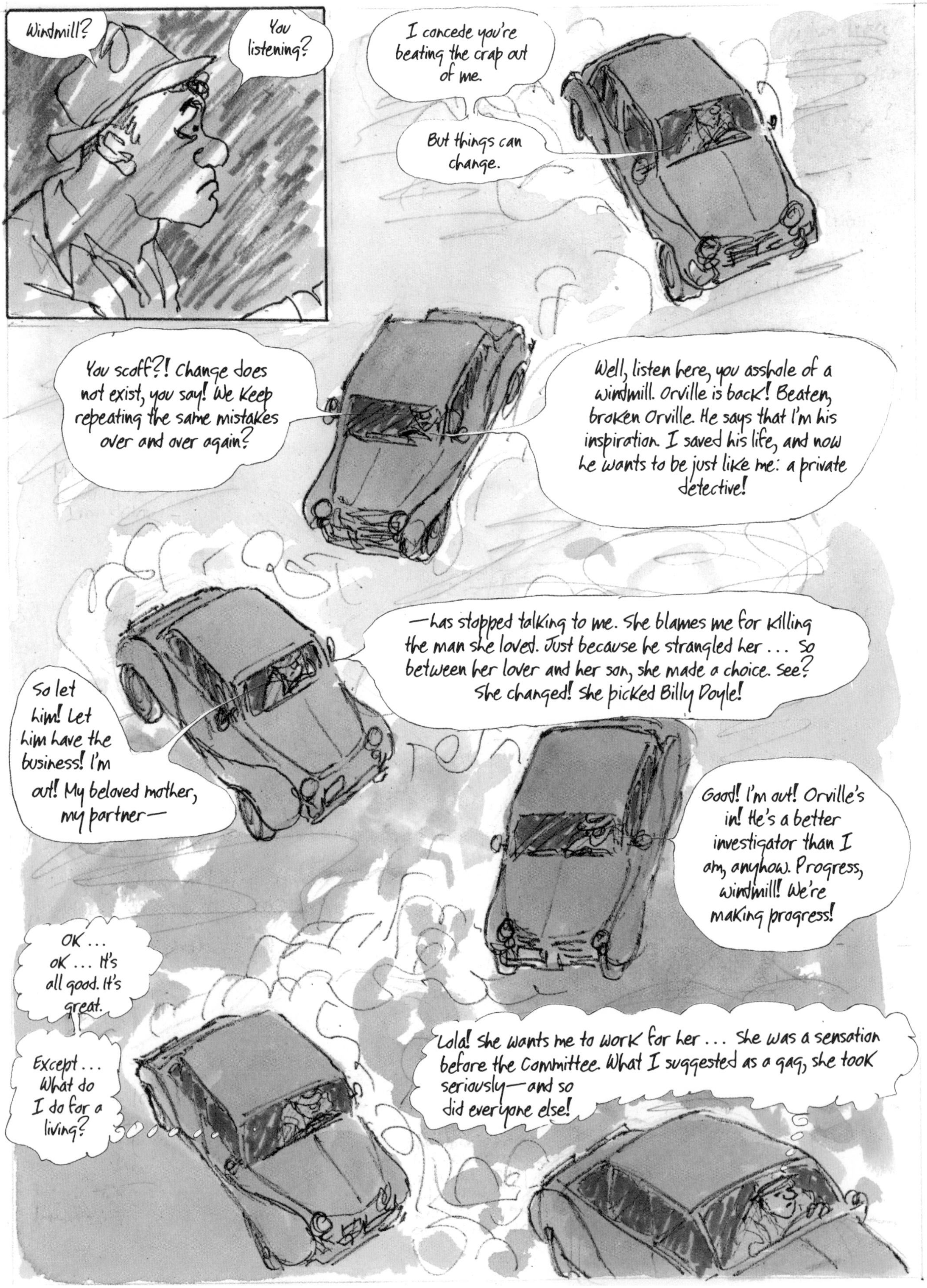
Windmill?
You listening?
I concede you're beating the crap out of me.
But things can change.
You scoff?! Change does not exist, you say! We keep repeating the same mistakes over and over again?
Well, listen here, you asshole of a windmill. Orville is back! Beaten, broken Orville. He says that I'm his inspiration. I saved his life, and now he wants to be just like me: a private detective!
So let him! Let him have the business! I'm out! My beloved mother, my partner—
—has stopped talking to me. She blames me for killing the man she loved. Just because he strangled her . . . So between her lover and her son, she made a choice. see? She changed! She picked Billy Doyle!
Good! I'm out! Orville's in! He's a better investigator than I am, anyhow. Progress, windmill! We're making progress!
OK . . . OK . . . It's all good. It's great.
Except . . . What do I do for a living?
Lola! She wants me to work for her . . . She was a sensation before the Committee. What I suggested as a gag, she took seriously—and so did everyone else!

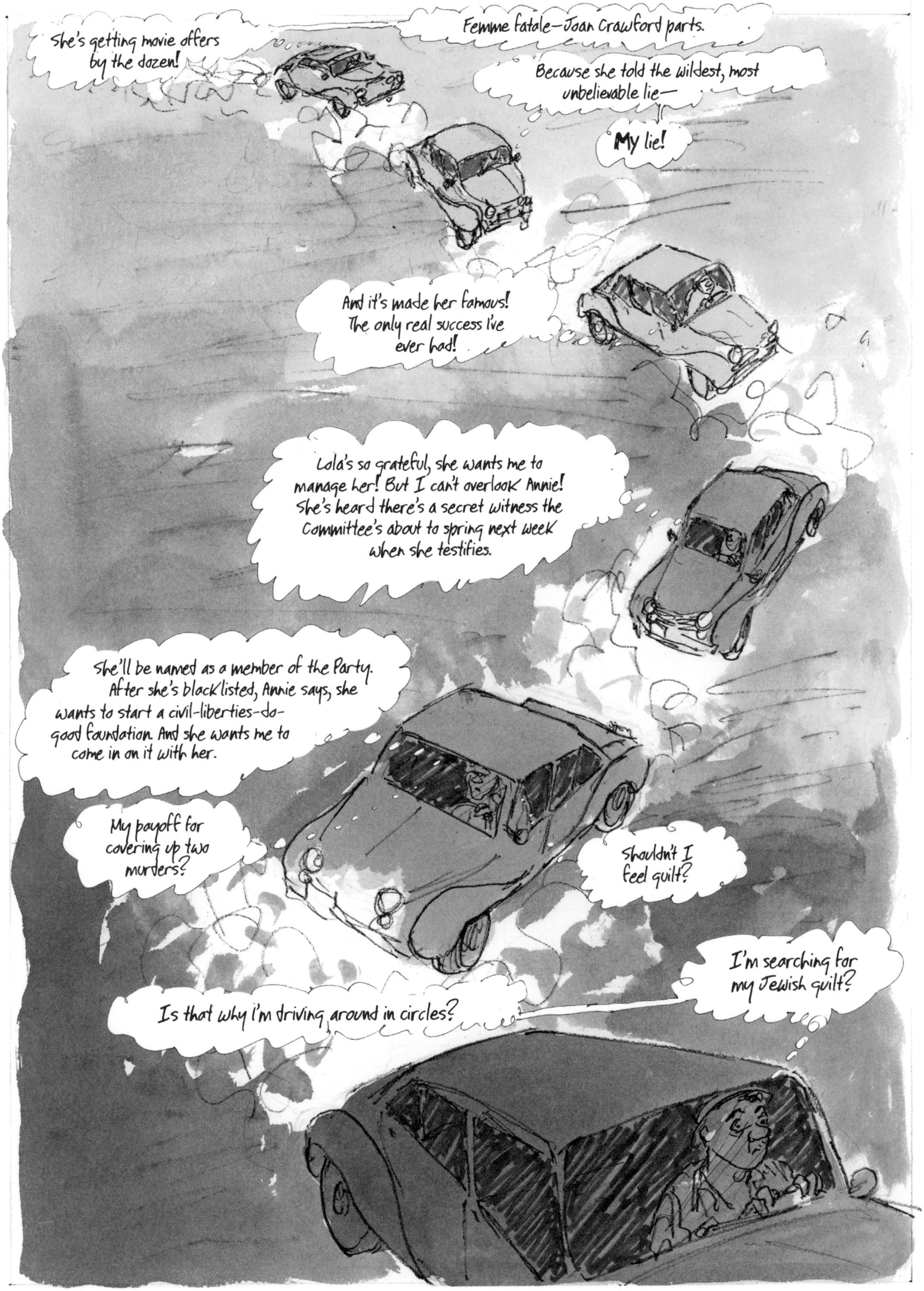
She's getting movie offers by the dozen!
Femme fatale—Joan Crawford parts.
Because she told the wildest, most unbelievable lie—
My lie!
And it's made her famous! The only real success I've ever had!
Lola's so grateful, she wants me to manage her! But I can't overlook Annie! She's heard there's a secret witness the Committee's about to spring next week when she testifies.
She'll be named as a member of the Party. After she's blacklisted, Annie says, she wants to start a civil-liberties-do-good foundation. And she wants me to come in on it with her.
My payoff for covering up two murders?
Shouldn't I feel guilt?
I'm searching for my Jewish guilt?
Is that why I'm driving around in circles?

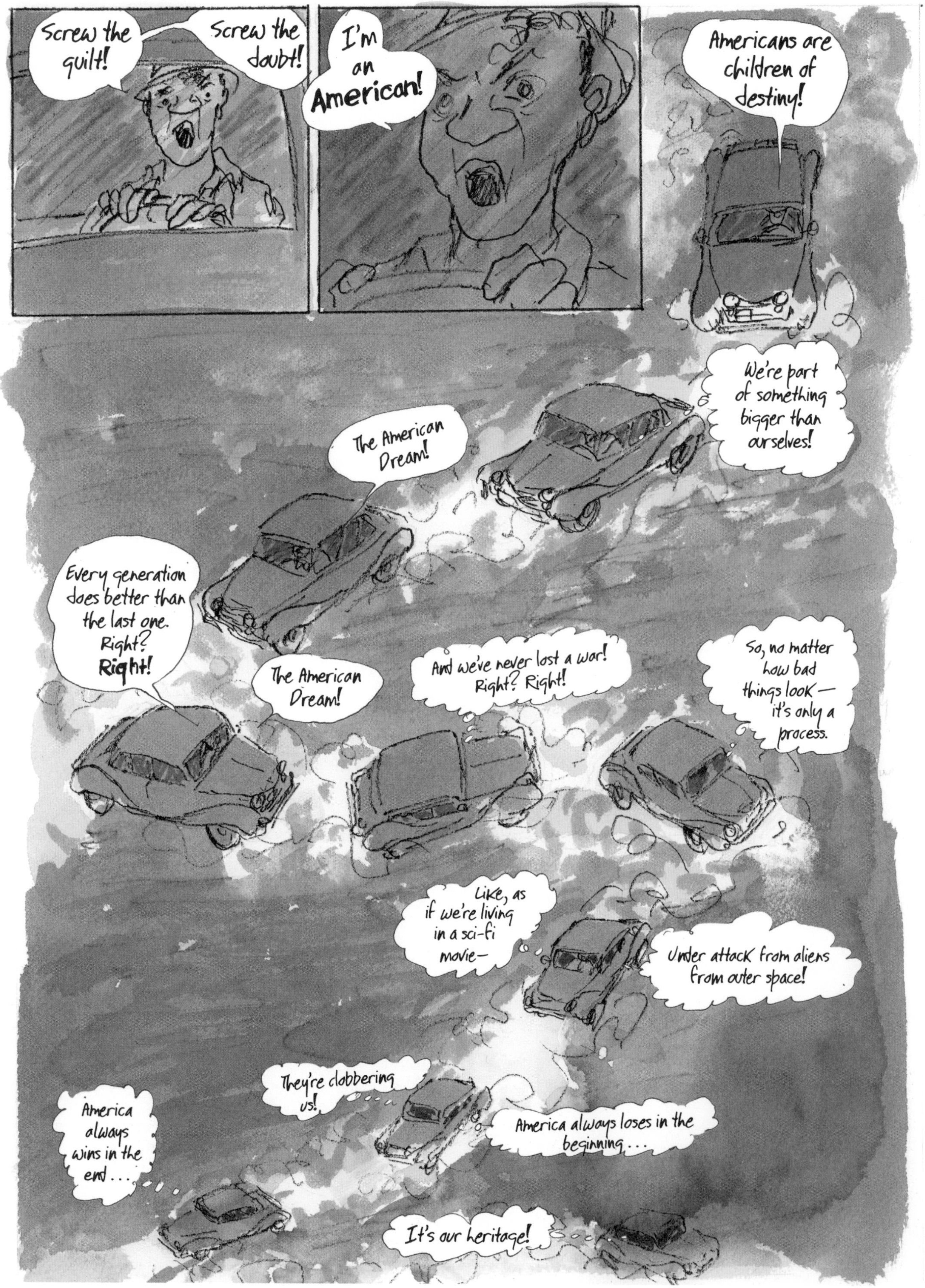
Screw the guilt!
Screw the doubt!
I'm an American!
Americans are children of destiny!
We're part of something bigger than ourselves!
The American Dream!
Every generation does better than the last one. Right? Right!
The American Dream!
And we've never lost a war! Right? Right!
So, no matter how bad things look— it's only a process.
Like, as if we're living in a sci-fi movie—
Under attack from aliens from outer space!
They're clobbering us!
America always loses in the beginning . . .
America always wins in the end . . .
It's our heritage!

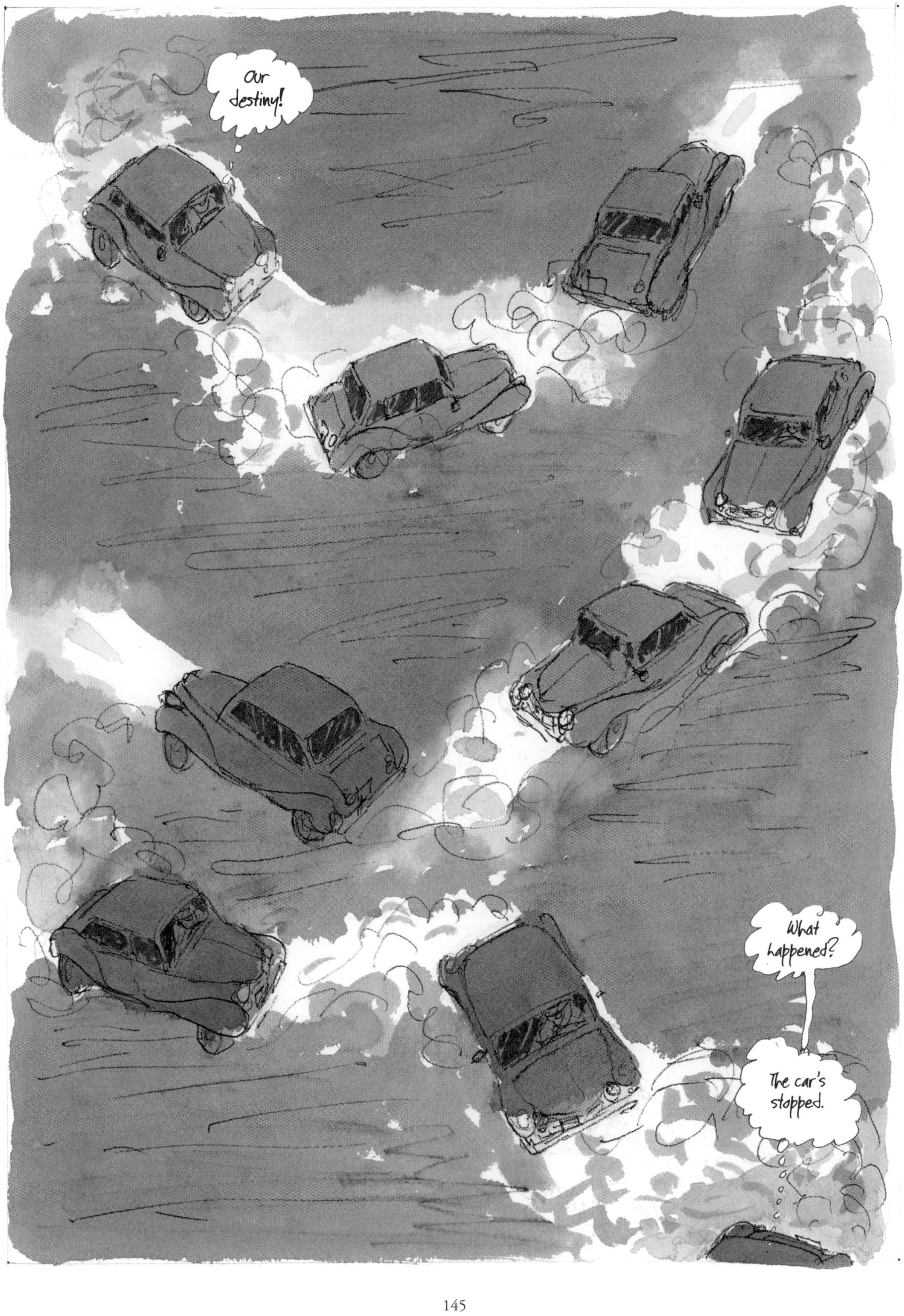
Our destiny!
What happened?
The car's stopped.

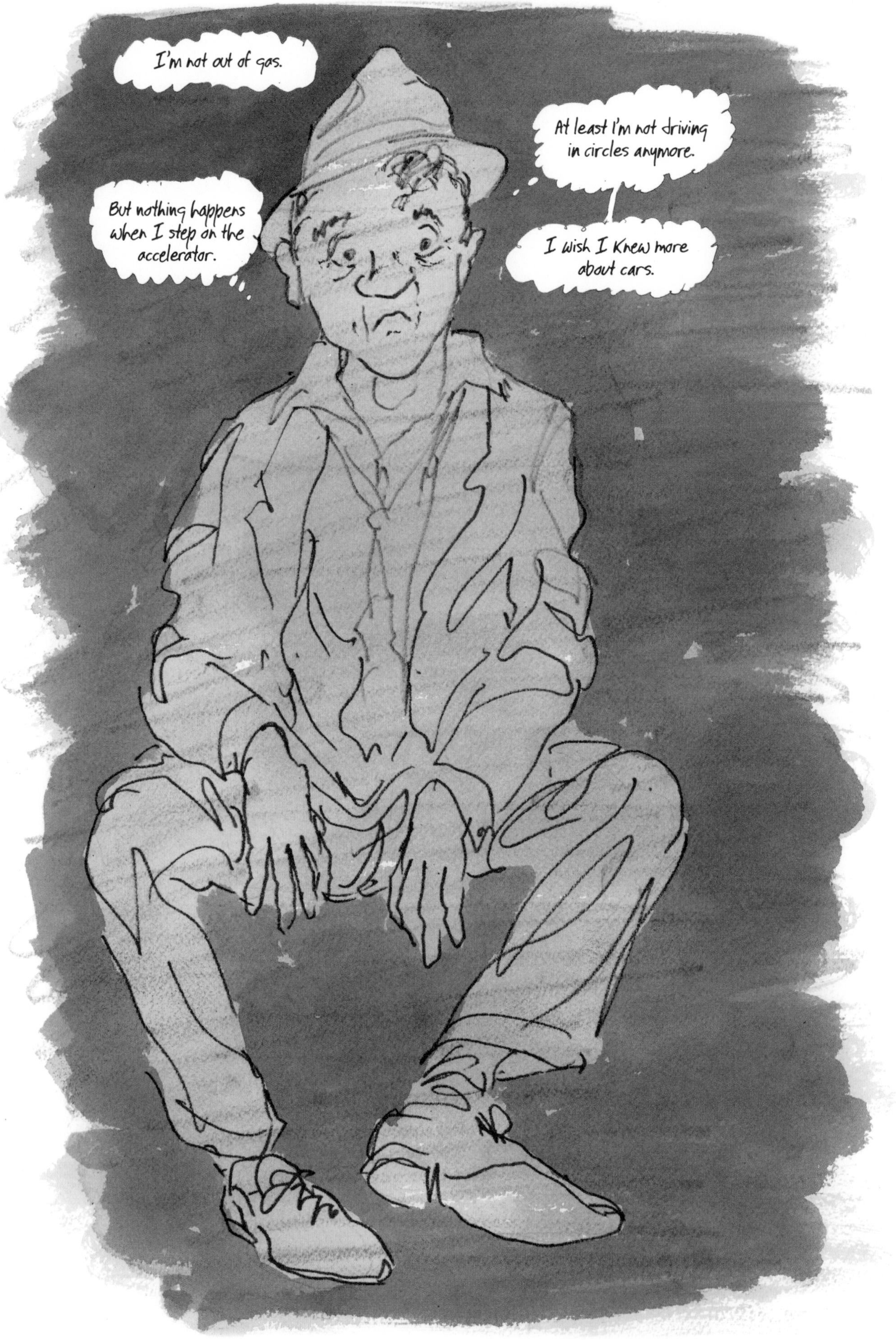

I'm not out of gas.
But nothing happens when I step on the accelerator.
At least I'm not driving in circles anymore.
I wish I knew more about cars.

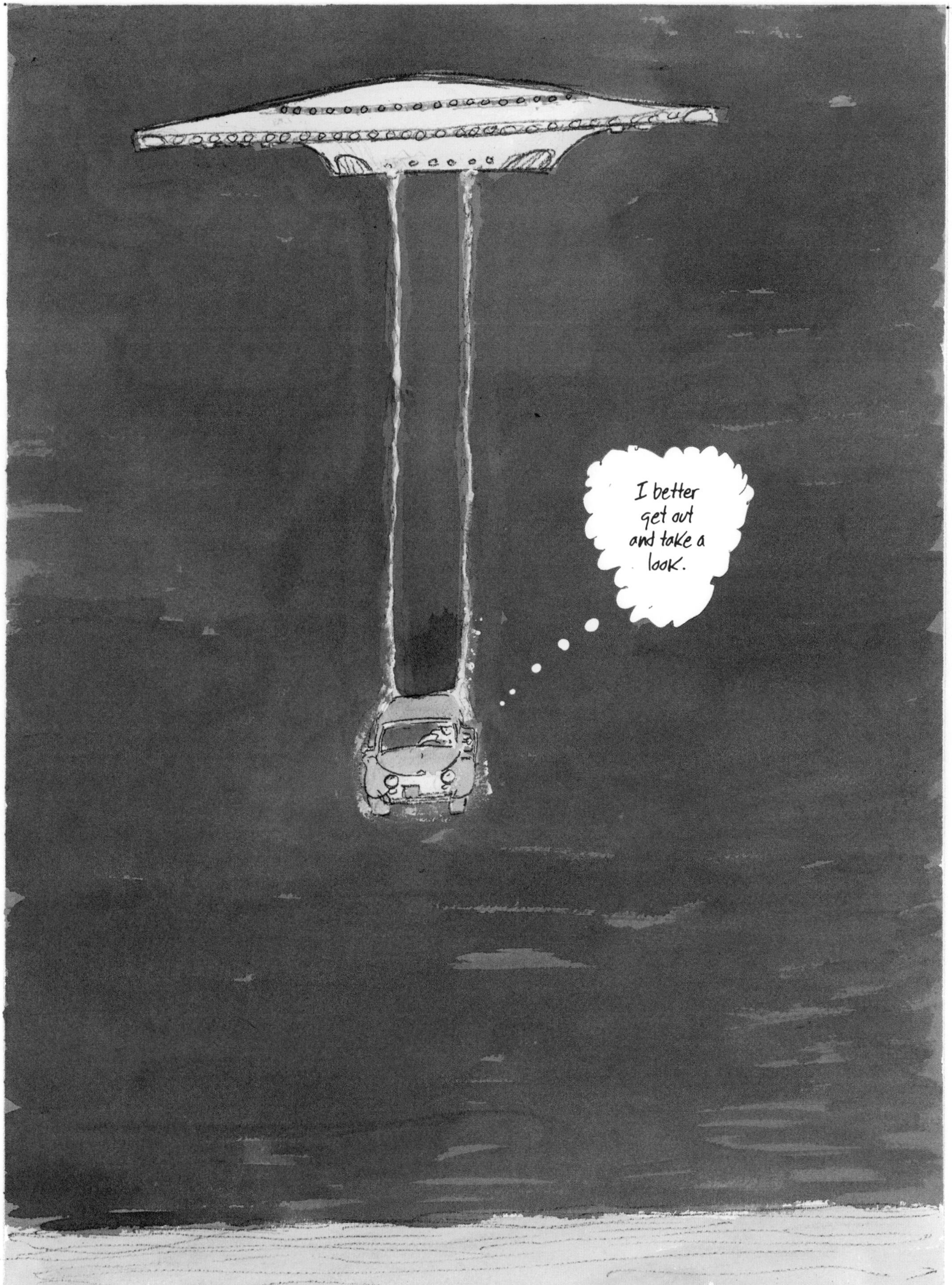
I better get out and take a look.

Chapter Sixty-Three: Kill My Mother

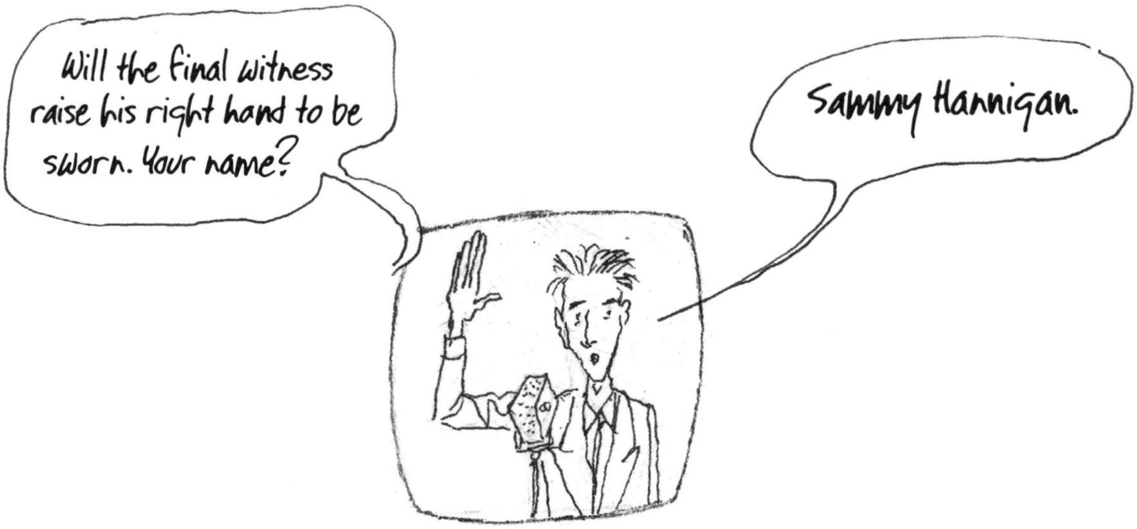

Will the final witness raise his right hand to be sworn. Your name?
Sammy Hannigan.

Acknowledgments

Two books helped me onto the path of this story: *The Hollywood Writers' Wars* by Nancy Lynn Schwartz and Sheila Schwartz and *Tender Comrades* by Patrick McGilligan and Paul Buhle. I did a lot of other reading and browsing, but these two helped most to solidify my point of view and provoke me into the reflective insanity that I chose as my goal. Old and valued friends were never far from my mind: the blacklisted writers Studs Terkel, Lillian Hellman, Walter Bernstein, Ring Lardner Jr. And add to that a much-admired acquaintance, the actress Lee Grant.

But I am not beyond personal weaknesses. As a distant cousin of Roy Cohn, how could I not be? So there was a mixed assortment of finks with whom, from time to time, I enjoyed myself: Robert Rossen, Abe Burrows, Budd Schulberg, and Jerome Robbins, whom I knew slightly and liked. And then there was the God-awful Harvey Matusow, not involved with film, but who ratted on everyone else. Still and all, Harvey and I had a brash, two Jewish wise guys bantering relationship.

But more than all the others, I owe this book to Kazan and Odets, who caused in me an undiluted rage, new to me in the 1950s, and almost as vivid today for the life-souring lessons they taught me about America, and political and personal betrayal.

The incredible Jackie Henry typed and retyped the many drafts of scripts, which laid the groundwork for the two years of illustration that followed. In which almost everything got changed. And the no less incredible Meg Larsen, my assistant, who organized and photographed and made order out of chaos (which is my habitual approach to functioning).

And to my friend and agent, Gail Hochman, as well as my friends at Liveright—my editor, Bob Weil; his assistant, Marie Pantojan; jacket designer Kelsie Netzer; production manager Anna Oler, publicist Peter Miller: I thank you all.

And how can I not name-drop my two brilliant daughters, Kate and Halley Feiffer, who validated their father by following him into different branches of his several careers. And repeatedly come up with highly original, and successful, creations, far beyond their old man's imaginings. And Kate and Chris's Maddy, my beloved granddaughter. Look out, world!

And at last, there's my wife and my life, Joan (JZ) Holden, brilliant in ways I still haven't begun to fathom, and the sole reason I'm still around. Beginning.